Changing the Paradigm of Homelessness

Changing the Paradigm of Homelessness offers a comprehensive look at family housing distress related to the homelessness epidemic in the United States. This book explores the causes and consequences of this epidemic and proposes drastic changes in America's historically ill-fated approach to family homelessness. By describing this crisis in detail, the authors enlighten readers to the scope of this issue, describe those impacted by it, and outline ways to shift public policies and public perceptions. The authors interweave scholarly concepts with insights of those who are currently or previously homeless, and, in doing so, they show the importance of academic knowledge influencing policy decisions and the ways in which these influences impact the lives of real persons. This book, then, uses pedagogy, policy, and pragmatism to critique the United States' approach to family homelessness.

Yvonne Vissing is a Professor of Healthcare Studies, and previously Professor and Chair of Sociology, at Salem State University, where she is the Founding Director of the Salem State University Center for Childhood and Youth Studies. She was appointed Policy Chair by the United Nations for child rights under the Convention on the Rights of the Child, and she is a long-term board member of the National Coalition for the Homeless.

Christopher G. Hudson is Professor Emeritus in the School of Social Work at Salem State University. In addition to his responsibilities at Salem State, he has been elected as the President of the 7,700-member Massachusetts Chapter of the National Association of Social Workers. He is the recipient of numerous awards, including the NAMI-MA Research of the Year Award, and two William J. Fulbright Senior Faculty Awards, one in Hong Kong (2002/2003) and the other in Prague, CZ (2017/2018). He has also taught and conducted research in international mental health at universities in Auckland, Hong Kong, Jerusalem, and London.

Diane Nilan is the founder and president of HEAR US Inc. and has three decades of experience running and managing homeless shelters and advocating for improved state and federal homeless policies. She has filmed and produced two award-winning documentaries – *My Own Four Walls* and *On the Edge: Family Homelessness in America*, wrote the book *Crossing the Line: Taking Steps to End Homelessness*, and has given numerous university and congressional addresses on homelessness.

Changing the Paradigm of Homelessness

Yvonne Vissing,
Christopher G. Hudson,
and Diane Nilan

Routledge
Taylor & Francis Group

NEW YORK AND LONDON

First published 2020
by Routledge
52 Vanderbilt Avenue, New York, NY 10017

and by Routledge
2 Park Square, Milton Park, Abingdon, Oxon, OX14 4RN

Routledge is an imprint of the Taylor & Francis Group, an informa business

© 2020 Taylor & Francis

The right of Yvonne Vissing, Christopher G. Hudson, and Diane Nilan to be identified as authors of this work has been asserted by them in accordance with sections 77 and 78 of the Copyright, Designs and Patents Act 1988.

Library of Congress Cataloging-in-Publication Data
A catalog record for this title has been requested

ISBN: 978-1-138-36295-6 (hbk)
ISBN: 978-1-138-36298-7 (pbk)
ISBN: 978-0-429-43181-4 (ebk)

Typeset in Bembo
by codeMantra

Contents

Preface

Why is there so much homelessness when the nation has been addressing it for years? This is the underlying question that will be answered in this book. A second question addressed is "What can we be doing better to prevent homelessness, especially for families?"

Homelessness is both a personal and social problem. A national dilemma exists on how to address homelessness, confusion about how to feel about homeless people, and about what to do for, with, or about them. When we pass by them on the street, part of us feels pity and compassion, believing that "we are our brother's keeper" and have a moral obligation to help those in distress. Another part feels antipathy, disgust, even anger as we hustle past them. Simultaneously, we see them as both victims and perpetrators of their homelessness. We may feel a tinge of guilt for not sharing and caring, but often this guilt is offset by moral indignation, questioning why they aren't doing more to live like "good, upstanding members of society." Despite excuses to the contrary, homelessness is evidently a problem that we don't actually want to get rid of. If we did, as a nation we would be taking very different courses of action than the path we've created.

As your authors, we've worked for decades with homeless people, analyzing policies and conducting research, and we're concerned that the rhetoric about homeless people, especially homeless families, doesn't fit reality as we see it. "Misinformation" is so common that it has been designated the 2018 word of the year (Diaz 2018). Erroneous assumptions have become egregious social policies. The conditions for people who are homeless, or on the brink of homelessness, are only going to get worse unless we change how we view and help them.

Policy makers and scholars rely on research to guide understandings and decisions. Studying homeless people is challenging in both definitional and methodological ways. Official reports state homelessness is declining; others report it is increasing. Which is it? There is hidden homelessness: couch-surfing, people over-staying welcomes with good-hearted people who haven't (yet) thrown them out. Counting people is problematic. In New Hampshire, a school counselor provided accurate accounts of homeless students only to be criticized because it made the community look bad. The next year, she wasn't allowed to do the count, and amazingly the number of homeless students had plummeted (Vissing 1997). The numbers game behind homelessness is a big concern.

The paradigm the nation is using to address homelessness isn't working, especially for children, youth and families (Bassuk Center 2018b; Bassuk and Olivet 2016; Bassuk et al. 2014; Baumberg and Gaffney n.d.; Biello 2016). There are many different things that we could try that might prevent homelessness or help people to gain more stable, secure housing arrangements. In this book, we will analyze the current paradigm, explain how we got to it, and explore alternatives that may be more effective, both in human and economic terms.

Part I

Background of Homelessness in the US

1 The Dilemma

In 1991, Gregg Barak, in his book *Gimme Shelter*, predicted homelessness would skyrocket unless we changed our housing and social policies. He advocated for a paradigm change that has obviously gone unheeded. He was correct – homelessness has grown as predictably as was obvious 30 years earlier. While few could argue he was wrong, systems continue to operate as they always have – which don't prioritize the needs of families and especially of those who are down-and-out. Today the housing crisis in America is "a ticking time bomb that's only going to get worse," according to a Harvard University study (2018; Hobbes 2018). America can't solve homelessness because we cling to limited policy ideas and quick fixes (Hobbes 2019).

Homelessness has long been a part of "the land of the free and home of the brave." Today it is a normalized feature of US society (Da Costa Nunez 2017b). Homelessness has become an industry that has ensured a steady production of homeless people, as well as a plethora of disjointed social services that often pathologize individuals instead of housing them (Beck and Twiss 2018). Homelessness organizations don't eradicate homelessness – they manage it in what is called the "homelessness industrial complex." Entire networks of professions have been built around homelessness. While ostensibly here to help, they aren't designed to actually eradicate it. If they did, they would also eliminate their jobs. Therefore, there is a structural dis-incentive to getting rid of homelessness. Causes of homelessness are social and systemic, and people end up without housing due to constrained forces over which they have virtually no control (MacKay-Tisbert 2016).

Such facts don't seem to get in our way of refusing to let go of assumptions that belie the dominant paradigm – that there is really something fundamentally flawed about people who become homeless (Hoffer 1951). The word "homeless" evokes images of single adults, alcoholics, drug abusers, dirty, lazy, doesn't have a job, doesn't want to work, may be criminal, violent, mentally ill, unhealthy, bad teeth, inappropriate or outlandish behavior, uneducated, inarticulate, not trustworthy, has lice or disease they could spread to us, and sleeps on sidewalks or places they shouldn't. Good-hearted people accept these stereotypes without question (Friedrich 2019).

We are regularly confronted by data, hard facts about the sorry state of the economy for the poor and middle classes (American Institutes for Research 2018, b), yet we tend to believe things aren't really so bad. When we look at those who suffer, we may believe they had a hand in the creation of their own misery. Humans rely on biased sets of cognitive processes to arrive at a given conclusion or belief (Friesen et al. 2015); this tendency to cherry-pick and twist the facts to fit with our existing beliefs is known as motivated reasoning (Wier 2017). Some scholars think we are hard-wired to believe what we want to believe. People routinely use mental shortcuts to understand what happens around them; there are so many things occurring in the world simultaneously that we don't make or take time to examine them. We use quick and largely unconscious rules of thumb to decide what to believe. People overestimate the frequency of an event when that event is more "available" in our memory – so if we see a news article about a homeless person being mentally ill, we tend to believe it even though most homeless people are not mentally ill. Sometimes we rely upon emotional reasoning to justify or defend a belief. We are more alert to information that justifies a position we already hold, a process called "confirmation bias" (Feldman 2017). It's harder to know what facts are these days, since in the media and everyday conversation "the capacity to inject poison into the political bloodstream – in the form of lies and falsehoods, crazed conspiracy theories, smears and dehumanizing attacks – is unprecedented" (Wehner 2018).

A Huffington Post (Ruiz-Grossman 2018) article listing "5 things that people get wrong about homelessness" included the following:

1 It's easier to look at people on the streets as the problem instead of a system that is broken.
2 It's easier to think that people who are homeless are addicts instead of thinking that they might be like you and me.
3 It's easier to think that people become homeless because they have substance problems or mental illness instead of blaming our poorly functioning systems for supporting people having a mental health or substance problem.
4 It's easier to think if we gave people jobs they wouldn't be homeless instead of looking at the fact that most homeless people work, at least part-time.
5 It's easiest to think that homelessness is their fault instead of that they are good, decent, hard-working people who are more like us than different from us.

Blaming homeless people for their lot in life masks the role social structures play (Ryan 1971). It hides how criminal justice systems swallow up poor people, how healthcare systems underserve the poor and mentally ill, how housing markets don't provide enough safe and affordable options. Framing homelessness as a personal pathology, rather than a social one, reinforces the legitimacy of the industry and places the blame for housing deprivation on the individual (MacKay-Tisbert 2016).

When you hear the word "homeless," what doesn't come to mind are people who are employed, clean, educated, dependable, honest, responsible, reliable nice people who go out of their way to help others, with families they work hard to take care of. These are people with hopes and dreams that routinely get crushed by the weight of poverty. They are the growing population of homeless people, the ones that we don't see because in most ways they are like us.

There is the erroneous assumption that homeless people are lazy – if they would just get a job, they wouldn't be homeless anymore. Many homeless people work but don't earn enough to afford decent housing. People can work full-time and live with a partner who works full-time, but if they are making minimum wage, two full-time salaries aren't sufficient to afford housing, food, transportation, and other necessities.

Homeless families provoke our fear and disdain; the working poor evokes our sympathy and sense of camaraderie. We shy away from homeless people, as if they are going to contaminate us. The invisible homelessness inspires the public to believe they aren't really homeless. We tend to deny or downplay their financial distress because their reality is a little too close for comfort. Even saying that homeless people could be kind, loving, thoughtful, and hard-working seems to defy what we have come to believe is true. As long as we can mentally compartmentalize them to be sub-human and not-the-same-as-us, the more we can justify not caring about them or doing for them. Things switch in our brains when the distance between us and them disappears.

The down-and-out today include middle-class families and children of all ages. Families are a different category of homeless people than those seen in stereotypes. They aren't likely to be visible, identifiable, or receive government assistance. This is partially because parents go out of their way to be independent, to care for their children and create as normal a life for them as possible. (Brown et al. 2018; Nunez and Sribnick 2013). Being defined as homeless may yield some benefits, but stigma accompanies that label, and every one of every age learns that being regarded as homeless is not a good thing. Homeless families and children are often omitted from official definitions and counts. By not helping people who are going through hard times (GTHT), a down-hill slide is almost inevitable when one-crisis-too-much becomes unbearable. Waiting until people have become destitute with no economic, social, or emotional resources to call upon help is a fool's errand. Prevention always costs less and yields many more benefits (Institute for Children, Poverty and Homelessness 2012).

Targeting assistance to people who currently meet the definition of chronically homeless does nothing to prevent chronic homelessness from happening in the first place. While some of today's chronically homeless adults are receiving supportive housing to end their homelessness, by relegating children and youth to the end of the queue in the nation's plan to end homelessness, and failing to promote assistance that meets their unique needs, we ensure a continuous flow of homeless young people falling through the cracks, many to become "chronically homeless" themselves as the system continues to fail them over time (Duffield 2016).

The economic and personal tragedies we are creating by our homelessness policies are not in anyone's best interests. Other options are available. There are a variety of different paradigms we could be following, alternative models, approaches, systems, and ways of contextualizing and addressing poverty and homelessness. It's time to take a thoughtful, considered look at them. The paradigms that we highlight in this book are seeds to be planted, nurtured, to grow what would be good for us as individuals and for us as a society.

Let us get right to the point – how the nation is addressing homelessness isn't working. Unless we change the course of action, it's going to get much worse. This isn't new news – those in the know have been predicting this for half a century. But what is new is that we're going to highlight what is happening in the backrooms that the public never gets to see. What we are going to say is going to create controversy. Agencies that are dependent upon Department of Housing and Urban Development (HUD) money are afraid to speak about what isn't working because they may see their funds dry up. When push comes to shove, none of us wants to be homeless. Workers protect their jobs and income streams because they know what can happen if they don't. This isn't fantasy – programs have closed or shifted their service focus to chronic homelessness rather than family homelessness; programs that focus on treating the destitute get more assistance than those trying to prevent people from going under. And the way those guidelines are constructed these days creates a very narrow road of possibilities that must be followed if to receive federal funding.

HUD-affiliated agencies and consultants publicly announce what a good job they are doing, how numbers of homeless people are going down, their programs are successful. Indeed, if they ceased to exist and there were no other options available, poor and homeless people would be up the creek without a paddle. Something is better than nothing. Instead of bucking the system, they play the game, follow the rules, and make others follow them too.

But behind closed doors, those working in the shelter-industrial complex are conflicted. They work hard and must believe in their mission to come to work each day and try to help people whose horrific stories can break one's heart. But staff realize what recipients know all too well – how homeless people are treated and piecemeal services they receive are so far from being adequate that there is no way that things are going to get much better unless a miracle occurs.

HUD's famous Continuum of Care model turns out to be a shell game, telling communities they can decide for themselves how they want to spend funding to help the homeless, but only programs scoring high on

HUD's funding rubric will get the money. On the surface, it appears communities have choice and free-will to design as needed. But in reality, only programs that adhere to HUD definitions and agendas will get funded. If agencies want to serve homeless people, they have to modify what they intend to do to meet official guidelines. While guidelines can be helpful to ensure that funding meets goals, one has to assess whether HUD's goals for helping homeless children, youth, and families are high priority. We attest that they aren't.

Nonprofit, charity, and religious organizations pose a conundrum as well, because they are filled with good-hearted people who contribute a great deal of social good. But there is a dark side that doesn't get talked about. Their manifest mission may be to help the poor, but as observed in cushy corporate offices and gourmet dinners paid for by donations, if homelessness ceased to exist, so would their businesses and profits.

Like any business, there is significant variability in the quality of programs, staff, and outcomes for homeless individuals. These include poor or biased leadership, wrong-headed program avenues, questionable management or mismanagement, inadequately trained personnel, underpaid staff, insufficient funding, and antiquated facilities with scarce resources. From a cost-benefit analysis, a lot of money is being spent on outcomes that could be better.

Below are real-life examples from actual people, Tilly the provider and Sophie the recipient. Both point to the need for a different, better paradigm to address homelessness:

Tilly was a shelter director who shared her story: Her HUD transitional housing program and flexible funding for construction programs, a full set of services, good record-keeping for people who could stay two years and get their lives together worked pretty well. But HUD cut the transitional housing budget to fund Housing First programs. HUD now makes families prove they are homeless before they can get shelter. They don't consider being doubled-up or sleeping on a cousin's couch as homeless, so families have to have virtually no resources and sleep in their car or go to the emergency room before getting help. Once in the shelter, families must adhere to strict rules in order to stay. There are multiple hoops to jump through, time to come, time to go, what you can and cannot do when you are in the shelter, and if you fail to comply, out you go. Expectations imposed upon them are ridiculous, oppressive, nothing like one would have in one's own home, but you have to put up with it and play the game to get help. In order to stay in the shelter, you lose your identity and how you can parent your children or care for your family. Most shelters run with patchwork-quilt funding, so staff don't get paid much. Staff vary from being trained or not, and being well intentioned or not. Whoever is managing the staff doesn't have time to supervise, train, or monitor them. Power can be abused by workers who thrive on the little authority they have. Workers may oppress others because they can and rail against minor infractions or rip into folks in front of others for things that they were incapable of doing. Staff can be brutal and dehumanizing. Those who fund and work with homeless people have their own agendas, and the vulnerable people are those that pay the price. Once you enter the shelter, it's like going down a rabbit hole, full of twists and turns that you can't see, and you have no idea where you'll come out. Ultimately Tilly was fired because she asked too many questions, pointed out too many flaws...

Sophie used to be a stay-at-home mom before her husband left her for another woman. When he left, so did the family's income. Alone, she could not manage the house, two children, and all the expenses, so she was awarded a housing subsidy and food-stamps. She didn't receive other aid because she "messed up the application and they wouldn't reconsider me for a year." She had no family, few friends, and didn't have good job skills or a baby-sitter, so her isolation grew along with her depression, which she tried to manage through drinking alcohol. The intake worker did a home visit and decided Sophie should go into detox. Her children were put into foster care, but her housing subsidy ended because she didn't have the children. When she got out of rehabilitation, the state wouldn't return her children because she didn't have money for housing, and the bank had foreclosed on it when she was in treatment. She had to move to the shelter, which didn't allow children. The staff weren't sympathetic that a mother would lose her children because she became a drunk. When Sophie's frustration skyrocketed, her outburst was deemed unacceptable and she was told she had to leave the shelter. Dismayed, Sophie couldn't comprehend how her once-functional life had tanked as both she and her children had become homeless, apart, through the act of her husband leaving her to have an affair. At last contact, she had no idea if she could ever get her children back, given she had no place to live, no job, and now a history of substance abuse and mental illness.

Top-down funder and administrative agendas may have good intentions but be ill-conceived. Bottom-up system distress and workers who are supposed to care end up engaging in exploitation that squeeze vulnerable homeless people who get stuck smack in the middle in ways where there's no way for them to win.

Current homelessness policies could be reconsidered to determine if they meet the actual need of the nation's most vulnerable populations – and those that can fall into that category if preventive mechanisms aren't put into place. There are lots of well-intended, hard-working, smart people to be complimented and honored trying to come up with some alternatives. We will explore some of those paradigms in this book.

2 The Definitions to Numbers Debacle

In Congress's backrooms there are heated debates about exactly who can be considered to be poor or homeless.[1] Definitions influence policies and funding for programs that will determine who gets help and who doesn't. Definitions determine research methodologies used to conduct counts on how many of what kinds of people are homeless. Numbers are then used to make political and administrative decisions of who gets what at the federal, state, and local levels. All this trickles down to the individual level, where real people's everyday lives are impacted.

First definitions and counts of poverty will be explored, which leads into the issue of homelessness. "When you count [poor or homeless people or] unemployment levels, you are counting the wrong thing. You are not counting dignity of people. You are counting exploited people."[2]

Poverty's Definitional Conundrum

Poverty is determined by a poverty threshold, a statistical calculation of a 28-cell matrix of indicators like family size, number of children, and so on. Poverty guidelines are simplified versions of the federal poverty thresholds used for administrative purposes – for instance, determining financial eligibility for certain federal programs (U.S. Department of Health and Human Services 2019). Definitions influence criteria for people's eligibility for services. Peter Rossi's classic work *Down and Out in America* (1990) identifies homelessness not as a housing problem but as one created by keeping people in poverty. He sees little difference between the person who is homeless on the street and the person who has a home but lives in the chaos of poverty, who could lose their ability to shelter themselves in the blink of an eye. His work highlighted how millions of people get along on virtually no income with very precarious ability to secure housing, food, health care, transportation, and things most people take for granted. He views poverty as the root of literal homelessness and those just above the margin of it.

The government calculates poverty with a 1963 formula, using a 1955 Household Food Consumption Survey that defines poverty for a family of four at three times a typical family's food budget. Without question, daily life and costs have changed significantly since 1955/1963. Food prices have increased, people eat out more, transportation costs have grown, medical care costs have ballooned, and housing/utility payments have skyrocketed. Poverty needs to be realistically redefined (Uchitelle 2001). No longer is one just "poor"; poverty is subdivided into categories so some poor people aren't regarded as poor as others. There are severe, absolute, or extreme poverty where one lacks basic necessities (living on under $1.25 a day), and relative poverty, or being unable to meet a society's average standard of living. Data indicate there are Third World levels of poverty in the US, especially for Black Americans (Baldari 2019; Edelman 2017; Gould and Schneider 2018). The Children's Defense Fund (2016) reports that while median incomes of families are around $66,557, distributions vary by race, ranging from $95,000 for Asians, $83,000 for Whites, $44,000 for Hispanics, and $39,000 for Blacks (Figure 2.1).

Alternative measures of poverty exist (Froelich et al. 2018). A 2011 Supplemental Poverty Measure was introduced that takes into account noncash resources from government assistance programs (tax-credits, food stamps, child support, shelter, etc.). The National Academy of Science's and Economic Policy Institute's family budget–based measurements to secure a "safe and decent, yet modest, living standard" includes housing, food, childcare, transportation, health care, and taxes. The Brookings Institution's Hamilton Project endorses a poverty threshold that's twice the official poverty level. The European Union determines poverty rates by counting all those living in households with incomes that are equal to or less than 60% of the respective national median income. The National Poverty Study (American Institute for Research 2018b) seeks to redefine

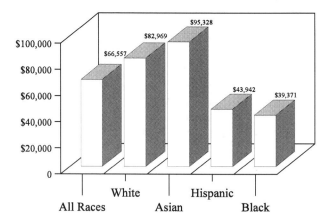

Figure 2.1 Median Family Income: Families with Children.

Source: Data from Edelman, M. (2016, Sept. 16). *Ending child poverty: A moral and economic necessity.* Downloaded from: www.childrensdefense.org/child-watch-columns/health/2016/ending-child-poverty-a-moral-and-economic-necessity/.

poverty in ways that could better address homelessness. Their indicators include:

- Validity of poverty measurement: How are low-income people actually living? Does the Supplemental Poverty Measure accurately represent who is/isn't experiencing deprivation?
- Gradations of poverty: What are qualitative differences between various poverty populations? Do extreme-poor, middle-poor, and near-poor populations have different lives, experiences, and strategies for making ends meet? Do existing poverty policies address their needs equally well?
- Hidden poverty populations: How do subpopulations that have remained largely hidden in other studies, including families and children, experience poverty?
- Retesting key conclusions: Can inferences made from classic and highly influential qualitative studies stand up to rigorous tests based on systematic samples?
- Early warning system: What do real-time assessments show about how the poverty population is dealing with national emergencies (e.g., recessions) and sweeping new policy (e.g., health care reform, school reform)?
- Develop new theories and interventions: How can new interventions be developed on the basis of qualitative evidence on (a) the everyday lives of the extreme poor, moderately poor, and near-poor, (b) how they react to immediate or long-term need, and (c) how they engage with the formal/informal safety nets?

The World Inequality Database reports that if rising inequality is not properly monitored and addressed, it can lead to political, economic, and social catastrophes. The US poverty rate is among the highest of all developed nations. According to the World Bank, 3.2 million of the world's 769 million people who lived on less than $1.90 a day in 2013 live in the US, and 5.3 million people in the US are absolutely poor by global standards (Deaton 2018). The biggest nay-sayers about economic inequality who blame victims of poverty for their economic distress tend to come from the upper 1%, who are chief beneficiaries of income inequality. Business and political leaders would lose money if inequality was eliminated and have "loudest megaphones in media and the most assiduous supporters in government" (Hiltzik 2018). With economic policies that support the rich, Trump is seeking to redefine poverty to cut the numbers of people on welfare and what the government would have to spend to help them (Sink 2019).

Today's poverty threshold is a statistical calculation of a 28-cell matrix of indicators, such as family size and number of children, but there are simplified versions used for determining financial eligibility for certain federal programs (U.S. Department of Health and Human Services 2019). A family of four living on less than $24,858 and an individual earning less than $12,488 are considered poor (Froelich et al. 2018).

People working part-time or who have special conditions, such as those with disabilities and their caregivers, or students are more likely to be poor (Bauer 2019).

Of those living in poverty, 2016 figures show 13.3 million children, 4.6 million over-65ers, and 23 million age 18–64 constitute the parent-pool of homeless families. The Brooking Institution's Hamilton Project found that four in ten working-age adults are poor, and having a job doesn't keep one out of poverty. Black Americans are more likely to be unemployed than White Americans and have a poverty rate that is twice as high; Latino Americans have a poverty rate that is approaching that of Black Americans. Native Americans and Alaskan natives have the highest poverty rates. Women are more likely to be poor than men, and women with a high school education or less are most likely to be out of the workforce. Poverty risks can be compounded – young Black Americans have a poverty rate in excess of 30%, and among single Black mothers, the poverty rate exceeds 40%. The Urban Institute's Well-Being and Basic Needs Survey (Karpman et al. 2018) found that 40% of non-elderly adults reported difficulty meeting basic needs such as food, health care, housing, and utilities while geographic variation exists: with New England costing more to live than the South (Froelich et al. 2018; Shambaugh 2017). The 2017 US Census reported the national poverty rate at 12.3%, with 39.7 million people meeting the government's definition of poverty. The median household income was $61,372 (Fontenot et al. 2018). Census data indicate men's income increased over 3% in the past year while women's income (at average of $10,000+ lower) fell 1.1%, suggesting that economic gender equality continues to be a myth.

While government leaders tout economic growth (Casselman 2018), the Economic Policy Institute finds US wage growth has been slow and uneven, with African-Americans and women at a clear disadvantage while the wealthiest are accumulating more money than ever (Eidelson 2018). Median real wages grew only 0.2% over the past year, and wages for African-Americans declined; wage-earners in the 95th percentile saw average pay hikes of 1.5%. Even when women had graduate degrees, they still made less money than men with only undergraduate degrees. While racism and poverty are correlated, poverty's adverse effects impact everyone; poorly educated whites also have poorer health and low-life options. The poorest of the US poor are located generally in Appalachia and the Mississippi Delta area, as well as in the Southwest (Korten 2019).

Rising inequality is found in every part of the nation, from cities to rural areas. States with the greatest amount of economic inequality vary; California, Colorado, Connecticut, Florida, Massachusetts, Nevada, and New York populations have the most; Iowa has the least. Poverty and inequality set the stage for homelessness (Martin 2018b).

Defining Homelessness: The Root of the Problem

What is homelessness? This question sounds obvious and benign. Homeless is homeless, or so the unenlightened, including the bulk of Congress, would reply. As 1964 Supreme Court Justice Potter Stewart is famous for saying, "I know it when I see it" (Find Law 2018). Not so fast. Homelessness could be lack of a stable conventional dwelling, but this definition is hardly satisfactory. Rossi (1990) notes the term "homeless" is ambiguous and can refer to different things.

There is a definitional conundrum about what homelessness is and who homeless people are. It's essential to identify exactly who and what we are talking about. Etiology and consequences must be identified. Definitions we employ shape how we get numbers, which shape what we think about homelessness. How we think about homeless people influences what we will do for and about them. Despite rhetoric to the contrary, the nation seems to have made a decision deeming homelessness to be acceptable. In short, definitions create numbers, and numbers create mind-sets that go on to create homelessness itself.

The national definition of homelessness, hence the subsequent methodology, resultant numbers, and what we believe to be true, is inaccurate. Change the definition, change the methodology, and the numbers will change, which will alter our understanding of what homelessness is and who homeless people are. Paradigms determine what we believe homelessness to be and what we do about it. If we change our paradigm, we could change how we view the social phenomenon of homelessness and the way we look at those who are in housing distress. A different paradigm would allow us to take a different approach to preventing or eradicating homelessness.

Many definitions focus on location. Locations range from staying in shelters, on the street, in one's car, in tents or campers, in nontraditional locations, with friends or relatives, doubled (tripled or quadrupled) up with others, having a roommate, bouncing around motels, in tunnels under highways, in caves or underground areas beneath buildings. If someone is in foster care, jail, hospital, or a residential facility, are they homeless? What about truckers who live in their cabs and have PO boxes for mail? Are students who live in dorms and have no other home homeless? The consensus isn't clear when it comes to location as criteria for establishing a homeless designation.

Other definitions consider time. Temporally, chronic homelessness can last years, short-term homelessness may be days, weeks, or months in duration, and intermittent homelessness occurs unpredictably and periodically (Vissing 1997). When someone is homeless, they may be uncertain how long the housing distress is going to last. If housed, will homelessness occur again? Long-term homelessness is viewed differently than short-term homelessness. There is an assumption that people who experience short-term housing dislocation aren't "really" homeless. How many days of being homeless are enough to destroy someone's sense of stability? Such things are unclear.

There are situational parameters to consider in our definition of when someone is homeless or our willingness to help. There are "acts of God" that render 14 million people a year homeless, from fires, hurricanes, earthquakes, tsunamis, or natural disasters (Statista nd; Suliman 2017). There are "acts of man" that may force people to become homeless, such as the northern Massachusetts gas explosions that impacted thousands of people in 8,600 homes and businesses (Sellars et al. 2018); or the countless electric, smoking, or cooking fires that force people out of their homes. It is assumed, perhaps erroneously, these people have insurance and will get into new homes before long. There are acts of man such as urban renewal, residential gentrification, or destruction of available housing to make way for businesses or fancier housing units that leave people with no affordable places to go (Crane et al. 2005; Powell and Spencer 2003).

People may have personal problems that contribute to their becoming homeless. Health problems, injuries, physical, cognitive, or mental illnesses can result in homelessness. Addiction problems can result in losing homes. Divorce, job loss, domestic violence, criminal justice problems may render people homeless. If people don't have money to get their own place while they figure out what to do, are they considered homeless in the same way that someone who lost their job or benefits might be? If someone has financial resources but doesn't have a regular place to stay, how are they similar to, or different from, someone who doesn't have a regular place to stay because they don't have money? Do we feel kinder toward people we perceive to be innocent victims and more willing to help them than those who we perceive to be responsible for their problems? While "acts of God" homelessness result in a community's outpouring of help, when you become homeless because of an alcohol or opiate problem, health condition, or bad relationship, you get less sympathy. In those allegedly personally caused problems, you're pretty much on your own until you find someone to help you.

If youth and parents have conflict, "my way or the highway" situations and run away, are they homeless if they could return but only if they "straighten up and fly right"? Many prefer uncertainties of the street to known certainty of maltreatment at home (Vissing 1997).

Homelessness is a process, not just an outcome. It seldom occurs overnight, unless there is a fire or natural disaster. If it is a process, where is the exact cutting point between people who are "going through hard times," living in "housing distress" and "barely making ends meet" compared to folks who have crossed into what is considered homelessness? Counting only people who are in shelters or living on the street misses those who are invisibly homeless or in the process of falling downward. Using more fluid definitions of homelessness can result in dramatically different numbers.

Official Definitions

Government organizations employ strict definitions, and they take precedence when determining who qualifies for services. There has been heated disagreement among authorities about which definition should be the dominant one. The National Health Care for the Homeless Council (2018) states there is more than one "official" definition of homelessness. Health centers like it are funded by the US Department of Health and Human Services (HHS), which uses the following:

> A homeless individual is defined in section 330(h)(5)(A) as an individual who lacks housing (without regard to whether the individual is a member of a family), including an individual whose primary residence during the night is a supervised public or private facility (e.g., shelters) that provides temporary living accommodations, and an individual who is a resident in transitional housing. A homeless person is an individual without permanent housing who may live on the streets; stay in a shelter, mission, single room occupancy facilities, abandoned building or vehicle; or in any other unstable or non-permanent situation [Section 330 of the Public Health Service Act (42 U.S.C., 254b)]. An individual may be considered to be homeless if that person is "doubled-up," a term that refers to a situation where individuals are unable to maintain their housing situation and are forced to stay with a series of friends and/or extended family members. In addition, previously homeless individuals who are to be released from a prison or a hospital may be considered homeless if they do not have a stable housing situation to which they can return. A recognition of the instability of an individual's living arrangements is critical to the definition of homelessness.
>
> (National Health Care for the Homeless Council 2018)

The definition of "homeless" used by the US Department of Housing and Urban Development (HUD) is the one most often employed. HUD's focus has been on serving the chronically homeless adult population. It has been adopted by the US Interagency Council on Homelessness (USICH) and Department of Veteran Affairs (VA), drives the requirements for the Shelter Plus Care (S+C) Program, the Supportive Housing Program (SHP), the Continuum of Care (CoC) Program and the Rural Housing Stability Assistance Program (RHSP), and funds the National Alliance to End Homelessness (NAEH) (2012), which summarizes HUD's definition of homeless as:

- People who are living in a place not meant for human habitation, in emergency shelter, in transitional housing, or are exiting an institution where they temporarily resided…people will be considered homeless if they are exiting an institution where they reside for up to 90 days and were in shelter or a place not meant for human habitation immediately prior to entering that institution.

- People who are losing their primary nighttime residence, which may include a motel or hotel or a doubled-up situation, within 14 days and lack resources or support networks to remain in housing.
- Families with children or unaccompanied youth who are unstably housed. This applies to families with children or unaccompanied youth who have not had a lease or ownership interest in a housing unit in the last 60 or more days, have had two or more moves in the last 60 days, and who are likely to continue to be unstably housed because of disability or multiple barriers to employment.
- People who are fleeing domestic violence, have no other residence, and lack resources or support networks to obtain other permanent housing.

The HUD definition is generally considered restrictive, especially to families and youth and those who are not identified to be in chronic conditions.

The major competing definition of homelessness comes from the McKinney–Vento Act and the Department of Education (DoE). DoE's *definition* includes students who "…lack a fixed, regular, and nighttime residence" or an

> individual who has a primary nighttime residence that is a) a supervised or publicly operated shelter designed to provide temporary living accommodations; b) an institution that provides a temporary residence for individuals intended to be institutionalized including welfare hotels, congregate shelters, and transitional housing for the mentally ill; or c) a public or private place not designed for, or ordinarily used as, a regular sleeping accommodation for human beings.

Table 2.1 shows the different definitions used by educators, HUD, the Homeless Emergency Assistance and Rapid Transition to Housing (HEARTH) Act, and runaway youth. It highlights how differently homelessness is defined by organizations that serve children and youth. Different government agencies use different definitions to define who is homeless. Definitions dictate policy, which often eliminate identifying young people as homeless.

HUD's definition has been criticized for being too restrictive; public outcry against the limited chronic homeless adult definition resulted as economic conditions plummeted and unveiled rising homelessness in families and youth. HUD responded by changing its definition in 2011 to include programs serving families with children and/or unaccompanied youth. According to the HUD Exchange (2018), the HEARTH Act amended the McKinney–Vento Act, which consolidated HUD's "competitive grant programs," created Continuums of Care (CoC), and broadened services into rural areas. The HEARTH Act defined people who were "at risk of homelessness" to be eligible for services, as shown in Table 2.2, with attention to families and youth. It created guidelines for

Table 2.1 Definitions of Homelessness for Federal Program Serving Children, Youth, and Families

	EDUCATION DEFINITION	HUD DEFINITION – PRIOR TO 2009	HUD DEFINITION – HEARTH ACT – CURRENT	RHYA DEFINITION
Statutory Reference:	Section 725 of Subtitle VII-B of the McKinney-Vento Act	Section 103 of Subtitle I of the McKinney-Vento Act	Section 103 of Subtitle I of the McKinney-Vento Act	Section 387 of the Runaway and Homeless Youth Act
Federal Programs and Agencies Using This Definition:	– Elementary and Secondary Education (ED) – Individuals with Disabilities Education Act (ED) – Higher Education Act (ED) – Head Start Act (HHS) – Child Nutrition Act (USDA) – Violence against Women Act (DOJ)	– Homeless Assistance Programs (HUD) – Emergency Food and Shelter (Homeland Security) – Department of Veterans Affairs (all programs) – Department of Labor (all programs)	– Homeless Assistance Programs (HUD)	Runaway and Homeless Youth Act Programs (HHS)
		LIVING SITUATIONS COVERED BY THESE DEFINITIONS		
Unsheltered Locations	Yes: "(ii) children and youths who have a primary nighttime residence that is a public or private place not designed for or ordinarily used as a regular sleeping accommodation for human beings (within the meaning of section 103(a)(2)(C)); (iii) children and youths who are living in cars, parks, public spaces, abandoned buildings, substandard housing, bus or train stations, or similar settings"	Yes: "an individual who has a primary nighttime residence that is a public or private place not designed for, or ordinarily used as, a regular sleeping accommodation for human beings."	Yes: "an individual or family with a primary nighttime residence that is a public or private place not designed for or ordinarily used as a regular sleeping accommodation for human beings, including a car, park, abandoned building, bus or train station, airport, or camping ground;"	Yes, if the youth cannot live with relatives and has no other safe place to go: "a youth… for whom it is not possible to live in a safe environment with a relative, and who has no other safe alternative living arrangement."

(Continued)

	EDUCATION DEFINITION	HUD DEFINITION – PRIOR TO 2009	HUD DEFINITION – HEARTH ACT – CURRENT	RHYA DEFINITION
Emergency Shelters and Transitional Housing	**Yes:** "children and youth who are living in emergency or transitional shelters"	**Yes:** "a supervised publicly or privately operated shelter designed to provide temporary living accommodations"	**Yes:** "an individual or family living in a supervised publicly or privately operated shelter designated to provide temporary living arrangements"	**Yes, if the youth cannot live with relatives and has no other safe place to go:** "a youth… for whom it is not possible to live in a safe environment with a relative, and who has no other safe alternative living arrangement."
Motels and Hotels	**Yes, if there are no appropriate alternatives:** "children and youth who are living in motels, hotels, trailer parks, or camping grounds due to the lack of alternative adequate accommodations" (emphasis added)	**No, except for "welfare hotels":** "an individual who has a primary nighttime residence that is a supervised publicly or privately operated shelter designed to provide temporary living accommodations (including welfare hotels, congregate shelters, and transitional housing for the mentally ill);"	**Generally, no, except for the following situations:** – "hotels and motels paid for by Federal, State, or local government programs for low-income individuals or by charitable organizations" – "an individual or family who has a primary nighttime residence that is a room in a hotel or motel and where they lack the resources necessary to reside there for more than 14 days, who has no subsequent residence identified; and lacks the resources or support networks needed to obtain other permanent housing;" – "any individual or family who is fleeing, or is attempting to flee, domestic violence, dating violence, sexual assault, stalking, or other dangerous or life threatening conditions in the individual's or family's current housing situation, including where the health and safety of children are jeopardized, and who have no other residence and lack the resources or support networks to obtain other permanent housing"	**Yes, if the youth cannot live with relatives and has no other safe place to go:** "a youth… for whom it is not possible to live in a safe environment with a relative, and who has no other safe alternative living arrangement."

Staying with Others ("Doubled-Up")	Yes, if it is due to loss of housing, economic hardship, or a similar situation (within the definition of lacking fixed, regular, and adequate situations):	No	Generally, no, except the following situations:	Yes, if the youth cannot live with relatives and has no other safe place to go:
	"…individuals who lack a fixed, regular, and adequate nighttime residence (within the meaning of section 103(a)(1)); and (B) includes — (i) children and youths who are sharing the housing of other persons due to loss of housing, economic hardship, or a similar reason;"		"an individual or family who will imminently lose their housing, including housing they are sharing with others, as evidenced by credible evidence indicating that the owner or renter of the housing will not allow the individual or family to stay for more than 14 days, and who has no subsequent residence identified; and who lacks the resources or support networks needed to obtain other permanent housing; – "any individual or family who is fleeing, or is attempting to flee, domestic violence, dating violence, sexual assault, stalking, or other dangerous or life threatening conditions in the individual's or family's current housing situation, including where the health and safety of children are jeopardized, and who have no other residence and lack the resources or support networks to obtain other permanent housing"	"a youth… for whom it is not possible to live in a safe environment with a relative, and who has no other safe alternative living arrangement."

– "unaccompanied youth and homeless families with children and youth defined as homeless under other Federal statutes who have experienced a long term period without living independently in permanent housing; and have experienced persistent instability as measured by frequent moves over such period; and can be expected to continue in such status for an extended period of time because of chronic disabilities, chronic physical health or mental health conditions, substance addiction, histories of domestic violence or childhood abuse, the presence of a child or youth with a disability, or multiple barriers to employment.

(Continued)

	EDUCATION DEFINITION	HUD DEFINITION – PRIOR TO 2009	HUD DEFINITION – HEARTH ACT – CURRENT	RHYA DEFINITION
			– "unaccompanied youth and homeless families with children and youth defined as homeless under other Federal statutes who have experienced a long term period without living independently in permanent housing; and have experienced persistent instability as measured by frequent moves over such period; and can be expected to continue in such status for an extended period of time because of chronic disabilities, chronic physical health or mental health conditions, substance addiction, histories of domestic violence or childhood abuse, the presence of a child or youth with a disability, or multiple barriers to employment."	
"At Risk of Homelessness"	No such definition.	No such definition.	**Defines "at risk of homelessness" to include all families with children and youth defined as homeless under other Federal statutes.** (1) AT RISK OF HOMELESSNESS.–The term 'at risk of homelessness' means, with respect to an individual or family, that the individual or family–	**No such definition. However, RHYA does define "youth at risk of separation from family:"** YOUTH AT RISK OF SEPARATION FROM THE

FAMILY.—The term 'youth at risk of separation from the family' means an individual—
(A) who is less than 18 years of age; and
(B) (i) who has a history of running away from the family of such individual;
(ii) whose parent, guardian, or custodian is not willing to provide for the basic needs of such individual; or
(iii) who is at risk of entering the child welfare system or juvenile justice system as a result of the lack of services available to the family to meet such needs.

(A) has income below 30% of median income for the geographic area;
(B) has insufficient resources immediately available to attain housing stability; and
(C)(i) has moved frequently because of economic reasons;
(ii) is living in the home of another because of economic hardship;
(iii) has been notified that their right to occupy their current housing or living situation will be terminated;
(iv) lives in a hotel or motel;
(v) lives in severely overcrowded housing;
(vi) is exiting an institution; or
(vii) otherwise lives in housing that has characteristics associated with instability and an increased risk of homelessness.

Such term includes all families with children and youth defined as homeless under other Federal statutes.

Note: The two major definitions of homelessness in use by federal agencies are the education definition in Subtitle VII–B of the McKinney-Vento Act, and the Housing and Urban Development (HUD) definition in Section 103 of Subtitle I of the McKinney-Vento Act. The following chart illustrates the similarities and differences between federal agencies' definitions of homeless. In December 2011, HUD issued complex regulations on the HEARTH definition of homelessness.

Table 2.2 HEARTH Act

Criteria for Defining At Risk of Homelessness

Category 1	Individuals and Families	An individual or family who:
		Has an annual income below 30% of median family income for the area; AND
		Does not have sufficient resources or support networks immediately available to prevent them from moving to an emergency shelter or another place defined in Category 1 of the "homeless" definition; AND
		Meets one of the following conditions:
		  Has moved because of economic reasons 2 or more times during the 60 days immediately preceding the application for assistance; OR
		  Is living in the home of another because of economic hardship; OR
		  Has been notified that their right to occupy their current housing or living situation will be terminated within 21 days after the date of application for assistance; OR
		  Lives in a hotel or motel and the cost is not paid for by charitable organizations or by Federal, State, or local government programs for low-income individuals; OR
		  Lives in an SRO or efficiency apartment unit in which there reside more than 2 persons or lives in a larger housing unit in which there reside more than one and a half persons per room; OR
		  Is exiting a publicly funded institution or system of care; OR
		  Otherwise lives in housing that has characteristics associated with instability and an increased risk of homelessness, as identified in the recipient's approved Con Plan

Category 2	Unaccompanied Children and Youth	A child or youth who does not qualify as homeless under the homeless definition, but qualifies as homeless under another Federal statute
Category 3	Families with Children and Youth	An unaccompanied youth who does not qualify as homeless under the homeless definition, but qualifies as homeless under section 725(2) of the McKinney-Vento Homeless Assistance Act, and the parent(s) or guardian(s) or that child or youth if living with him or her.

who constitute being "homeless," "homeless individual," "homeless person," and "homeless individual with a disability" that are to be contained in recordkeeping requirements and one's case file.

Government criteria that someone must meet in order to be considered "at risk" is challenging for many parents and youth to prove. Meeting government definitions is another road-block that plagues people who need help. What exactly are the cut-points that make people at risk? They aren't clear. Inherent in this determination is the notion that housing isn't a right; avoiding "scamming the system" requires that someone must meet arbitrary criteria to be deemed "truly needy" to get assistance.

How HUD and McKinney–Vento came to choose their definitions involved agenda-setting, financial considerations, policy making, turf-staking, and advocacy selection. While schools tend to use McKinney–Vento's, HUD and the National Alliance to End Homelessness (NEFH) use a definition designed to undercount children and families as it focuses on chronically homeless adults with substance or mental illness challenges. Since underlying situations differ for families and adults, it's important to have different definitions for each. The NAEH provides technical assistance to HUD as a paid contractor and plays a major role in defining, explaining, and helping implement HUD's homelessness policies. One could say HUD, the NAEH, and other HUD financially supported agencies have an intertwined, vested interest. While the McKinney–Vento definition is designed broadly so schools can help more children who are in housing distress, the HUD definition is designed to keep people out, not let people in, unless they meet rigorous standards of "truly needy." The HUD definition requires families become destitute or in dire conditions before aid will be awarded. This type of strategy is terrible for children's healthy development and ensuring that parents can support their children in ways that contribute to their success and well-being. Even so, HUD's definition, reports, methodology, and counts are used by almost everyone as the official designations of homelessness in the US. It is showcased in the annual Conference of Mayors Task Force on Homelessness and Hunger reports representing cities larger than 30,000.

The Child Trends database reports that available data on child homelessness are a gross undercount for many reasons and there are no comprehensive, reliable data about the numbers or impact that homelessness has on the developing lives of young children (Shaw 2019). Federal programs lack reliable data on young children's housing status. Federal agencies collect aggregated data from states and communities on housing/homeless programs and rely upon fragmented, uncoordinated data systems, making it especially hard to estimate the number of young children experiencing homelessness. They report that different data collection strategies used by HUD and the DoE make it impossible to compare estimates across the two agencies' datasets, and both agencies' systems show only a segment of the young children experiencing homelessness. HUD misses the bulk of homeless children, since most are doubled-up or not identified. Preschool-child data include those attending public preschools *(1.4 million children in fall 2018)*, which is only 18% of the *8 million 3- to 4-year-old children in the US*. While early care and education (ECE) programs buffer some negative effects of homelessness on children's development, providers often have difficulty identifying families eligible for slots reserved for homeless children.

Homelessness might be the wrong concept to focus upon if we want to prevent people from living in precarious housing arrangements that lead to poorer physical, emotional, and social well-being. The difference between someone who is just getting by and someone who becomes homeless is slim indeed. The problem is definitions determine how homeless people are counted. Counts determine funding. Different agencies use different definitions of homelessness, which affect how various programs determine eligibility for individuals and families at the state and local levels (Katayama 2017). When we look at how to fix homelessness, we have to start with how it is defined.

Sociologists identify front-stage and back-stage behavior; front-stage is what we want people to see and back-stage is what's really going on. HUD's numbers are front-stage by painting a picture of what they want the world to see about family homelessness; back-stage data tell a different story than what's in HUD's PIT count. Boone (2019) reflects on how individual homeless people are counted one by one and a multiplier used to estimate how many people might be living in a car or tent.

> PIT counts are widely understood to undercount the number of people experiencing homelessness by a significant margin—some experts say by half or more. After spending a few hours scouring the predawn streets of Oakland, I have a better understanding why critics of the count say its numbers are both far too low and too unreliable to be used as a sole basis for understanding a region's homelessness service needs.

He found that enumerators missed homeless people who didn't fit HUD's definition, that unless seen, homeless people weren't identified or counted, and counting people at 6 am at the end of January missed many homeless people, especially families with children, who were more likely to be hunkered down in alcoves, cars, or couch-surfing than being on the street. HUD counts only people who are literally homeless, so if someone stayed in a motel or someone's couch for the night, they are not considered homeless. Big counts are discouraged at the federal level, since it means the more homeless people identified, the more money they have to pay for services. Local organizations may actually get a monetary bonus if they can demonstrate their numbers went down since a decrease can convey they were effective in reducing homelessness, and they were therefore a good use of HUD dollars. HUD provides the major funding for assisting homeless people. Organizations understand the politics of the count and may lowball numbers to show they're making progress even if it's not the case.

Welfare: Another Definitional Pothole

Welfare pertains to community well-being and is ideologically a positive concept. Welfare programs are broad and help people across the income spectrum. Some best-known ones include Temporary Assistance for Needy Families, Medicaid, Medicare, Supplemental Nutrition Assistance Programs, Supplemental Security Income, Earned Income Tax Credit, and housing assistance, childcare, Head Start, WIC, heating assistance, Pell grants for college education, school lunch programs, adoption and foster care services, Job Corps, weatherization and energy assistance, disability services, and health care, education, and transportation services. But welfare has become associated with hand-outs to poor people and has taken on negative connotations.

Welfare to the rich costs the taxpayer more than welfare to the poor but ironically isn't viewed as welfare. That is reframed as incentives, benefits, or positive distribution of people or organizations (since tax laws now regard organizations as people). Welfare to the rich include government subsidies to corporations that cost taxpayers billions annually. Wealthy tax breaks cost taxpayers over $100 million each year, most going to the wealthiest 1% (Quigley 2014). Unlike welfare to the poor, wealthy welfare recipients are praised for their work and contributions to society.

Welfare to the poor is now associated with fraud and criminality.

> Many of the current welfare policies and practices are far removed from promoting the actual welfare of low-income parents and their children. The public desire to deter and punish welfare cheating has overwhelmed the will to provide economic security to vulnerable members of society. While welfare use has always borne the stigma of poverty, it now also bears the stigma of criminality.
>
> (Gustafson 2009: 644)

Welfare practices involve stigmatization, surveillance, and regulation of the poor. They assume a latent criminality among the poor. Yet hard-to-prove white-collar crime costs taxpayers much more while penalties for violators are usually minor.

The point is that the definition and perception of welfare vary depending on who is doing the labeling and who is being labeled. The amount of money that taxpayers spend is viewed in a disparaging way when it comes to the poor but seen as deserving when it comes to the rich. Definitions, methodologies, and data interpretations are part of the game that leaders use to keep the status quo intact and homelessness viable.

The Politics of Methodology

Definitions influence methodologies, which influence counts, which influence our understanding of homelessness, which influences policies and funding, which influence services, which influence whether we have homelessness or not. Got all that? That's why understanding definitions and methodologies is important.

Pleace (2016: 25) asserts that "homelessness research....is still uncomfortably close to being a conceptually inconsistent mess." Evidence about homelessness has undergone radical change in the last 25 years, but both scholars and the public often fail to comprehend its current form. Causal sequences need to be updated, since analyses show that support needs and problematic behaviors associated with long-term homelessness don't always predate homelessness but can arise during, and as a result of, homelessness. Relying on administrative data, service contract evaluations, funding reimbursements, and focus on subgroups aren't reflective of the whole homeless population (Culhane and Byrne 2010).

The US Census is supposed to count everyone but doesn't (Frey 2010). It has been faulted for years because it failed to count certain groups of people, especially those who are homeless, immigrant, or refugees. Other studies have been criticized for making sampling decisions that include some groups but not others. Going into nontraditional housing locations to count or study homeless people has been unnerving for some researchers, who are unfamiliar with locales and accepted stereotype of homeless people as dangerous. Many are oblivious to where homeless people (especially youth) might be found. Thus the Census has not been an accurate measure of homelessness individuals.

The definition by HUD is designed to undercount people while DoE's definition is designed to include them. HUD's definition has greatly reduced the population of homelessness without spending a cent. Lower numbers convey HUDs programs are successful. HUD figured out that if you eliminate on paper who is counted, they won't show up in HUD's Annual Homeless Assessment Report (AHAR) (HUD Exchange 2017), and if they don't show up there, Congress will be none the wiser, eliminating their guilt over not appropriating more funding for homelessness prevention. To illustrate the number confusion:

> On a single night in 2017, 553,742 people were experiencing homelessness in the United States. For every 10,000 people in the country, 17 were experiencing homelessness. Approximately two-thirds (65%) were staying in emergency shelters or transitional housing programs, and about one-third (35%) were in unsheltered locations.
>
> (Henry et al. 2017; HUD Exchange 2017)

While HUD's Point-in-Time (PIT) Count sounds like a legitimate way to count people experiencing homelessness at a point in time, the public doesn't understand why its numbers are flawed. Numbers of homeless people vary over time and location, and many homeless people will not be identified, so are not included in the counts. Therefore, any PIT number is going to be a gross underestimation of the actual number of people who are homeless. The PIT count is required by communities to get HUD funding. In mid-1990s, HUD began requiring communities to submit single applications for homeless assistance under McKinney–Vento Homeless Assistance grants. Now local jurisdictions must participate in HUD's CoC to bring together players to address how they are going to deal with homelessness in their communities. Those at the CoC table tend to be those with vested interests in how funding is distributed locally. Since 2013, their emphasis focuses on Permanent Supportive Housing (PSH) and Rapid Rehousing (RR), especially for those who exhibit mental and physical conditions who might be seen as problematic in downtown areas and contribute to patrons of local businesses to feel uncomfortable. HUD has barely addressed the housing needs of families and youth experiencing homelessness. The dissolution of transitional housing – the mainstay of housing assistance for families – as PSH and RR became the solution du jour is evidence of HUD's disdain for addressing housing needs of families. The lack of priority given to families, reducing the chance on the local CoC level that a program serving families or youth will be funded, is another dead giveaway of their disdain.

A review of the PIT methodology by the National Law Center on Homeless and Poverty (NLCHP), *Don't Count On It*, calls the PIT count "severely flawed." NLCHP dissects the methodology and points out the ultimate flaw of this count and the AHAR report created from the tainted data:

> HUD refers to data from the counts to inform Congress about rates of homelessness in the U.S. and to measure the effectiveness of its programs and policies aimed at decreasing homelessness...many interpret the count as a comprehensive depiction of the crisis and rely on it to inform policy design and implementation decisions.
>
> (p. 9)

But the reality is that bad data = bad decisions.

On the surface, a half million people being homeless sounds like a lot. What HUD failed to admit, and media did not uncover, was behind-the-scenes tinkering with the homeless definition and methodology used to acquire data. Few question the number, most accept it at face-value. Its blanket acceptance reflects HUD's reluctance, and Congress' complicity, to challenge policies and funding for those who need it most. These data indicate that for every 10,000 people in the country, 17 were experiencing homelessness. From our observations, that figure seems unreasonably low. Our previous research indicated that 5–10% of high school students reported being homeless or in serious housing distress (Vissing 1997). In everyday conversation, we encounter people who candidly discuss how hard it is to make ends meet and to afford their homes. HUD's report cited two-thirds (65%) of homeless people were staying in emergency shelters or transitional housing programs, and one-third (35%) were in unsheltered locations. Thirty percent of those in shelters were listed as families, and only 10% of unsheltered people were families. These data don't jive with our understanding of the reality of homelessness. The majority of homeless families we studied were never in shelters. Rather, they lived with other financially marginal people who joined forces just to get by, or with others who put them up so that they wouldn't be on the street. It was common for grandparents or siblings to take in housing-distressed relatives, especially when there were children involved. The low HUD figure is a manifestation of both definitional and sampling decisions.

Findings may be cherry-picked so that certain conclusions are reported that show a particular trend, where other findings are downplayed or not mentioned. Controversial conclusions may be strategically downplayed because of repercussions either for certain organizations or special interest groups with vested interests and agendas. HUD's focus on chronic homelessness is a small part of the population of people in dire housing constraints. As shown in the following figure, while homelessness may be a national problem, chronic homelessness is concentrated in particular geographic areas. These tend to be urban with Florida and California, followed by Texas, New York, and Georgia reporting the highest amounts (Carrier 2015). Family homelessness hasn't received the same attention.

The 2017 PIT counts report that the number of people experiencing homelessness in families with children declined by 5% between 2016 and 2017. They reported 184,661 people in families with children were experiencing homelessness, or 33% of the homeless population. They also reported that there were 40,799 unaccompanied youth (under age 25), with most (88%) being between 18 and 24. Unaccompanied youth were more likely to be unsheltered (55%) than both, all people experiencing homelessness (35%) and all people experiencing homelessness as individuals (48%). They reported 12% more individuals with chronic patterns of homelessness in 2017 than in 2016, but has declined by 27% since 2007, thereby still pointing to HUD's success.

Missing or hidden data could provide a more complete picture of reality. This is true in almost any research project but is especially the case reporting about homelessness. As pointed out, HUD's definition misses huge numbers of people who are homeless or in severe housing distress, and many are not counted. Those staying in motels on their own dime, who lost housing, don't count. Those who were homeless (doubled-up or in motels) before landing in hospitals and jails aren't counted. Those not seen by the enumerators, either because they don't want to be counted or because they're out of view, don't get counted. Babies, toddlers, kids, young adults, parents, and other individuals don't get counted. Estimates range as high as 10 million, as proffered by Nan Roman, NAEH executive director, at a Congressional hearing in 2007:

> We did some preliminary analysis of the Census' American Community Survey data on this issue. It shows that between 2.4 and 10 million individuals are doubled-up for economic reasons. That is 4 to 15 times as many people as are currently considered to be homeless.
>
> (Roman 2007)

Ironically, Ms. Roman's homelessness advocacy organization led the charge against expanding HUD's definition, thus denying millions of people hope for assistance while keeping Congress and the public in the dark about the true scope of homelessness. The gist of the argument was expanding the definition would open floodgates, enabling millions more to qualify for housing assistance.

The US Conference of Mayors has been issuing annual reports on homelessness since 1982, in a well-intentioned effort to highlight hunger and homelessness across America. Their *Report on Hunger and Homelessness* looks at the scope of these issues and describes local and national responses from a selection of 30,000 cities in 24 states. It is released during the Christmas holiday season and is heavily cited in feel-good news stories about hunger, homelessness, and poverty during the season of giving. Methodologically, the survey is only sent to participating cities and is constructed so that questions about homelessness take up about ½ of a page while hunger questions take up 3½ pages. The task force uses HUD's data and interpretation assistance from NAEH in formulating their report. This is an example of how the arbitrary definition taken by HUD has gone forth to shape what others identify as homelessness. It should therefore be no surprise that "trends in the study cities followed the same pattern" (p. 20), which reported a decrease in homeless children and families. HUD's assertion of an 18.5% reduction in family homelessness (2009–2016), which gets picked up in the Mayors' report, is inconceivable: in the aftermath of the Great Recession, which found millions on the street after losing their housing; when the nation reels from an opioid-heroin outbreak that destroys families in every community; when there are record increases of students experiencing homelessness nationwide; staggering income inequality; housing affordability versus family income gaps that have reached record levels; and state budgets that have been ravaged (for a variety of reasons), forcing cutbacks in human services and housing. Few, beyond incensed activists, question data, given the media attention it generates.

As HUD funding failed to dent HUD's signature "chronic homelessness" push, critics accused HUD and Congress of focusing on those individuals exemplifying the extreme characteristics of homelessness– mental illness, addiction, lack of hygiene – typically seen on streets in larger cities and the sample in most studies. Visible in shelters, tent-cities, or soup-kitchens, these, mostly men, are blamed for creating a negative impact on downtown businesses, tourism, and community climate. From the early 1990s to present, families and unaccompanied youth have been all but totally ignored by HUD. Even as DoE identifies 1.3 million homeless students, they remain a minor emphasis of HUD. HUD is criticized for playing a numbers game to show its alleged successes, despite the rise of more families and children living in housing distress. It invented the term "functional zero," which makes it seem like it is successful when the availability of resources in the community exceeds the size of the population needing the resources. Whether homeless people use those resources or are successful from them is irrelevant, since under "functional zero," people remain chronically homeless on the streets even after their communities have "ended" chronic homelessness because there are designated resources that supposedly exist (Duffield 2016).

HUD-funded entities must develop criteria to serve prioritized homeless populations, which excludes the bulk of the homeless population and those at risk of homelessness. Local communities' Coordinated Entry System, by virtue of questions asked, makes it almost impossible for families to get help, including shelter. Instead, those in families and unaccompanied youth who experience homelessness must wait until they fit the definition of "chronically homeless" before getting help. In another example of how HUD prevents people in need of help getting it, its HEARTH Act requires grantees to operate within localized CoCs to match programs and people to end homelessness. But this requires collecting and sharing data, which concerns domestic violence and victim service providers. Preventing domestic violence means not just removing someone from a dangerous housing situation, it requires making sure they have socioeconomic resources needed to maintain safety. HUD's system-wide collection of data conflicts with the Violence against Women Act that prohibits sharing personally identifying information. Shelter providers find it hard to give victims services and protection while complying with two contradictory policy mandates (Duchscherer 2016). Congress is fed flawed data that (only) about 500,000 mostly single people are homeless, omitting millions of families and unaccompanied youth.

The data game boils down to this – if there aren't many homeless people (according to the counts), then we won't think of homelessness as a social problem. By stereotyping individual people as contributing to their own poverty, misery, and housing distress, then we can blame them, not society, for homelessness. But if there are big numbers of homeless individuals, and the numbers reflect demographic characteristics that are similar to the majority of the population – meaning that homelessness could happen to anyone – then chances are increased that the public might demand that something be done. Government and taxpayers don't want to pay more, so it's easier to promote data that pigeonholes homeless people as causing their own distress or that they are somehow different from "the rest of us good, hard-working Americans". It's also more politically efficacious for organizations to tout reductions of homeless people to show that they are effective and are worthy of sustained funding, respect, and support (Loehwing 2018).

How Many People Are Homeless?

Numbers of people who are homeless are symbolic of whether our systems are working. The more homelessness, the greater the proof our systems preventing it has failed. For instance, since Trump has become president, numbers of homeless people have increased, thus an indicator that his economic policies have not been good for the poor and middle classes (Filipovic 2018; Ruiz-Grossman 2018). On the other hand, if reports indicate low numbers, it can be said that homelessness isn't a major problem, that it's more a personal problem than a system problem, and that systems to prevent poverty or help those in need are working.

One of the biggest challenges faced by homelessness researchers is the dominant theory used. Research oft assumes homelessness is a relatively simple, relatively small-scale social problem with clearly understood causes.

> There are concerns that the political right has sought to narrow the definition of what homelessness is, emphasizing only visible homelessness that can be easily linked to individual pathology and drawing attention away from wider structural problems with affordable housing supply and inequity...Beyond this, there is the view of homelessness as individual pathology that dates from before the nineteenth century – a mass cultural understanding of homelessness encompassing only a self-inflicted state found among people in emergency shelters and on the street.... Assumptive research must be challenged because it is based on a clearly false construct of what homelessness is and lacks any social scientific foundation.
>
> (Pleace 2016: 34)

An examination of theory is in Chapter 4.

How many people are homeless? HUD has announced "good news: Homelessness in the U.S. is down," In the mid-2000s, HUD's "Housing first" program made *substantial inroads* against the problem and continued with the Homeless Prevention and Rapid Re-Housing Program. As a result, the nationwide homeless population is reported to have fallen according to their data (Smith 2018a). But has it really?

Both President Bush and Obama were credited with the reduction of homelessness, but few ask "what kind of homelessness" or what sampling and data collection mechanisms were used to come up with the numbers. The push under their programs was on chronic homelessness of single adults. Government data announced homelessness in families with children declined by 5% between 2016 and 2017 – 10,055 fewer people and 3,294 fewer family households. As of 2017, 184,661 people in families with children were reported homeless, 33% of the homeless population. In 2017, 40,799 people under the age 25 experienced homelessness on their own. Most unaccompanied youth (88%) were between the ages of 18 and 24. Unaccompanied youth were more likely to be unsheltered (55%) than both, all people experiencing homelessness (35%) and all people experiencing homelessness as individuals (48%). The report cites an increase of 12% more individuals with chronic patterns of homelessness in 2017 than in 2016 but declined by 27% since 2007. In 2017, HUD reported 554,000 people were homeless, ending six straight years of decline when 637,000 Americans were homeless. This reflected a 9% increase in the number of people experiencing homelessness in unsheltered locations. It also shows that the number of chronically homeless individuals – those who have been without a home for at least a year – increased for the first time since 2008 and jumped by 12% over the prior year (HUD Exchange 2017; Wilson 2017). Reports from the same year (2016) say it's increased (Day 2017), while others say it's decreased (Henry et al. 2017). Either way, officials state that reported estimates are low (Dickrell 2016). Frequent estimates range widely: half-million (Henry et al. 2017); 2–3 million people; 13.5 million (Link 1995); and in a single article, statistics range from 64,708 people, 206,286 people in families, 358,422 individuals, 83,170 individuals considered "chronically homeless," 47,725 homeless veterans, 1.4 million veterans at risk of homelessness, 550,000 unaccompanied, single youth, and young adults under the age of 24, 380,000 of that total are under the age of 18, 110,000 LGBTQ youth in the US are homeless, and 50% of the homeless population being over the age of 50 (Social Solutions 2016).

Eyes blurred and confused yet? If you have problems making heads-or-tails about how many people are homeless in the US, you're not alone. As you see from those numbers, the "how much" question morphs into "what kinds of people" and data are all over the board. Some data indicate that 40% of homeless people are addicts and another 25% have severe mental illness – constituting 65% of all homeless people (Gatto 2018), while others point out that these figures reflect counting stereotypes, especially those that correspond to HUD's definition – and don't reflect the majority of homeless families and youth.

HUD's 2016 Annual Homeless Assessment Report to Congress counted 64,197 homeless family households while the Department of Education counted 1.2 million homeless children. Annual counts of homelessness are important because data are used to make funding and policy decisions, like which states and organizations get funding, what services are needed, what prevention programs hold the most promise, and so on. If Congress is looking for justifications on how to cut the budget and not spend more than they have to, they may find HUD's numbers appealing. If they are looking at how to shore up families so that children will have a fighting chance to be healthy and successful, then DoE numbers would be chosen – which could result in greater expenditures.

Family and Child Homelessness Counts

When it comes to family homelessness, all researchers agree that they are undercounted for a variety of reasons (Bassuk Center 2018a; Doorways 2018; Green Doors 2019). Their numbers point to similar trends – that family and child homelessness is a significant problem.

The Bassuk Center on Homeless and Vulnerable Children's letter to the Boston Globe (2018a) points out data typically used by US authorities to count homeless people vastly underestimate the number of homeless children and families:

> HUD's flawed methodology does not account for hundreds of thousands of children or their parents who have become invisible to the system. The agency's "Point-in-Time" approach counts only people in shelters, in transitional housing, or seen on the streets. Of the 1.3 million homeless school-age children and youth, more than 80% are missed, since only 13.9% of these kids are staying in shelters and just 3.7% are in the streets.

Among industrialized nations, the US has the largest number of homeless women and children; not since the Great Depression have so many families been without homes. Homeless families are estimated to comprise 37% of the homeless population. Over 84% of families experiencing homelessness are female-headed. Among homeless women, 60% have children under age 18, but only 65% of them live with at least one of their children, while among all homeless men, 41% have children under age 18, but only 7% live with at least one of their children. Half (42%–51%) of children in homeless families are under age six. Studies report that families of color are over-represented in the homeless population and mothers may have limited education – 53% of homeless mothers don't have a high school diploma and only 29% of mothers work (Green Doors 2019).

But these numbers are derived from visible, obtainable homeless families – not the ones who fly under the radar. While helpful, they point to a visible homeless population. It doesn't jive with other data that include a more diverse, educated, employed, and once-middle-class group of people. Families who are counted are those for whom the bottom has fallen out completely; figures and profiles may not include those who are less visible and exist just above the official cut-point for poverty or homeliness designations. Just because they aren't counted doesn't mean they aren't there.

Child homeless data are particularly subject to the methodological biases discussed earlier in this chapter. The article *Public Schools Report Highest Number of Homeless Students on Record, While HUD Claims Reduction in Family and Youth Homelessness* (Family Promise 2018) finds HUD's 2018 Annual Homeless Assessment Report Part I (AHAR) estimates that on a single night in January 2018, 180,000 parents and children were experiencing homelessness. According to HUD's numbers, this is a 2% decrease from 2017, and a 23% decrease since 2007. However, other studies report significant increases in child and family homelessness. For example, the DoE (National Center for Homeless Education 2019) reported that 1,354,363 homeless children and youth were identified in the 2016–2017 school year by public schools, a 4% increase from 2015–2016 and a 70% increase from 2007–2008. Head Start programs also reported record levels of homeless children, from 26,200 homeless children in 2007–2008 to 52,764 in 2016–2017 – a 100% increase.

State homeless liaisons who know the children, their districts, and the data recognize this disparity. In Davie County, NC, there has been a 38% increase in homeless students from 2015–2016 and a 98% increase from the 2009–2010 school year (NCHE 2019). Data from the New Hampshire Department of Education report that there has been a steady increase in numbers of reported children in recent years. Three-quarters (72%) of these students live doubled-up with others. Only 14% live in shelters. Relying upon shelter data as an indicator of actual numbers of homeless children undoubtedly represents just a fraction of the actual numbers of homeless children (Elliott 2018).

The 2018 AHAR claims that 36,361 unaccompanied youth under age 25 were experiencing homelessness – but public schools reported 118,364 unaccompanied homeless youth, an increase of 6% since the 2015–2016 school year, the highest number on record. A first-of-its kind study on unaccompanied youth homelessness in America, *Missed Opportunities: Youth Homelessness in America* identified 4.2 million young people experienced unaccompanied homelessness over a 12-month period. The National Center for Homeless Education (2018) found 76% of students experiencing homelessness double-up with others due to loss of housing, economic hardship, or family issues. Shelters are the next most commonly used type of housing, but only 14% of homeless students resided in shelters. Six percent had a primary nighttime residence at hotels or motels, and 4% were identified as unsheltered. Unsheltered student numbers grew the most, with a 27% increase. Staying in hotels and motels increased by 10%, continuing a trend, while doubled-up students increased by 7%. The number of students staying in shelters only increased by 3% over the three-year period. The change in unaccompanied homeless youth was the most marked of the subgroups, with an increase of 25%. Additionally, unaccompanied youth make up 10% or more of the homeless student population in 28 states, up from 20 states in the previous school year. Students who are English learners increased by 19% and now account for 16% of students in homeless situations. The category for homeless students with a disability saw an increase of 14%. While only 13% of all students have an identified disability, nearly 62% of states reported a proportion of homeless students with disabilities of 20% or more. According to data from the National Center for Homeless Education at University of North Carolina Greensboro (2019), states provided an average per pupil amount of $79.61 in federal McKinney–Vento funding to school districts for additional supports needed by homeless students in 2016–2017.

In 1998, the National Survey of Homeless Assistance Providers and Clients estimated families comprised 34% of the homeless population; 23% were children and 11% were adults in homeless families (Burt 1999). Since that time, estimates are all over the board, including 420,000 families and 924,000 children. Schools are regarded as the one institution that has contact with all school-age children and are in the position to come up with more accurate figures than other organizations. Since 1987, schools have been required under federal law to monitor homelessness, and the DoE requires schools include families that have "doubled-up" among their counts of homeless students. That's critical because doubling-up is an enormous, hidden portion of America's homeless population. But while DoE tracks this data point, HUD's point-in-time survey doesn't (Institute for Children, Poverty and Homelessness 2018a). As shown in Figure 2.2, many homeless children are living doubled-up with others families, especially in the middle and western part of the US.

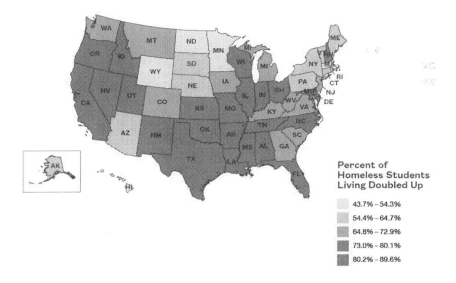

Percent of
Homeless Students
Living Doubled Up

43.7% – 54.3%
54.4% – 64.7%
64.8% – 72.9%
73.0% – 80.1%
80.2% – 89.6%

Figure 2.2 Where Doubled-Up Homeless Students Live.
Note: "Doubled-Up" refers to homeless students identified by schools as staying with others when they were initially found eligible under the McKinney-Vento law.
Source: U.S. Department of Education, "ED Data Express," http://www.eddataexpress.ed.gov.

Separating number of homeless families from numbers of homeless children is very challenging. Counting children (anyone under age 18) who are with their parents, grandparents, extended family, guardians, in foster care, or unaccompanied is really complicated. School-based data are useful but only for those who are in school and identified as homeless. Younger children and those whose housing distress is hidden are undocumented. Safe to say, there aren't accurate figures on most any of those categories of young people, and the numbers available are likely gross undercounts. National data point out the increase of all children who are homeless, even those who are in kindergarten and primary school (Figure 2.3.)

Under the DoE definition, schools identified 1.3 million homeless students in 2015–2016, doubling since 2006 when schools were first required to tabulate the number of homeless students. The number of young homeless children enrolled in Head Start increased by 92% over approximately the same period, and these are primarily children from poverty-stricken homes (Duffield 2016; Duffield and Lovell 2008). The DoE definition reflects the reality for most households that become homeless – few head directly to shelters and many communities lack shelters anyway. Staying with family/friends is typical. Bouncing in and out of motels is common. Avoiding the authorities who might pose a threat to families staying together isn't unusual. Hiding your circumstances because of shame or embarrassment is normal. Sometimes people may not identify they are homeless but on "hard times." Many districts fail to identify homeless students, either because the educators don't recognize signs of homelessness or because students/families don't identify as homeless when registering. Schools occasionally turn away homeless

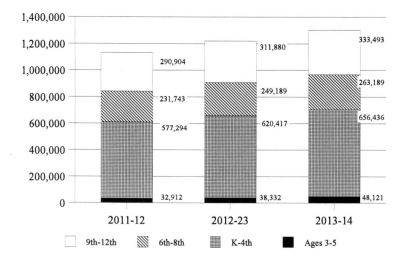

Figure 2.3 Increases in Homelessness among Students, by Grade Level.

Source: National Center for Homeless Education, Federal Data Summary: School Years, 2011–12 to 2013–14, November 2015.

students, illegally, for a number of reasons, including the stigma of having homeless students, the financial burden districts may incur serving students without housing, or fear standardized test results could be negatively impacted. All these reasons put districts in violation of the federal law guaranteeing educational rights to students experiencing homelessness. The numbers don't report babies, toddlers, or youth not attending school. Thus even the DoE numbers are a significant undercount.

The Institute for Children, Poverty and Homelessness (2018 b,c) finds that child homelessness is both an urban and a rural problem. As examples, New York State is home to two-thirds of reported homeless students in the Northeast. In Washington, DC, the homeless student population grew by 66% over three years. While rural homelessness increased by 11% nationwide, states like Minnesota experienced a growth of over 50%. The number of homeless students living in shelter in South Dakota doubled over three years, while New Mexico's unsheltered homeless student population quadrupled during the same period and over one-third of homeless children in Georgia live in rural areas. New Jersey's student homelessness grew fastest of any state in the past three years; 10% is a conservative estimate of how many students might be homeless based on the free lunch number, which indicates that there are probably 45,000 homeless students in New Jersey – but the school reported only 12,000. The gap of 33,000 students means many students aren't receiving services for which they are entitled under McKinney–Vento (Duffield 2016). Two-thirds of Maryland's homeless students live in the suburbs. From Seattle to Philadelphia and New York, from Texas to Ohio to Virginia to California, homeless students are flooding schools and communities (Institute for Children, Poverty and Homelessness 2018a). It's time to pay attention to their presence and what it means for them today and for all of us tomorrow.

In sum, estimates of homeless children range from 1.3 to 2.5 million annually. Researchers estimate that over 200,000 children have no place to live. The Institute for Children, Poverty and Homelessness (2018a) points out the difference methodology makes:

- HUD reported that there were 460 homeless people in families in St. Louis, MO. But St. Louis's public schools reported to the Department of Education that 5,451 children were identified as homeless in 2016 – more than 1000% more.
- San Diego, CA, reported 1,714 homeless people in families to HUD last year, but the San Diego City School District alone reported 7,082 homeless students.
- Tampa, FL, counted 533 homeless people in families in their HUD count, but Tampa's schools found 3,311 homeless students in the district.

Data from schools counted 1,065,794 homeless students during the 2010/2011 school year. Four years later, the same survey found 1,263,323 homeless students – a 19% increase. But the US Interagency Council on Homelessness, which uses HUD's numbers, claims a "steady reductions of people experiencing homelessness," including a "23% reduction in family homelessness" from 2010 to 2016.

Changing Our Understanding of Family Homelessness

If we want to understand how to "fix" homelessness, we have to start by fixing the definition. Current definitions have been designed to limit the numbers of homeless people – especially children and families. The amount of distress that families are experiencing is real, and likely to get worse, despite what partisan pundits portray.

If we see homelessness as a condition that begins and ends with housing, then housed people are no longer homeless. This could mean that people couch-surfing at the home of others aren't homeless, neither are those who are in winter-rentals, or those in shelters, foster care, residential facilities, or any number of temporary housing conditions. Rapidly rehousing a homeless child, family, or adult does not guarantee that the reasons for their housing, economic status and instability will be resolved just because they have a roof over their head. When we spend half of our income on housing costs, when our salaries can't finance necessities like food, transportation, medical care, or shoes, homelessness becomes both predictable and inevitable. No one making $13,000 a year and spending $9,000 on housing can make ends meet. Add in one unexpected crisis, illness, domestic violence, divorce, job loss, or "straw that broke the camel's back," people are thrust into homelessness. "It's one thing to want to ensure that no one lives on the streets. It's entirely another to aspire to get at the root of the problem by providing families with stability and opportunity" (Institute for Children, Poverty and Homelessness 2018a).

Since 2007, a piece of bipartisan legislation has held a significant solution to this homeless definition issue: the Homeless Children and Youth Act (HCYA). The bipartisan HCYA, H.R. 1511/S. 611, addresses shortcomings in HUD's counts and makes improvements in federal policies to serve homeless families and youth. It aligns HUD's definition of homelessness with those of other federal agencies and permits communities to use HUD homeless funding more flexibly to assess and serve the most vulnerable homeless children, youth, and families identified in their area.

Advocates have steadfastly pursued developing support for the bill, which would, in essence, align HUD's definition of homelessness with the more comprehensive one used by the DoE and other agencies (Bassuk Center on Homeless and Vulnerable Children 2018c). At a congressional hearing held in June 2018 to examine the merit of the HYCA, compelling testimony was provided by Kat Lilley, Deputy Director of Family Promise of Colorado Springs, who was previously homeless with her six children:

> Expanding the PIT count brings families out of the shadows and aligns the public perception of homelessness with the reality. In addition, it would allow for more accurate trend tracking for children and youth homelessness. It would also expand private funding opportunity by demonstrating the need and demand for assistance for children and youth experiencing homelessness and help mobilize community responses for the currently invisible homeless population.
>
> (Newswires 2018)

HCYA was approved by the House Financial Services Committee on a bipartisan basis in 2018. While the legislation focuses on children and youth, it could reduce homelessness among all populations by helping to prevent today's homeless children and youth from becoming tomorrow's homeless adults. The hundreds of organizations supporting HCYA – service providers, educators, and child advocates – urge Congress to approve the bill without delay, allowing communities to accurately identify the children, youth, and adults experiencing homelessness and to tailor local responses to effectively serve their needs.

If we continue to follow historical and current trends, we can anticipate more poverty, more homelessness, more severe situations for children's development, more people needing help as social structures become designed to keep people out instead of letting people in as a way to curb skyrocketing government expenditures. It could become normative if we don't change our definitions, methodologies, and paradigms for understanding and addressing family homelessness.

Notes

1 www.schoolhouseconnection.org/house-hearing-on-homeless-children-and-youth/.
2 Winnie Byanyima. https://blogs.oxfam.org/en/blogs/19-02-01-video-inequality-has-gone-viral-so-what-next.

3   Why Did We Get Here

Theoretical Explanations of Homelessness

How we choose to address homelessness isn't random – it stems from a long history of theoretical and situational underpinnings. How one goes about addressing a problem depends on why you think it's happening. People have different ideas about why homelessness is occurring and what should be done. This explains disagreement about what homeless people are like and how to address homelessness. Understanding theory helps elevate one's discourse on the issue.

Stratification Theories

Socrates and Plato's Republic introduced the notion that God created people from the earth and each person's soul has mixed into them a metal that reflects their worth. Sometimes referred to as "the noble lie" or "the myth of the metals," people born of gold were destined to be leaders, those of silver were to be soldiers – the protectors of the state, and those of the least desirable metals, bronze and iron, were doomed to be laborers who produced things for the better metals (Stanford 2018). This notion that some people are worth more than others continues into today. The idea that rich people (gold) are more valuable than those who labor (iron) can be seen in contemporary stratification and social class systems.

People get stratified, or ranked, into social categories from high to low, which impacts access to wealth, prestige, and power. This theoretical approach assumes that resources are not evenly distributed and that one's placement, or social class, on the stratification spectrum influences their quality of life. Designation of social class includes factors like education, lifestyle, and reputation. Money tends to be the primary variable influencing social placement. People's ascribed and achieved statuses influence placement within these different strata and our success, marginalization, or oppression. For instance, men continue to have a higher status than women, whites more than nonwhites, people from Judeo-Christian faiths more so than other religions, college graduates over high school drop-outs, and so on. Republicans are more likely than Democrats to see the economic system as fair and rich people having earned their wealth, and that poverty is the result of people not working hard enough, rather than having unequal advantages (Dunn 2018).

Data from a variety of sources show that the top 1% wields the most power, while 85% of the population scrambles to "make-it." The top 1% of wealthiest Americans inherited their money or obtained it from investments or entrepreneurial endeavors. The middle class is shrinking from around 30%, while the lower half of the social classes have increased in number as financial struggle and poverty have increased. Once homelessness was territory of the lower strata, but it has crept into the middle class. Today, almost nobody is immune from potential housing distress. Add into the mix the intersection of social-placement variables and the risk for homelessness increases exponentially. If someone is a nonwhite, poorly educated single mother with no savings, childcare challenges, and a job that doesn't pay a livable wage who lives in a community where there is little available, affordable housing, these ingredients combine to make poverty and homelessness almost an inevitability.

There is an attitudinal dimension of social class. Our experience colors the way we see the world and others. As long as there are others beneath us in the strata, we share a warped sense of comfort, an "at least I'm not on the bottom" mentality. But it is accompanied by fear that if something unfortunate happens, we could fall downward. When you're barely hanging on to what you have now, the loss of income, status, respect, and opportunity is a real concern. Mutz (2019) points to fear people have over losing status to explain the outcome of the 2016 presidential election; in this social dominance theory, while economic loss was a concern for middle- and working-class voters, fear of losing their social position and influence attracted them to Trump because he spoke to their concern over losing social positions and privileges to nonwhites and immigrants.

There is a method to the madness of keeping others oppressed. If women, nonwhites, immigrants, and the poor rise up and claim limited resources, then middle and upper classes could fall down the stratification ladder. Hence, they need to be kept down "in their place." Many imagine that there is a "fixed pie" of social and economic resources; that is, if one person or group gets a larger slice, others will necessarily get less. This ignores the fact that the total size of the pie can decrease or increase depending on many factors, including the levels of social cooperation and technological innovations.

Meritocracy raises people's anxiety about receiving money, respect, or social rewards. Those who "earn" them through talent, effort, or achievement are viewed more positively than those who fail to achieve them. People who don't are viewed as failures who don't deserve assistance. This meritocracy view fails to consider how huge segments of the population experience institutional discrimination, socially structured inequality, and don't have avenues that allow them to succeed. The saga that "anyone can make it if they try hard enough" just isn't true, especially for nonwhite youth (Anderson 2016). Hiring people on the basis of established merit instead of potential results in replication of the traditional status quo.

A Massachusetts Institute of Technology study of 9,000 employees suggested that meritocracy reinforces bias; while performance is supposed to be the basis for salary increases, women, minorities, and immigrants have to work harder and obtain higher performance scores in order to receive similar salary increases to white men. Studies repeatedly show that stereotypes of all kinds (gender, ethnicity, age, disability, etc.) are filters through which we evaluate others that advantage dominant groups and disadvantage lower-status groups (Cooper 2014, 2015; Young 1958).

Social Drift Theory

The fact that some people have easy, abundant lives while others experience challenge and scarcity isn't new. Some religions view people living "the good life" as deserving and blessed by God; those without are seen as forsaken. Max Weber (1905) thought the Protestant ethic reinforced the development of capitalism; since one couldn't know if they were to be "saved" in the Kingdom of God, they looked for tangible indicators here on earth. People who had big families, money, fine homes, and influence must be blessed, whereas the sick, poor, with no one to care for them, must be cursed. People were likened to milk, where the rich *crème de la crème* floated to the top and the less desirable milk sunk to the bottom. Being "cream of the crop" was socially desirable. There must be something inherently less desirable, or bad, about those who couldn't make it. There must be something wrong with those at the bottom of the barrel, where those who drifted to the top must have something very special about them.

During the Victorian era, poor and homeless people were viewed as blameworthy for their distress. Moral lapses, criminal activity, choices not to work honestly, or drinking too much caused their tragedies (Higginbotham 2014; Kelleher 2019; Kennedy 2015; O'Sullivan 2008; Pleace 2016). This approach is still embedded into cultural perceptions of homeless people. This view holds that those who are homeless must be dumb, lazy, mentally ill, addicts, sick, or deficient in some way. It's seen in views that homelessness is caused by "the ravages of substance abuse and mental illness" (Baum and Burns 1994). One finding in social sciences is the negative correlation of mental illness with socioeconomic status, with those in the poorest social strata having two to three times the risk of mental illness compared with those in the highest strata (Dohrenwend et al. 1992; Scott 1993). Data tend to show the poverty's prevalence of comorbid diagnoses, including substance abuse, physical and mental illness (Kessler et al. 2007).

Data suggest that personal dysfunction does not accurately portray homeless children or families (Burt 1999; Pleace 2016; Vissing 1997). Homeless children and families haven't been researched as much or provided needed services because they don't fit the mentally ill, substance abuser typology. When they are discussed, there is a tendency to view them as dysfunctional and blamed for their homelessness. This is why advocates for homeless children, youth, and families have become incensed over this wrong-headed application of research at one level being applied to another.

Two general hypotheses occur to explain homelessness. One is that people who are mentally ill or drug users become poor and homeless because of their infirmities. The other is that when typical people are confronted with toxic stress, whether prolonged or traumatic, that mental illness or drug use is a reaction to that stress. This causal link is often misunderstood in the general public's eye. It is easy to look at homeless people and assume mental illness or drug use is the cause, rather than the effect, of poverty and stress. If one starts with the domain assumption that homeless people have something wrong with them, samples and methodologies get constructed that ensure that those findings emerge. This bias is undoubtedly at work with studies on the chronically homeless and homeless families and children.

Focusing on personal, rather than social-structural, dysfunction obscures social and economic issues that set the stage for developing such troubles. Contemporary research has mostly supported the hypothesis that social stress, lack of supports, and other forms of social marginalization lead to mental illness. Only limited data are available on the social drift hypothesis, that mental illnesses develop endogenously, due to biological and genetic causes, that causes people to become poor and homeless (Hudson 2012).

Social factors like economic inequality, gentrification of skid row neighborhoods, criminalization policies, lack of access to services and affordable housing, or blaming the victim for being deficient, disabled, and destitute continue to be stereotyped explanations that don't fit homeless individuals and families. While the public and pundits gravitate to the drift explanations, data don't uphold its validity.

Functionalism

Basic premises of this theory are what's good for society is more important than what's good for particular individuals, the existing social order is supported by the status quo and challenging the way things are done will cause disruptions, and rules are created that people are supposed to follow because it will allow society to run more smoothly. Theorists see institutional connectedness – if times are good for the economy, families and businesses tend to flourish; during economic depressions, people may lose their homes, health care, and jobs.

Functionalists tend to defend the status quo, avoid social change, and believe people should cooperate to support the existing social order. Leaders rise to high positions because they allegedly have insights and abilities to lead a society forward in certain directions. Functionalism sees societies operating best when there is stability leading toward advancement of society.

Social cohesion is important; challenging the status quo may upset the apple cart and cause disruptions. Things that aren't in the best interest of the status quo may be deemed dysfunctional.

Early functionalists lived during a time of growing industrialization, capitalism, and innovation. Contributing to the advancement of society was a priority. Communities created institutions that promoted greater functionality. Emphasis was on helping to maintain the status quo and creating homeostasis to move society forward in a smooth fashion. Having a job, a home, being a productive member of society, taking care of yourself, and not asking for help were seen as admirable qualities because they moved a society forward without requiring outside interventions. People who are hard-working and compliant with the demands of authorities receive positive reinforcements in the forms of wealth, prestige, and power, while negative reinforcements are directed to those who don't to keep them in line.

As social change occurred, not everyone advanced, so theorists identified individual and social explanations. Homelessness can be seen as socially dysfunctional because it violates the assumption that a community is a place of care and opportunity for everyone. Societies may feel obligated to "do something" about homelessness, which costs money and effort. By giving poor people aid, it may send the message that people can get help even if they don't work, thereby undercutting the requirement that everyone works and is productive.

Homelessness, like wealth or poverty, is a product of social construction. Herbert Gans (1971, 2012) alleges that poverty is functional for society – or at least for people who stand to benefit from it. These may be taxpayers, corporate and political leaders, and even the general public. There are economic benefits that elite groups gather. There are also socio-emotional benefits that the public gains from knowing that there are people below them on the social stratification ladder. This is observed in attitudes such as "I may be poor, but at least I'm not homeless." We see it in the job sector where workers feel emboldened when they learn they make more than another employee or that they get a bigger bonus than others. It is seen by people who proudly announce they live in certain residential neighborhoods or that their houses are worth a large amount of money. Poor people recognize they have limited options and provide a labor pool to do the dirty work for low wages that others don't want to do, whether it's waiting on or cleaning up after them. A mother from New York City begged us for suggestions for what her son could do because he felt the only way for him to get food and shelter was to join the Army; she feared her son would be sent away to front lines and be what poor people have been for years – fodder for the military.

It has been also proposed that extreme poverty, and especially homelessness, serves a disciplinary function (Hopper and Hamburg 1986), in that it functions as a public "exhibit" of what may happen to a person should they not adhere to conventional social norms. This is not unlike practices of public shaming conducted in the colonial era. In this way, it is believed that the wider society has a vested interest in maintaining a focus on the suffering of the homeless, and their more bizarre behaviors and symptoms. One of the first to study homelessness was Nels Anderson (1923), who studied "bummery" or "hobohemia" in Chicago. Transient men were regarded as lesser than those who were stably housed and employed. While environmental influences, like lack of jobs, contributed to homelessness, people didn't blame the social structure since many people had jobs – rather, they blamed individuals for their lack of well-being.

This position is seen in the Welfare to Work programs – unless you show you are trying to better yourself and do something for society, you won't receive benefits. Having a home, health care, food, or modest life-style aren't entitlements – they are privileges that one has to earn. It embodies an assumption that people asking for aid are lazy and could work if pushed. It fails to take into account that the majority of homeless people and people who are in need of assistance are working, single moms, sick, disabled, elderly, children, or cannot work jobs most available to them (Dupere 2015; Godoy and Aubrey 2017).

This theory assumes that we don't end homelessness or poverty because it is so emotionally beneficial and financially lucrative for some groups. We may provide a little help to the poor in order to make ourselves feel better about helping the needy, but we seldom take measures that would truly lift them out of poverty. This notion that we don't want to get rid of poverty is essential to understanding why big business is allowed to rake huge profits from those kept impoverished.

While homelessness is dysfunctional for individuals, changing institutional policies, laws, and services to assist them will have ripple-out effects on other institutions and the government, the family, and the use of goods and services. People are expected to bend to meet the needs of institutions, rather than institutions bending to meet the demands of the individuals. Conversely, if institutions can see change will benefit them and help them to function better, shifts may be accomplished. This is why cost-benefit analyses are used to show society that preventing homelessness may inevitably cost less and yield better outcomes than models currently used.

Conflict Theory

Conflict theories suggest that capitalism is the main cause of homelessness; homelessness is not a consequence of individual shortcomings but flaws in society itself. Power struggles between social classes are a result of the capitalistic society. While functionalists try to co-opt people's behavior and attitudes in order to run a smooth running society, conflict theorists think by challenging the status quo and the social order they created, beneficial change can occur. People in power must be challenged or overthrown in order to bring justice

to the oppressed. People in power (bourgeoisie) create and promote structures, rules, and ideologies that benefit them, while workers and those without power (proletariats) have their lives formed around normative exploitation
(Marx 1964). Conflict, not homeostasis, is seen as essential to the development
of society. Rich and powerful people force the poor and weak to do their
bidding; business owners exploit workers by not giving them resources to
get food and shelter. The power elite develop alignments with others, sub-
sidiaries of organizations, and convoluted systems that are not transparent to
the public's eye in order to maintain wealth, prestige, power, and control of
financial assets and people's maintenance of the status quo (Mills 1956).

People in charge don't just manipulate people's jobs, incomes, and
opportunities they also manipulate the way they want people to think.
Workers are under the impression that they are taken care of properly,
because their bosses say so. They rely on business owners to take care of
them. The theory suggests that the bourgeoisie, or people in power, do
not have the working class' best interest at heart; their goal is simply to
accumulate wealth by any means necessary. They may use media or other
means to denigrate people who don't work or comply with the rules they
create, rules designed to keep people in line. Bourgeoisies argue wealth
is earned through hard work, dedication, and determination, and not be
handed over to others (unless they are family members, who are regarded
as justified to inherit the wealth of their forbearers). People in positions of
power regard the poor and homeless as unmotivated, uneducated, lazy, and
willing to be taken care of by others. This way of thinking is called false
consciousness and is inherent in keeping the stratification system intact.

The Declaration of Independence states that it is the right of the people
to alter or abolish governments that aren't adhering to honoring the needs
of all citizens. However, proletariats lack power, can't access information
that could help them, and have lives so filled with struggle and strife that
they are beaten down and emotionally subjugated, all of which make it
difficult for them to challenge the existing social order. Under-dogs are
not in positions where they can change laws or funding streams; they are
too busy trying to survive to do so. In this view, few people in authority
listen to a homeless person or regard them as equal partners. Homeless
people need advocates to speak for them. Elites occupy positions of leadership within dominant social institutions. They develop alignments with
leaders in other institutions who share belief systems, resources, and agendas. The result is that ordinary people are rendered impotent, powerless,
with lives manipulated by elites. Leaders are far removed from the daily
struggles common people face and insulate themselves with views that
justify their oppression of others (Mills 1956). For example, many organizations that serve homeless people don't have poor or homeless people
on their boards or staff. Homeless people may be regarded as objectified
commodities that provide jobs for others who gain social credibility for
their willingness to help the unfortunate destitute.

The conflict approach has variants to it that are worthwhile to consider. These include gender and racially based approaches. Structural discrimination against women prevails, especially in the employment, childcare, and economic sectors, which results in single mothers being a large proportion of homeless families. The feminization of poverty theories helps to contextualize the important impact of gender on homelessness (Fukuda-Parr 1999; Pearce 1978). Similarly, critical race theories are essential in understanding why nonwhite individuals experience higher rates of poverty and homelessness (Crenshaw 2010, 2019; Lewis 1994). Institutionalized racism has embedded racism in minds, structures, and policies impacting everyday life and interactions. This results in the allocation of economic, political, and social resources, such as housing, jobs, respect, and fair wages, in unequal ways. Unless massive grass-roots efforts are well mobilized, their efficacy may be limited, as we see from the current women's, LGBTQ+, Black Lives Matter marches or Poor People's Campaigns (n.d.) occurring around the nation. Intersectionality, gender, and race theories help to explain and sensitize us to how changing social structures and their practices could result in more equitable arrangements.

Symbolic Interaction/Labeling Theory

According to the symbolic interactionist perspective, people attach subjective meanings to symbols and act according to the interpretation of these symbols. How people interact with each other around them, verbally and nonverbally, convey messages of worthiness. The words we use, facial expressions, body language, what we wear, how we style our hair, what kind of job we have, the meaning of our race or gender all have symbolic meanings to both senders and receivers.

Houses are symbols to which we assign meaning – is living in a McMansion, penthouse apartment, third-floor walk-up or mobile home a mark of distinction or embarrassment? We are judged by how we look and how we act. People may act nicer to individuals who are wealthy than those who are poor – but why? Are homeless people not as good as others? It depends upon who you ask. We assign labels to people all the time, arbitrary, subjective opinion-based labels that have emotional, social, financial, and structural implications.

If we accept stereotypes to be real, such as wealthy people are better or work harder, then labels that poor people are worse or deficient must be real as well. As people like Joselyn, who was once a home owner and ended up living in the car with her kids, realized, the difference between "us" and "them" is arbitrary indeed. One day we may have a job, a home, and respect and the next we may be unemployed, homeless, and stigmatized as a deplorable or "trash" (Feeding America 2014a, b; Goldberg 2015).

Homelessness, like all "deviant" behaviors, gets defined to be a social problem when significant numbers of people experience housing distress, when homelessness becomes visible and unavoidable, or when people who aren't expecting to be homeless find themselves in situations when they are. How the public and policy makers perceive and label the lack of housing is a determining factor on whether homelessness is regarded to be a personal or social problem. How people are labeled when they apply for assistance may determine their eligibility and whether they actually get help. Labels are a big deal. Those who do the labeling, like authorities, have the power. It doesn't matter how legitimate the circumstances are for the person needing help – once you've been branded an outcast, it's hard to get rid of that label.

We hold on to stereotypes even when they're wrong because we're getting something out of believing or promoting a stigmatized view of the homeless. Homeless children and families are much different from the chronically homeless single adult. Morality-directed, patriarchal stereotypes created years ago continue to be embraced and applied to people for whom they are irrelevant. Studies repeatedly report that homelessness is a product of institutional and structural arrangements over which individuals have little control (Barak 1992; Super Scholar 2018). Homeless people generally do not pose a serious danger to society and are vulnerable to interpersonal and social violence, yet the public tends to be afraid of them. Homeless persons are seen as responsible for their housing distress and treated with scorn.

Re-defining the label for homeless families is needed if a new domestic policy is to address the underlying structural nature of the problem (Barak 1992). Unless we change how we label the causes of homelessness and how distressed people are treated, we can predict the creation of more, and more severe, homelessness in years ahead.

The New Orthodoxy Theory

What is referred to as the "new orthodoxy" in theorizing about homelessness emerged in the 1990s and influences the way homelessness can be understood and measured (Caton 1990; Farrugia and Gerrard 2015; Pleace 2012). This model alleges that homelessness is neither individual nor structural in nature but a consequence of interaction between micro and macro factors (Fitzpatrick 2005; O'Flaherty 2004). Structural factors as housing, economic, political, and cultural factors contribute to inequality through the way institutions like welfare, public health, and housing discriminate on the basis of gender, race, and ethnicity. It includes individual factors like needs, characteristics, and behavior (Pleace 2016).

This theoretical framework emerged in response to what theorists regarded as fundamental flaws in how homelessness was understood. One flaw was on observable individual traits, such as gender, behavior (mental illness or substance use), or locations where they could be found (shelters, sleeping on the sidewalk). This observable trait approach gives little reference to the context or situation where people find themselves. Another flaw was homelessness seen as solely a consequence of capitalism and economic exploitation, and the failure of systems, like HUD or welfare systems, to serve individuals in need. Homelessness was seen as inflicted on powerless people by forces that were, literally, beyond their control. Essentially, housing markets, welfare agencies, health and human services, education, business all combined to cause homelessness. Structural and personal factors in combination could assemble and intersect to create housing distress. The new orthodoxy model focuses on personal capacity and access to both informal and supports (Pleace 2016).

Homelessness increases when people lack personal capacity, including resilience, coping skills, and access to financial resources. People are disadvantaged when having low levels of schooling, limited job skills, illness (physical or mental), disability, a disrupted childhood, problems with the law, or substance abuse. Limits to personal capacity could be countered if people have access to informal support systems, including family, friends, and partners. The informal network may provide housing, food, healthcare, negotiate with systems, and provide emotional, physical, social, and financial support that can buffer them from homelessness. Access to formal support systems are key; services for health, housing, welfare, and others could counteract limits to both personal capacity and informal supports (Pleace 2016). This model presupposes that structural factors that contribute to inequitable resources cause homelessness only when someone has limits to their personal capacity and insufficient access to informal support. If people have high capacity and an informal support system that can intervene on their behalf, homeless may be kept at bay. But lacking those resources, people need formal support to prevent or exit from homelessness. When formal systems are under-resourced, unavailable, or people can't qualify for them, this increases chances preventable homelessness will occur.

All theories contribute to our understanding of homelessness. If homelessness is the result of the accumulation of individual and structural factors, exactly how this happens and what it looks like is an area for the future development.

Systems Theories

Over the years, there have been a variety of efforts to develop broad theories of systems but only occasional efforts to apply these to understanding homelessness. Although many of the original sociological theories, such as functionalism, have been regarded as early systems theories, the first generation of systems theory was introduced by Ludwig Bertalanffy in the 1940s, and known as general systems theory (1974). General systems theory is based on the assumption that there are universal rules, laws, or processes common to systems in a wide range of domains and scales. It assumes the desirability of maintaining equilibrium and existing social structures.

It focuses on single well-defined systems, such as a person, family, organization, or community, and defines a system as a collection of interacting elements that have a meaningful boundary separating it from its various environments (Bertalanffy 1974).

Individual aspirations, capabilities, disabilities, and economic opportunities do not exist in a vacuum but are defined and molded by a range of historical, cultural, political, environmental, and interactional conditions (Melton 1976). Capabilities and opportunities self-organize out of those created by past generations. A few of these conditions critical to understanding homelessness include racism and the epidemiological transition involving the aging of society. Globalization impacts manufacturing, servicetization (development of the service economy), technological innovation, and general economic restructuring, which impact those struggling to survive. Boundaries may be permeable or impermeable, flexible or rigid. What passes into and out of every system are combinations of information, energy, matter, verbal/nonverbal statements, reports, funds, motivation, waste, and so on.

The overarching paradigm for understanding what happens within a system is a three-part process: input, process, and output. Inputs in social systems may involve people, whether clients or workers; intervening processes may include therapies, support groups, and administrative procedures; and outputs might involve homeless people who are housed, with a general education diploma or better work skills (Hudson 2010).

A particularly important part of systems theory is the way that the intervening processes are conceptualized. These processes are often thought of as being controlled by implicit or explicit rules that are combined to form various procedures or algorithms. With homelessness systems, such as those driven by professional social workers, these processes are usually both iterative and transactional. They are iterative in that many actions are repeated until some goal or desired state is successively approximated. They are transactional in that they involve back-and-forth communications (feedback loops). Negative feedback loops serve to maintain equilibrium and have traditionally been emphasized in general systems explanations of dynamic processes, often at the expense of understanding how systems change, for better or worse. Positive feedback loops are interactive patterns in which processes become amplified (Arthur 1990). One problem inflames another until there is a complete breakdown, or a client learns new problem-solving skills that reinforce one another and permit him or her to transition to a more effective level of adaptation, breaking out of lower equilibria governed by positive feedback loops. "Positive" or "negative" feedback loops do not mean good or bad, functional or dysfunctional loops; either may be desirable or undesirable.

Families may vary based on the responsibilities of children, parents, and grandparents, and organizations may have various different departments. All systems have multiple levels of organization: For example, in education, there are systems involving individual students, classrooms, schools, and larger school systems, each system nested within a more encompassing system. In social work, microsystems refer to individuals and families; mezzo-systems, larger groups, organizations, and local communities; and macro-systems, larger policy making and other national and international systems, each with associated practices (Bronfenbrenner 2005).

When systems theory has been applied to understanding homelessness, it's focused on the use of ecomaps to capture the range of risk factors surrounding homeless people. Risk factors include low education, substance abuse, mental illness, domestic victimization, as well as structural factors like depressed job markets or unaffordable housing (Nooe and Patterson 2010). Occasionally, a system dynamics perspective (Radzicki and Taylor 2008) is applied to understanding the intersection of a small subset of these risk factors in terms of the flow of people at risk who are entering the population of homeless and eventually moving into temporary and possibly permanent housing. One study (Stroh and Goodman 2007) found the two greatest opportunities for intervention with the homeless involved either reducing the number of people entering the risk pool or increasing getting people back into the permanent housing market.

As useful a general systems approach is for understanding dynamic social processes, it needs further development in addressing problems of nonlinearity, interactions of multiple systems, actors with ambiguous or conflicting goals, and long-term social forecasting. "Complex systems" (CS), "complex adaptive systems" (CAS), or nonequilibrium theories have emerged to provide rich models and methods for the understanding of human and system behavior, particularly nonlinear dynamics, chaos theory, self-organization, and autopoietic theory (Hudson 2004). "Sensitivity to initial conditions" (Lorenz 1972) explores how positive feedback processes may lead to either precipitous regressions in individual or social functioning ("when it rains, it pours") or development of more adaptive levels of functioning and underscores importance of beginnings, whether of an interview with a homeless person, a staff meeting, or a program development initiative to create positive or negative feedback.

Hudson (1998) used this approach to study why some communities see more homeless individuals than others. He explored fragmentation, the breakup of economically, socially, and psychologically interdependent relationships which sustain people and systems. These relationships consist of ongoing transactions and multiple and reciprocal dependencies. Employers are dependent on employees for services, who are dependent on employing organizations for income and benefits. The concept of interdependency is central. Individuals are neither victims of circumstances nor the primary instigators of their failures. Hudson's model proposes a reciprocal relationship between individual capabilities and job opportunities. The presence of many job opportunities provides job experience and training; alternatively, a capable workforce attracts and creates business

(Reich 2010b). The absence of business activity and high unemployment and a supporting culture leads to anomie, increased rates of mental illness, and a workforce with minimal education or high levels of disability, which risks the exodus of business to competing locales (Brenner 1973). Development of technology, driven by the dramatically increased capacities for information processing and communication, has led to a misfit between

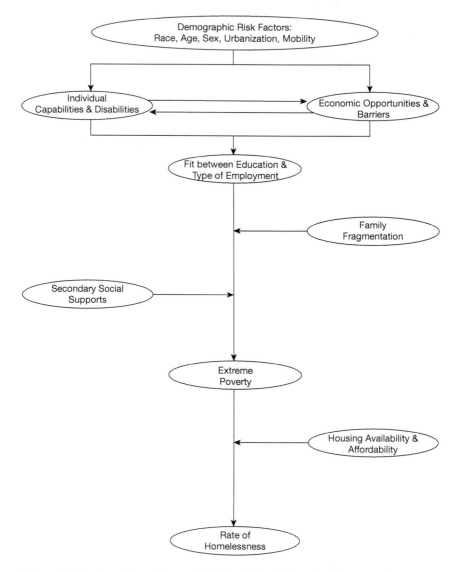

Figure 3.1 An Interdependency Model of Conditions Predictive of Rates of Homelessness.

Source: Adapted from Hudson, C. (1998), p. 16.

available jobs and the skills of those who have completed minimal levels of education, ultimately, reflecting the failures of our educational and employment systems.

The outcome between an area's workforce and its employers is thus moderated by the presence of both primary and secondary social supports. Families provide support and buffering against the economic and emotional assaults of unemployment and under-employment, especially when there are two wage earners in a family. Without support from other family members or savings, under-employed individuals rely upon mental health services, unemployment compensation, social security disability, or other supports, which in turn modify their job capabilities and opportunities. Family support engenders heightened motivation for career advancement; similarly, the availability of rehabilitation and training services creates feedback loops involving enhanced job capacities.

The extent that income and resources are generated through reciprocal transactions between an area's business and family determines someone's ability to rent or purchase housing. Low wages and high unemployment, with few family supports, and scant support from income maintenance programs make housing unaffordable. Figure 3.1 provides a simplified rendition of the most central concepts and relationships proposed in this model. Those causal relationships included, as indicated by the lines, represent the most critical ones. Others could be included that explain the level of community homelessness.

Chaos Theory

Another theoretical approach for in-depth understanding of complex systems like homelessness is chaos theory. The theory was developed to deal specifically with systems characterized by the mathematical notion of "chaos" (Hudson 2010). Chaos refers to systems which can be found at an intermediate point in the continuum, which ranges from the completely periodic and predictable to the totally random. Mathematical chaos exhibits three features: sensitivity to initial conditions, in which small differences in initial conditions lead to dramatically different results; patterned processes, in which behaviors are repeated but only within general bounds; and nonrepeating processes, in which exact trajectories are never repeated.

At the heart of chaos theory is the notion that complex systems can be characterized by fairly simple mathematical equations (Mandel 1995). These are typically iterative equations that describe feedback loops (Heiby 1995). By using iteration or feedback, relationships that underlie complex or chaotic behavior can be identified. For instance, the complex behavior of flocks of birds or crowds of people can be characterized through the repetitive application of simple decision rules used by each individual: "… global structure emerges from local activity rules, a characteristic of complex systems" (Lewin 2000).

Just as in general systems theory, the notion of feedback is central to chaos theory, especially in nonlinear relationships. Feedback processes may be either negative or positive, deviation-reducing or deviation-amplifying. Such amplification may result from the operation of a single variable or the combined effects of several variables. In any case, time series which settle down to a regular linear or periodic pattern are often characterized by negative feedback, whereas those which never settle into a completely predictable pattern are likely characterized by positive feedback processes (Arthur 1990). Feedback processes involve two or more variables. Whereas certain attitudes or availability of resources may become part of positive feedback loops, intolerance or resource constraints may become part of negative feedback loops that maintain the status quo.

One of the concepts most closely associated with chaos theory in the social science literature is that of sensitivity to initial conditions (Galatzer-Levy 2016; Heiby 1995; Krippner 1994; Mandel 1995; Robinson 1993). This sensitivity, which is characteristic of all chaotic systems, is the basis of what has been referred to the "butterfly effect," as it has shown that a butterfly flapping its wings in Sumatra can result in a 5-degree centigrade change in temperature in Atlanta, Georgia, eight days later, or a tornado in some other part of the world (Galatzer-Levy 2016; Lorenz 1972). Small initial errors and perturbations sometimes endlessly magnify, through positive feedback loops, to create major changes.

There has been much speculation on the significance of sensitivity to initial conditions in the social sciences. Stanley Krippner (1994) suggests that "chaos theory holds that through amplification of small fluctuations, it can provide natural systems with access to novelty." Similarly, Duke (1994) points out that sensitive dependence leads to understanding that small things can have major repercussions; that we cannot over emphasize large traumatic events. (1994). Even a single act of kindness or well-timed social interventions can have major repercussions.

Also central to chaos theory has been the study of fractals, which are mathematically produced graphic patterns that contain boundary regions between periodic and random areas in which highly intricate chaotic structure can be found. This boundary phenomenon has been referred to as the edge of chaos (Lewin 2000; Packard 1988; Waldrop 1992). Lewin, for example, argues:

> The edge of chaos is where information gets its foot in the door in the physical world, where it gets the upper hand over energy. ...Being at the transition point between order and chaos not only buys you exquisite control – small input / big change – but it also buys you the possibility that information processing can become an important part of the dynamics of the system.
>
> (2000, p. 51)

Others, such as the psychologist Ruth Richards, argue that the ability to function at the edge of chaos is one of the most important conditions for creativity and effective problem-solving. Because chaotic processes never repeat themselves, they represent an endless source of novelty. The ability to maintain creative growth in nonequilibrium systems, combining negative and positive feedback, and balancing periodic and chaotic structures "at the edge of chaos," is no doubt a phenomenon which proponents of the general systems theory are liable to miss without the insights and tools of chaos theory.

Chaos theory is of particular significance for understanding homelessness for several reasons. As a theory about the transition from orderly to non-predictable and complex systems, it clarifies the processes through which deviation-amplifying feedback loops, involving the iterative and gradual snowballing of adverse events, result in expulsion from both housing and other social supports. It shows that while previous patterns of adaptation can never be exactly replicated, new levels of adaptation involving the balance between order and chaos, or the "edge of chaos," can be achieved. Research on the edge of chaos phenomenon illustrates how some of the most significant problem-solving and creativity potentially occur while individuals and groups develop such a balance. In general, each of the features of chaos, especially those involving sensitivity to initial conditions and the edge of chaos phenomenon, suggests the importance of balanced programs and policies for the homeless. These need to integrate, on the one hand, a bottom-up approach involving maximum choice for the homeless individuals involved, such as Housing First housing programs, and, on the other hand, should include some top-down structure and services that provide some predictability and ongoing supports.

Social Forecast Approach

Data, when collected using good methodologies and a triangulated approach, can provide insights to predict future trends (Denzin 1978; Encyclopedia. com 2001; Tetlock 2016). The purpose of social forecasting is to provide an analytical framework for helping decision-makers to make better judgments. Social forecasting relies on a complex matrix of both qualitative and quantitative data points that intersect to provide probability estimates of a phenomenon's occurrence. Based on sociological insights, it has become embraced by the business community. It recognizes pressures from social factors that determine success of an organization or social policy.

Homelessness is often studied using limited data points, such as HUD's PIT estimates of homelessness's occurrence on a given night. Such a technique does not reflect the actual number of homeless people, nor does it provide insight into how homeless people view causal factors, remediation strategies, or system operations that influence whether homelessness will continue or be curtailed. It is clear that the nation's current response to homelessness is neither preventing it nor giving individuals a life-course for success. Tetlock (2016) notes that data are often selected that enable reporters to root for their own team, data that support the position that they want to promote rather than looking at data from a comprehensive, neutral perspective. There are different sets of data to be considered, different ways to address homelessness.

We believe the current social forecast is increased poverty and homelessness, unless some things are changed. Data could help us to consider different possibilities society could use to address social problems like homelessness; if what we are doing changes, the forecast will change. A data-driven homelessness prevention social forecast model has not been developed yet, but could be. The challenge is not just to forecast what the future will be but to make it what it could be that is in the best interest of society (Enzer 1984). This may be hard to do because of vested interests, political agendas, and will require substantial restructuring of basic tenets and beliefs (Holroyd 1978).

Components of social forecasting include focusing on a targeted problem, what factors contributing to it will be studied, how those factors will be measured, and over what period of time. These will lead to a probabilistic calculation of outcome. Krishnamurthy (2010) provides a detailed variable check-list to be used in forecasting social outcomes that is worthwhile for anyone interested in developing this technique to review. It recommends cross-impact matrices, Delphi analyses, simulations, meta-forecasting, time-series, autoregressive moving average (ARIMA) models to name a few methodologies. Moving away from bias toward innovative measures of alternative options of how to address homelessness is an approach well-worth considering.

Summary

Homelessness is thriving in America and shows no signs of subsiding. This chapter has addressed different traditional and contemporary explanations for understanding homelessness. These include homelessness being beneficial to certain groups in society, a form of big business, being a way to punish people who can't adhere to norms of work productivity, labeling homeless people as deficient and unworthy, being a violation of human rights. They also include an understanding of homelessness and the possibilities of its elimination as a function of both dysfunctional interactions of various complex systems and the avenue for growth that they present. Movement toward multivariate mathematical models to help understand and alleviate homelessness is underway.

4   How Did We Get Here?
History of Homelessness
Policy

Homelessness is not a new phenomenon, but it has changed in how it has been perceived. Sometimes it is understood to be a personal problem that individuals are responsible for creating and managing. There have been other times when homelessness has been viewed as a social problem that requires social interventions. Often, there has been a tug-of-war about who caused it and who is responsible for addressing it.

In order to understand contemporary homelessness, it is useful to go back in time and see how it has changed and how homeless individuals have been viewed. This chapter reviews the relationship between social policies and the creation of homelessness. The underlying message in this chapter is that homelessness is a product of social construction. It sets the stage for understanding homelessness under the Trump era.

Homelessness in the Ancient Past

Anthropologists note that early people were homeless – nomadic hunters and gathers. Housing was portable and "home" was a fluid concept. As people settled into communities and built houses, a social stratification system emerged. When some people had more wealth and resource than others, money and materialism came to reflect a social position of value. People who didn't have access to high-status jobs, money, businesses, fine homes, and large families found themselves at the bottom of the heap. Meritocracy began. As people became more stable and communities developed, political, economic, religious, scientific, and technological institutions shaped what life should be like and what we expected from each other. Leaders debated the relationship between people, the state, the economy, and what the future should look like; some of the main idea-shapers included the Speenhamland system, Thomas Malthus, David Ricardo, Karl Marx and Friedrich Engels, and later Ayn Rand (Bregman 2016).

In some ways, street people who move from one location to another to find a safe place to sleep and carry their few possessions in bags with them could be regarded as contemporary nomads. The difference is that back in ancient times, everyone was homeless and the portable lifestyle was normative. Today, it's an aberration not to have an ongoing shelter with an address as a place to call home. The view that people with resources are better than those without is now embedded into common stereotypes. Policies impacting homelessness have arisen from social and economic transformations. Growth of capitalism during the 18th and 19th centuries, the Industrial Revolution, rise of corporate capitalism, deindustrialization, and emergence of the service sector influence our notions of social welfare (Katz 1996). Tension over the relationship between the state and people's well-being has never been resolved.

Founding of the Nation and the Founding of Homelessness

Being poor and without housing has long been stigmatized. As early as 1640, English "vagrants" were listed as outcast individuals and chased by police. These attitudes were brought to the Americas. A hypothesis exists that many who colonized America were outcasts, homeless, and willing to leave bleak futures for dreams of better opportunity in the New World (Fulton 2010). They arrived with nothing and were at the mercy of others, Native Americans especially, to help them build homes and find food to survive. Thinking of homelessness being a part of the building of the nation is an interesting spin to the traditional founding of America stories.

King Philip's 1675–1676 war against Native Americans drove people out of their homes to seek shelter in the forests or coastal areas. As war continued between the French and Indians, some families felt threatened and moved with no money or possessions to frontier areas or upstate New York. Baltimore and Philadelphia were thought to have more homelessness than other cities in America. Homeless people were regarded as "sturdy beggars" in the mid-18th century and found in most towns. A law was enacted to prevent "idleness" and idle people were made servants. During the Revolutionary War, itinerant workers became the "wandering poor" of an agricultural society reliant on worker mobility. Migrant workers and people who were without homes traveled from job to job, building transportation systems, cities, and towns. Their jobs were often lower class and temporary, and they slept where they could. In this way, homeless people may be maligned but were functional for the building of the nation (Kusmer 2003). Today, transient migrant workers are an essential part of the American economy (Higgins 2018). The book *Nomadland* (Bruder 2017) describes how employers discovered a new, low-cost labor pool of transient Americans who today live in travel-trailers and call themselves "workampers." Many are retired, but not all. They share that they can't afford houses, jobs aren't secure, and when their Social Security or savings are insufficient, these tens of thousands invisible casualties of the Great Recession take to the road.

Home ownership was important to Thomas Jefferson, who regarded yeoman farmers as the backbone of independence and democracy.

Being indebted to a landlord resembled the feudalism of Europe (Squire 2018). People generally want to work, and unless there is something "wrong" with them or they have enough assets to take care of themselves, homeless and unemployed people remain looked down upon. After the American Revolution, many individuals were forced into homelessness due to insufficient resources. Colonists brought with them a disdain for people who didn't work, but also an Elizabethan tradition that communities and the church had a responsibility to care for impoverished residents. "Settled" residents were entitled to more benefits than were "newcomers." The community had no obligation to help people who weren't accepted by vote as a town member or born into accepted families (Rossi 1989). Nonmembers of the community were encouraged to leave, as were those who needed benefits. Homelessness was seen as a moral deficiency. Good Christians, under God's grace, would naturally have their needs met, so people not getting that grace were seen as deserving of their plight, as God rendered justice accordingly and fairly. Widows, children, the disabled, and the elderly became transient poor denied settlement rights and shunted from community to community unless the "deserving poor" proved they were "truly needy" with the potential of being beneficial, productive members of the community. Otherwise, they were encouraged to go away. The pain of no relief was so great that many of them did just that (Fischer 2011; Rossi 1990).

The link between settlement and benefits has been long-standing. It can be seen as "Greyhound relief" where poor people are given one-way bus, boat, or plane tickets to other communities instead of receiving aid where they are. Homeless people may be given transportation out of cities like San Francisco and New York to Atlanta, Orlando, or even Puerto Rico (Guardian 2017). Hawaii is known for shipping homeless people to the Lower 48 so not to disrupt their desirable tourist image (Couch 2014). It is not a dissimilar strategy to the intentional hardships faced by immigrants at the US–Mexico border in 2019 to encourage them to go away (van der Leum 2018).

Work for Food

In 1704, Daniel Defoe introduced mercantilist ideas of "work for those who will labor, punishment for those who will not, and bread for those who cannot" (Himmelfarb 1983: 27). Productivity became a dominant theme, and education for children was seen as useful primarily for them to become economic producers for the public good. As the Industrial Revolution got underway, the value of work was elevated. Business owners thrive and workers paid little because "everyone but an idiot knows that the lower classes must be kept poor or they will never be industrious" (Himmelfarb 1983: 51). There were debates among economists like Adam

Smith about the importance of fair wages and education or Edmund Burke's view about not giving assistance to anyone who could possibly work. Paupers were sent to poorhouses.

The government has historically been the place where people could go for help, but when need grows bigger than the government's willingness to assist, limits got set. By the depression of 1857, most growing cities were full of homeless people, but there was no government intervention to help them. Private charities and organizations whose goal was to help emerged to fill the gap. One example is the Western Soup Society of Philadelphia that helped people with food during harsh winters. The organization tried to thrive, but without government funding it was hard. The government received criticism from many charity organizations but turned deaf ears to them.

The Industrial Revolution of the 1830s resulted in people migrating from farms to cities in search of jobs and eventually drew immigrants looking for work as well. Hunger led to pan-handling and jails became de facto shelters. Poor safety regulation contributed to deaths and disabilities, which led to widows with children they couldn't care for. The 1850s brought the first documented cases of homeless youth, many of whom were kicked out of their homes because their providers could no longer afford to raise them. By the early 1900s housing distress was such a problem that President Teddy Roosevelt in 1908 established a housing commission to figure out what was going on. In similar fashion, jails remain de facto shelters for those who are homeless (Greenberg and Rosenheck 2008) and thousands of youth are pushed out of home each year because their providers don't have the resources to raise them (NCSL 2016). It is no surprise that HUD is now being pressured to address the significant increase of unaccompanied youth who are homeless. This is another example of how things change and still remain the same.

Today, we see charities and nongovernment organizations (NGOs) running shelters, soup-kitchens, food-pantries, and stepping up to provide welfare services because the government won't (Camarota and Zeigler 2018; Lowrey 2017; Vissing et al. 2017). This view laid the foundation for today's SNAP recipients being required to work to "sing for their supper." As the US Department of Agriculture states on its requirement page to get food stamps:

> While SNAP is intended to ensure that no one in our land of plenty should fear going hungry, it also reflects the importance of work and responsibility. SNAP rules require all recipients meet work requirements unless they are exempt because of age or disability or another specific reason.[1]

The idea that one has to work to have food, housing, or other assistance is old indeed.

Housing and Homelessness History Timelines

Since those early days, the history of housing has been well studied, as exemplified by Barak (*Gimme Shelter* 1992), Rossi (*Down and Out in America* 1989), Kusmer (*Down and Out on the Road* 2003), Nunez and Sribnick's *The Poor Among Us* (2013), and a variety of others. Squire's history examines how race has long played a role in the nation's housing policies (2018). Here are some historical homelessness highlights:

1862: Homestead Act gave 160 acres of land to whites; 270 million acres given away if people built a house.

1866: Southern Homestead Act made land available to freed slaves and whites after the end of Civil War.

1867: The first tenement-law regulation in America is enacted in New York City.

1923: Socialist Mayor Daniel Hoan, Milwaukee, built the nation's first public-housing project.

1926: NY passes Limited Dividend Housing Companies Act offering subsidies for affordable housing.

1932: Federal Home Loan Bank System established.

1933: Home Owners' Loan Corporation (HOLC) authorized to refinance distressed mortgages.

1934: Great Depression; half of mortgages were delinquent; National Housing Act establishes Federal Housing Administration (FHA) to insure mortgages for families and Federal Savings and Loan Insurance Corporation (FSLIC); Catherine Bauer introduced Modern Housing to safeguard housing consumers from capitalist, commercial exploitations.

1937: Congress passes Housing Act, originally intended to create public housing for poor and middle-income families but whittled down to apply only to low-income people.

1942: Emergency Price Control Act establishes federal rent control for cities.

1944: GI Bill provides mortgage-loan guarantees for veteran home purchases. FHA created "redlining" giving white neighborhoods highest (blue) rating and black neighborhoods the lowest rating (red); loans and insurance would not be provided to homebuyers in red areas because they were labeled as too-risky.

1946: Farmers' Home Administration created U.S. Department of Agriculture.

1959: Section 202 of Housing Act implemented low-cost loans to nonprofits for elderly housing; most public housing units were built in slum areas and inhabited by non-white people, essentially warehousing vulnerable people least likely to qualify for mortgages.

1965: Congress establishes the Department of Housing and Urban Development (HUD) in a largely symbolic move to bring housing and slum-clearance programs to cabinet level.

1968: Congress passes the Fair Housing Act, outlawing discrimination in housing and mortgage lending after public protests demanded fair housing.

1973: Nixon administration issues moratorium on subsidized-housing programs.

1974: The Housing and Community Development Act creates Section 8 housing programs to replace public housing and consolidated grant programs into Community Development Block Grants.

1976: Supreme Court rules in Hills v. Gautreaux that Chicago Housing Authority contributed to racial segregation. HUD begins offering vouchers to address poverty and segregation.

1982: Under Ronald Reagan, HUD's budget is slashed to under $40 billion, a decrease of more than 50% from 1976.

1983: Housing and Urban-Rural Recovery Act begins Housing Development Action Grant and rental rehabilitation programs.

1985: Homeless advocate Mitch Snyder and members of the Creative Community for Non-Violence occupied abandoned federal building in Washington DC and housed hundreds to protest government's failure to care for homeless people. The Reagan administration agreed to lease the building to Snyder, which became the largest shelter in Washington.

1986: Reagan introduces the Homeless Persons' Survival Act, a low-income housing tax credit.

1987: The McKinney–Vento Homeless Assistance Act of 1987 provides federal money for homeless shelter and education programs.

1988: Indian Housing Act gives HUD responsibilities for housing needs of Native Americans and Alaskan Indians; Housing and Community Development Act authorizes Enterprise Zones and allows sale of public housing to resident management corporations; Fair Housing Amendments Act makes it easier for victims of discrimination to sue, stiffens penalties for offenders.

1990: Cranston-Gonzalez National Affordable Housing Act emphasizes homeownership and tenant-based assistance, initiates HOME block grant for housing; Low Income Housing Preservation and Residential Homeownership Act shows federal commitment to permanent preservation of assisted low-income, multifamily housing.

1992: Congress authorizes HOPE VI urban-revitalization demonstration program to provide grants for low-rise, mixed-income housing rather than high-rise public housing.

1996: Bill Clinton creates "one strike and you're out" initiative to evict public-housing tenants who have criminal convictions.

2005: HUD's first official point-in-time count of homeless people.

2007: Housing market crashes, 3 million homes are foreclosed in both 2009 and 2010.

2012: Obama administration authorizes Rental Assistance Demonstration program to change public housing into private-sector Section 8 housing.

2012: The Section 8 waiting lists are so long that half of them are closed.

2018: HUD Secretary Ben Carson proposes raising rents for tenants in subsidized housing as well as enabling public-housing authorities to impose work requirement (The Nation 2018; Squire 2018).

War, Mental Illness, Disability, and Homelessness

One legacy of war is the creation of conditions that foster homelessness for individuals and families. Bread-winners may be killed and their loss of income thrusts families into poverty and housing distress; houses may be destroyed through acts of war; homes may be taken over by the military and the owners cast into the street. Soldiers return home "shell-shocked," the old name for post-traumatic stress disorder. Homelessness among veterans have been documented since the Civil War, and that relationship continues to persist today. Many war veterans remained unemployed and others lost their properties to war and natural catastrophes; thus, they spent most of their times in the streets (McDonald 2017).

The military has long been an option for people with no place to go to secure a place to sleep and food to eat. After Civil War soldiers returned, many were transient workers on the railroad or as agricultural workers, moving with the seasons. When a credit-fueled railroad boom went bust, breaking banks and killing jobs, known as the "Panic of 1873," a depression occurred and a new group of homeless people emerged. These were freed slaves and veterans, whose used wartime habits of foraging or pillaging the countryside for food. This is when the terms "tramp" and "bum" were added to the lexicon (Roberts 2016).

In the years shortly after the end of World War II in the 1940s, fortunate soldiers returned from the war to build homes, families, and jobs in their communities. A boom of babies was born, industry thrived, and men came home to work minimum-wage jobs on which they could afford small, simple homes to raise families. But some came back from the war with emotional scars and didn't fit into this 1950s model of family, faith, and consumerism as the country got back on track.

Mental hospitals, which were always horrid places, became full with over a half-million people being hospitalized. The pharmaceutical industry grew and the drug chlorpromazine (Thorazine) became approved by the Food and Drug Administration as an anti-psychotic drug. This drug enabled some patients to not be institutionalized and live in the community. President Kennedy signed the Community Mental Health Act in 1963 to shift people with mental illness out of institutions and into the community where they could be cared for at community mental health centers.

These weren't adequately funded. Kennedy's proposal was historic because until then care of mentally ill individuals had been exclusively a state responsibility. The federal initiative closed many state hospitals and aborted development of state-funded outpatient clinics in process at the same time. Although community mental health centers were tasked with supporting seriously mentally ill persons discharged from hospitals, its focus quickly transitioned to the "worried well," people with less serious mental problems than had been in mental hospitals, an example of creaming. People with serious mental health issues were placed into the community without adequate care and supports. It is widely believed, rightly or wrongly, that deinstitutionalization of mental hospitals opened the floodgates of mentally ill people into the community who didn't have the resources they needed to survive well and live "normal" lives.

In 1965, Congress established Medicaid, to help people with low incomes and Medicare, to help people who were elderly, to obtain medical care and Social Security Disability Insurance (SSDI) and Supplemental Security Income (SSI). These increased federal oversight of healthcare under federal government oversight but never were designed to give comprehensive care. Because these systems were inadequately funded and administered, many people with mental illness ended up on the street, jails or prisons, nursing homes, and homeless shelters, never getting the help they need (Torrey 2013).

Soldiers continue to return from wars with physical and emotional disabilities for which they don't receive adequate care, which makes them and their families suffer. Today, there are over 120,000 homeless veterans, and only 8,000 beds to house them (Mo's Heroes 2019). There are around 40,000 veterans who are homeless on any given night and 1.4 million other veterans, at risk of homelessness due to poverty, lack of support networks, and dismal living conditions in overcrowded or substandard housing (National Coalition for Homeless Veterans 2019).

Communities continue to find themselves confronted with how to deal with single adults who are isolated, alone, with mental illness and substance abuse problems, and with no one to take care of them. Medicaid, SSI, and SSDI have failed to serve millions in need. Homelessness in families and children, like the single adults with trash-bag possessions, has become visible, thus harder for communities to deny. Yet no national system of comprehensive care exists to help any of them, making rising homelessness predictable.

The Roaring Twenties: 1920 and 2020

The 1920s was accompanied with an unprecedented economic boom. Science and technology were thriving, and innovations such as electricity, radio, telephones were commonly used. People enjoyed going to the theatre, and movie stars became household names. Automobiles went into mass production. Manufacturing was big business and factories drew new workers from rural areas and other nations. Unlike farming which led to erratic incomes, people working in factories gained steady incomes which allowed them to spend and invest. The banking and stock markets thrived. People did not imagine that around the corner their economic worlds would come crashing down.

Immigrants and transient workers came to seize the opportunity to work in factories and other industries that popped up due to this time of abundance. Most of them were men, not families. The men needed places to stay but often didn't have money to pay for them. There weren't many assistance programs and many didn't qualify for help. The public and police displayed a general lack of sympathy for these "bums," who were often blamed for crimes they did not commit. Because aid was often unavailable, shantytowns emerged where people constructed shelters out of scrap materials. Shantytowns became part of the "skid row," where transients looking for work would congregate together (Rossi 1990). These were the homeless of the 1920s. But shanty towns are popping up today.

Looking to 2020, we observe a time of immigration growth again. Many arrive with no papers, no money, and only the clothes on their backs. They need housing and resources essential to survival. There is a national debate about whether they should come or what to do with them. Without documentation that complies with government rules, people may not sign leases, get loans, or receive survival assistance like housing, education, food, or healthcare (Stribley 2017). A Bush Center reports that the benefits of allowing immigrants in and helping them to establish homes, jobs, and good lives far outweigh the costs (Orrenius 2016). But as history has shown, whether outsiders will get the help they need remains to be seen.

The Great Depressions: 1935 and 2008

The economic depression that began in 1929 and ended in 1941 changed the nation's understanding of homelessness. The transient, single male worker who was homeless was replaced by young men pushed out of their families to fend for themselves while their resources were used for hungry mouths to feed at home. There were no jobs, the men had few marketable skills, and the fear that they could become long-term homeless was a distinct possibility. Families lost homes. Some packed up the few possessions they had to travel to where they hoped the grass, and incomes, would be greener. Destitute families' lives came tumbling down as a result of the national economic decline.

The Great Depression occurred as a result of structural factors brewing in the 1920s. The booming stock market crashed. The fast-growing banking industry didn't have in place rigorous monetary safety policies. Banks had been loaning money to people to invest in the purchase of stocks, and when the stock market started to tumble, people ran to take their money out of the bank. Banks didn't have adequate funds there to pay everyone who came to demand their money, so many closed their doors and stopped lending money to businesses. With the collapse of the banking industry, people kept their money at home in places like their mattresses. Unemployment skyrocketed, deflation occurred, and people couldn't pay their bills. By 1934, half of all home loans were delinquent and over 1 million families had lost their farms or were evicted. New home construction came to a standstill. Climate change contributed to the Depression too. In the heartland's Great Plains states, a severe drought occurred that parched fields so badly this area became known as the Dust Bowl.

The government did not step in to provide disaster relief. President Herbert Hoover was personally blamed for much of the intolerable economic and social troubles of the day. Hoover believed that people should rely upon themselves and their families, not the government, when they needed help. He didn't believe in government assistance or benefit programs. He thought people's economic problems could be addressed by hard work and people helping each other. Charity through private philanthropy increased but wasn't sufficient to make a significant impact. Many Americans believed the government needed to create assistance programs to help them, but Hoover refused (History 2010).

Because people were losing their homes and had no place to live, shantytowns began popping up across the country where poor people bonded together and shared meager resources and plentiful stories of despair. Shanties were constructed of whatever people could find to shelter themselves from the weather and afford them a smidgen of privacy. Cardboard, tar-paper, wood, tin, and cloth were common barriers, but many dug holes in the ground with makeshift roofs laid over them, or they tried to find empty conduits and water mains. Most were built near rivers or water supplies. While people tried to decorate or make their "homes" as hospitable as possible, most were grim and unsanitary. Unemployment was high as jobs were unavailable, and when they occurred they were often sporadic, as highlighted in John Steinbeck's book *The Grapes of Wrath*. Shantytowns posed a variety of health risks to both themselves and the communities, but government didn't do much for the residents. The people who lived in them received no sympathy and support from nearby housed residents. They tried to develop their own form of governance and social organization, with spokespersons, but they lacked meaningful power and were highly stigmatized for being poor. Periodically the shantytowns were raided by police, their dwellings torn down, or people beaten-up.

These shantytowns became known as Hoovervilles, in "honor" of President Hoover's failed housing and economic policies. Newspapers used to shield the homeless from the cold were called "Hoover blankets"; empty pant pockets pulled inside out – demonstrating no coins in one's pockets – were "Hoover flags"; shoes with worn-out soles that had cardboard put inside to protect feet were called "Hoover leather"; and cars pulled by horses because gas was an unaffordable luxury were called "Hoover wagons" (History 2010). It is interesting to note that around the country's 2009 economic depression when high rates of bankruptcy and housing foreclosures occurred, shantytowns again emerged around the country and were called "Hoovervilles."

Hoover was swiftly defeated by Franklin Roosevelt at the next election. Under the new presidential leadership, the government stepped in to help millions in crisis. It passed the Glass–Steagall Act, which banned connection between commercial banks and investment banking; Roosevelt enacted his New Deal legislation; the Federal Deposit Insurance Corporation was created to ensure all deposits at banks. Congress passed the Securities and Exchange Act, the Trade Agreement Act, the Social Security Act, the Works Progress Administration (WPA), and a bill establishing a minimum wage that workers could be paid. A growing number of people became hired in government jobs.

Perhaps the biggest contributor to ending the Depression was World War II. When Japan attacked Pearl Harbor in 1941, the government borrowed over 1 billion dollars to build its military and US manufacturing jumped by 50%. As part of the buildup to World War II, Congress approved the creation of 20 public housing complexes near private companies manufacturing military supplies (Griffin 2015). After the end of both the depression and the war, Americans looked to the government for a safety net. It delivered with federal assistance programs that helped the middle class as well as those struggling economically. After World War II, eight of ten American men were eligible for no-money-down home loans from the Federal Housing Administration under the G.I. Bill. President Truman approved the Housing Act of 1949 that authorized the creation of 810 public housing units. These included mega-public housing towers, like Philadelphia's Richard Allen Homes or Chicago's Cabrini-Green apartments that segregated poor people from their surrounding community. New home housing construction thrived. But while 40% of all mortgages issued in 1946 and 1947 went to veterans, white veterans received more housing mortgages than black veterans, who were subjected to racial discrimination like redlining (Callahan 2013). The relationship between homelessness and race was thus codified.

If we turn to the Great Depression of 2008, it was arguably worse than the depression that preceded World War II (Egan 2014). The head of the Federal Reserve, Ben Bernake, regarded it as the worst financial crisis in the world's history. However, the policy responses to it were different, which made the results bad, but less severe than they could have been. Under Bush's administration, the Great Recession or subprime mortgage crisis of 2008 occurred (History.com/Recession 2018). Subprime mortgages are home loans granted to borrowers with poor credit histories and are considered high-risk loans. In early 2000s, mortgage lenders seeking to capitalize on rising home prices were less restrictive in terms of the types of borrowers they approved for loans and banks acquired thousands of risky mortgages, hoping to turn quick profits. When subprime mortgage lender New Century Financial and American Home Mortgage Investment Corp declared bankruptcy, housing prices began to fall as a glut of new homes came on the market. Millions of homeowners became "underwater," meaning their homes were valued less than their total loan amounts. Net worth of American households declined over 20%, and there was a loss of $14 trillion to the economy. Bush signed the so-called Economic Stimulus Act into law, but then Bear Sterns and Lehman Brothers collapsed and investment company AIG, which was viewed as "too big to fail," was loaned $85 billion to remain afloat as Bush approved TARP – the Troubled Asset Relief Program that provided the government with $700 billion in funds to purchase the assets of struggling companies like General Motors, Chrysler, and Bank of America in order to keep them in business.

Housing foreclosures spiked 81% in 2008 (Christie 2009). Declining prices put many homeowners "underwater," which made them more likely to default on their loans. As banks owned more homes, it stripped demand, lowered prices, and resulted in more foreclosures. By 2011 over 1.57 million Americans had filed for bankruptcy (Cammarosano 2015). A temp worker was hired to do filing for two weeks at a Boston bankruptcy court. Corrine liked her supervisor and returned the following week to find she wasn't there. As Corrine did her filing, she accidentally found out why – the supervisor had herself filed for bankruptcy. As Northwestern University's Institute for Policy Research observed, the financial crisis may be over, but its long-term effects are not gone and will reverberate for years (2014).

Presidents Make a Difference

What presidents are credited for accomplishing, or failing to accomplish, depends on Congress, the public, and who is pushing agendas behind the scenes. Taking a quick look at the relationship between presidents and homelessness, some have helped, some have hindered, and most haven't done anything lasting at all.

Franklin Roosevelt and Lyndon Johnson are the ones who spring to mind as having taken action to address poverty, homelessness, and institute programs that were designed to improve the quality of life for everyone. Roosevelt's New Deal was a response to the financial catastrophe of the Great Depression. His administration created a series of programs to restore prosperity, stabilize the economy, and create job programs such as the WPA, Works Progress Administration, which hired artists, construction workers, writers, musicians to rebuild both the physical and emotional infrastructure of the nation. He decided he'd act swiftly to face the "dark realities of the moment" and assured Americans that he'd "wage a war against the emergency" just as though "we were in fact invaded by a foreign foe." Some of his programs continue to exist today, such as Social Security, the Federal Deposit Insurance Corporation (FDIC), the Federal Crop Insurance Corporation (FCIC), the Federal Housing Administration (FHA), and the Tennessee Valley Authority (TVA).

President Lyndon Johnson's administration started the Great Society programs, War on Poverty, and racial equality initiatives. Race and poverty and poverty and homelessness are obviously correlated. His Great Society programs resembled some of Roosevelt's New Deal, but society was different in the 1960s, being a time of economic growth and stability. Tax cuts across the board occurred while the GNP increased and unemployment decreased. His administration passed the Voting Rights Act of 1965, the Immigration and Nationality Services Act of 1965, the Economic Opportunity Act of 1964, the Primary and Secondary Education Act of 1965, and Civil Rights Acts of 1964 and 1968 – it's important to remember that the 1968 act banned housing discrimination. Programs like the Job Corps, Food Stamps, VISTA, Upward Bound, Community Action Programs, Medicare, Medicaid, Head Start and Public Television helped lower and middle Americans to gain healthcare, education, skills, and benefits that could catapult their lives forward. There were improvements to Social Security, environmental protections, cultural and arts programs, to name a few. His War on Poverty had the goal of eliminating hunger, unemployment, community development (especially in rural areas like Appalachia) and reducing literacy.

Both President Franklin Roosevelt and Lyndon Johnson's programs created safety nets that supported millions of middle- and lower-income people for the better. They were not necessarily programs that benefited the elite and there was conservative backlash to many of them. If these programs had been awarded adequate funding and allowed to continue at full steam, perhaps their programs would have been successful in reducing poverty and improving the educational level, health, and social climate of America. However, the presidents who followed were not committed to such programs. As a result, they were under-funded or eliminated, one by one, essentially creating so many holes in the safety net that many people fell through – which resulted in sentiments that the programs weren't working. It is possible that they could have worked if they had been adequately supported. But that's not what happened.

The years following LBJ were fascinating in how they increased homelessness but had opportunities not to. President Richard Nixon inherited a safety-net system from LBJ. Supposedly in 1969 he was on the verge of implementing legislation that would give basic income to poor families. This promised to be a revolutionary step that could have changed the course for the future, but it was boondoggled by political agenda-staking. The story goes that in the days following the Civil Rights movement, women's movement, anti-war protests, and the social changes of the 1960s, five economists – John Kenneth Galbraith, Harold Watts, James Tobin, Paul Samuelson, and Robert Lampman – wrote an open letter to Congress that was published on the front page of the *New York Times*, a letter signed by 1,200 fellow economists. "The country will not have met its responsibility until everyone in the nation is assured an income no less than the officially recognized definition of poverty." According to the economists, the costs would be substantial but well within the nation's economic and fiscal capacity. Nixon was ready to move ahead with this, until one of his advisors, Martin Anderson, an advocate of Ayn Rand's philosophy, saw where the universal income and negative tax movements were headed. Anderson believed in the smallest possible government and maximum individual responsibility and launched an offensive that resulted in the death of the initiative (Bregman 2016).

How did Anderson torpedo the basic income act? He promoted a 1944 book by Karl Polanyi called *The Great Transformation* in which the author asserted that a basic income would incite the poor to greater idleness, dampen their productivity and wages, and threaten the very foundations of capitalism. Reportedly Anderson gave him this along with a quote by the Spanish-American writer George Santayana: "Those who cannot remember the past are condemned to repeat it." Nixon called in his advisors to ask them what they thought. Senator Daniel Moynihan and economist Milton Friedman argued that the right to an income already existed and poverty simply meant you were strapped for cash, nothing more, nothing less.

Nixon reportedly felt caught; he wanted to make history and saw himself presented with a rare, historic chance to cast out the old system, raise up millions of working poor, and win a decisive victory in the War on Poverty and take credit for LBJ era programs. But as a conservative, he deplored the rise of big government, and while proposing a new kind of social provision to the American public he did not offer them a new conceptual framework through which to understand it. Nixon saw basic income as the ultimate marriage of conservative and progressive politics; he steeped his progressive ideas in conservative rhetoric and began speaking of joblessness as a "choice" since he thought that would win over hearts and minds of the public. He decided to attach an additional proviso to his bill that basic income beneficiaries without a job would have to register with the Department of Labor. If "welfare" had to be packaged as "workfare" to get basic income through Congress, then so be it. He presented his bill in a televised speech. What Nixon failed to foresee was that his rhetoric of fighting laziness among the poor and unemployed would ultimately turn the country against basic income and the welfare state as a whole. His dream of going down in history as a progressive leader forfeited a unique opportunity to overthrow a stereotype rooted back in 19th-century England, the myth of the lazy poor (Bregman 2016).

Some of the Great Society's legacy continued like the Housing and Community Development Act of 1974, which resulted in the creation of the Section 8 housing voucher program to provide rental assistance to poor Americans. Community Development Block Grants gave lump sums of money to local government to spend on programs like housing and community development. But Nixon also declared a moratorium on public housing in favor of a market-based approach (Griffin 2015). Princeton University historian Brian Steensland observed that had Nixon's universal basic income plan gone ahead, the ramifications would have been huge. Public assistance programs would no longer be seen as simply pandering to lazy opportunists; if it had passed, there would no longer be a designation between the "deserving" and "undeserving" poor (Bregman 2016).

On the other end of the helping continuum from FDR and LBJ was Ronald Reagan. He is unaffectionately regarded as the Father of Contemporary Homelessness. As a result of his economic policies, there was a sharp increase in homeless individuals and families (Bloom 2005). Reagan's legacy is our government's weakened ability to protect families, consumers, workers, and the environment. His policies have contributed to the financial distress of families and the epidemic of homelessness that we now observe.

Reagan took office during an economic recession. Previous administrations had made cuts of Great Society programs that were becoming apparent. People were out of work and homelessness increased in cities all across the nation, but the people who were homeless were different than what previous administrations had observed. Instead of single men with drinking problems seen after World War II, the new homeless were factory and office workers and families who had lost their jobs in the recent global recession. It was clear that the new poverty created by lack of government programs to support the middle and lower classes was resulting in escalating amounts of homelessness in populations not observed before (Roberts 2016).

Reagan used the economic recession as an excuse to cut spending on social services – like the safety net that existed since the Great Depression. The recession was used as an excuse to cut taxes and slash government spending to spark growth. This was called "Reaganomics." He downsized government contributions. His policies were presented as a solution to homelessness. He alleged that if only every church and synagogue would take in ten welfare families, then poverty and homelessness could be eliminated. This conservative approach was reminiscent of how homelessness was addressed in the 19th century. Reagan advisors saw homelessness as a temporary problem that would cycle itself away, just as it had several times before – they did not anticipate that the conditions that they were sowing would be the fertile ground for long-term homelessness. They also didn't anticipate backlash from religious communities who didn't want to be the ones held responsible if homelessness didn't go away.

Religious communities argued that it was the state's job to care for the poor – that housing the homeless and feeding the hungry is the responsibility of the public sector.

While HUD existed as the main federal agency offering housing and programs aimed at helping the poor, under Reagan (and continuing with the next presidents), HUD's funding was reduced by 60%. The years between 1979 and 1983 saw $54 billion a year in cuts to affordable housing, and by 1982 cities were opening up emergency shelter programs across the country (Bayer 2014). Reagan abdicated the federal government's role in managing homelessness and housing policies. He was so disengaged from housing programs for the poor and middle class that he reportedly didn't recognize Samuel Pierce, his own HUD secretary. To his administration's scandal where HUD money was funneled to Republican consultants rather than building and repairing low-income housing, he turned a blind eye. Under Reagan, federal spending on subsidized and public housing dropped from $26 billion to $8 billion. Reagan was regarded as a masterful communicator and he was effective in stigmatizing people who were homeless and blaming them, not the government, for their poverty and housing distress. He announced that people sleeping on park benches, doorways, or grates to keep warm are choosing that lifestyle. His attitude fostered a cultural climate where it became acceptable to arrest people who were homeless or tear down their temporary encampments. The public responded by dramatically increasing calls on police to do something to get rid of homeless people. As Hoovervilles are named for President Hoover, it has been alleged that every park bench in America on which a homeless person sleeps should have Ronald Reagan's name on it (Drier 2011; Roberts 2016). In short, no understanding of today's homelessness could be complete without remembering Reagan's contribution to it.

Most presidential administrations have been less than noteworthy about their support for homelessness programs, especially those that would benefit families, children, and youth. However, most still engage in claims-making about how helpful they were to the cause. Gerald Ford didn't do much to help people who were homeless. His presidency occurred during a time of economic stagnation, and Ford believed that inflation, not a recession, threatened the economy, so he tried to institute mechanisms to control public spending. His program Whip Inflation Now, or WIN, required that the public reduce their spending on things like gasoline. He proposed a tax increase, then withdrew it, then proposed a tax reduction plan. Ford was viewed as a flip-flopper because he alternated from promoting a tax increase and a tax reduction within months. A deep recession took hold. Congress took steps to try to help the economy recover, and in Ford's last budget request to Congress he asked for funds for 506,000 new low-income housing units, including 400,000 rent vouchers to pay for privately owned housing in the Section 8 program. That was a high watermark for federal assistance but it was short-lived because under

Reagan funding for new subsidies dipped below 100,000 units per year, and by the time President Bill Clinton signed the Welfare Reform Act in 1996, fewer than 9,000 units were funded (Callahan 2013).

President Jimmy Carter is known for his post-presidential interest in building homes for Habitat for Humanity and his view that housing is a human rights (Milligan 2018), but during his presidency housing protections were not a priority. Carter, a religious man from the South, had compassion for the poor but was fiscally conservative. His presidency is regarded as being largely ineffective. He was dealing with economic issues of stagflation and recession, and there were international challenges that he reportedly was ill-prepared to manage. While Carter tried to overhaul welfare programs, Congress rejected most of his attempts, such as a guaranteed minimum income, job guarantee for people who were unemployed, a negative income tax. Carter himself rejected welfare reform program ideas if they increased government spending. Some allege that the major trouble escalating homelessness started out in 1979 with deep cuts to affordable housing programs that started under the last year of Carter's presidency, when he made across-the-board cuts to all of federal programs to cope with the recession (Bayer 2014). Carter sought reforms to the country's welfare, health care, and tax systems but was largely unsuccessful, partly due to poor relations with Congress (Milligan 2018).

Presidents post-Reagan to the present day have made minimal erratic progress in addressing homelessness, despite their rhetorical concern for the poor. President George Herbert Walker Bush was more interested in foreign than domestic policy. His 1990 Omnibus Budget Reconciliation Act called for a sizable tax hike and increased spending on assistance programs, such as unemployment, but Republicans discontent for his administration grew following the Savings and Loan collapse when Bush called for a massive federal appropriations package that cost taxpayers millions of dollars. The Cranston-Gonzalez National Affordable Housing Act of 1990 presented a commitment to house all Americans but didn't include money to do so. His inability to address unemployment and economic issues resulted in his reliance on volunteerism as his touchstone to alleviate societal ills in his Points of Light endeavors. Volunteerism was to demonstrate the power of individuals to improve issues ranging from care for infants, teenagers with AIDS, adult illiteracy, gang violence, or job training for the homeless. His most notable social program was his signing of the Americans with Disabilities Act of 1990, which forbade discrimination based on disability in employment, public accommodations, and transportation.

Observing that the nation's public housing stock was deteriorating, around 1993 Congress created the Hope VI program (Homeownership and Opportunity for People Everywhere). Designed to deconcentrate where poor people lived, tower-type and project housing were razed and replaced with smaller public housing units that fit a new way to think about low-income housing.

This is at the time that President Bill Clinton's administration proclaimed that "the era of big government is over," which, like Reagan, resulted in slashing welfare benefits for poor children and their parents. This was accomplished by his 1996 signing the Personal Responsibility and Work Opportunity Reconciliation Act, which shifted the nation's public-assistance model from welfare to "workfare." In 1996, in cooperation with the Republican majority in Congress, Clinton fulfilled his campaign promise to "end welfare as we know it." His welfare reform approach was rooted in a culture of poverty argument that viewed poor people as dependent, lazy, and taking advantage of the system. The former cash-assistance program, Aid to Families with Dependent Children (AFDC), was replaced by Temporary Assistance to Needy Families (TANF). Intent on quashing government dependency, the new program limited lifetime assistance to five years and required parents to find work within two years (Gripp 2014).

President Clinton's legacy to "help" the needy was to gut welfare and criminalize the poor (Nadasen 2016). He allegedly continued and intensified the anti-poor policies of the Reagan–Bush era, especially for African-American women, and his Violent Crime Control and Law Enforcement Act is the largest crime bill in history which helped contribute to the criminalization of homelessness. This act built prisons, expanded the death penalty, eliminated federal funding for inmate education, intensified racial profiling, and ushered in an area of arrest for nonviolent offenses, such as homeliness. Members of Clinton's cabinet quit in opposition to his welfare policies. As Peter Edelman (1997) wrote in a scathing editorial about the president's welfare plan, it wasn't a welfare reform act but a bill designed to cut assistance programs that had been proven to be effective for decades to millions of vulnerable women and children. The magnitude of the dangers in this policy change was stunning and could be predicted to make life much worse for millions of people in the future.

> The best that can be said about this terrible legislation is that perhaps we will learn from it and eventually arrive at a better approach. I am afraid, though, that along the way we will do some serious injury to American children, who should not have had to suffer from our national backlash.

President George W. Bush followed Clinton's welfare to work model and cuts to the welfare system. Bush pledged support for faith-based organizations, charities, and community groups to take the lead in solving social problems as "armies of compassion" (Dilulio 2002). Seeing the rise of homelessness, Bush is credited for instituting HUD's shift to the Housing First program (Frum 2013). The Housing First approach was met with criticism by homeless advocates who observed that homelessness was just the most extreme form of a lack of affordable housing problem faced by most low-income people generally. Critics of the Housing First model were concerned that by focusing resources on the nation's chronic homeless that it would distract the federal government from subsidizing better housing for millions of people who did not literally live in the streets. But there was another concern about the Housing First program. Programs with many employees existed across the country to help the homeless, and there was concern that moving people out of shelters and into the community would ultimately cost less and people employed by the nonprofit and shelter-industrial complexes would lose their jobs. Data collected from HUD indicated that there was a reduction in the chronically homeless from Housing First, so the program was deemed a big success (Frum 2013). But others, including Ralph da Costa Nunez (2017a), thought that the Housing First program would actually end up increasing homelessness, not curtailing it.

Under Bush's administration, Section 8 program vouchers were cut dramatically – in 1976, 400,000 vouchers were provided, but by 2003 only 34,000 new vouchers were provided to families and his 2005 budget cut them even further. He sought reauthorization of the 1996 Welfare Reform law that would make it harder for single mothers because neither going to school nor caring for children counted as work-time, since the law required people work 40 house per week in order to qualify for aid. His proposed cuts to the Women, Infants and Children (WIC) nutrition program would eliminate almost 200,000 mothers from the program (Johnson 2006). HUD's emphasis on the chronic homeless, not families, has led critics to not necessarily think that Bush should be given accolades for his supposed elimination of homelessness.

Barack Obama inherited the economic woes of the Bush administration and signed a stimulus package into law, earmarking $787 billion for tax cuts as well as spending on infrastructure, schools, health care, and green energy. Whether or not these initiatives brought about the end of the Great Recession is a matter of debate. His campaign promoted "hope and change," but as it pertains to daily lives of the homeless, not much changed. He announced his intention to extend Housing First since "stable housing is the foundation upon which people build their lives...Without that, it is next to impossible to achieve good health, positive educational outcomes, or reach one's economic potential" (Christian Science Monitor 2010). However, under Obama the federal government continued to focus its attention and funding on chronically homeless adults, extending George W. Bush's goal of ending chronic and veteran homelessness in a restructured HOPE VI into a new program called the Opening Doors campaign. It set a five-year date for ending chronic homelessness and veteran homelessness and a ten-year date for ending family homelessness (Capps 2016). These campaigns did not achieve their goals. Obama's Opening Doors plan proposed to end youth and family homelessness by 2020, but it wasn't until 2016 that HUD's budget called for any focused effort on family homelessness. This came in the form of an $11 billion request in mandatory funding over ten years for housing assistance (mostly Housing Choice Vouchers and a bit for Rapid Re-housing) for families who meet HUD's limited definition of homelessness. HUD's FY 2017 family homelessness proposal was regarded by most observers as dead on arrival, due to the size of the funding request, the limited legislative calendar, and the current fiscal and political budget climate (Duffield 2016). Under Opening Doors and HOPE VI, razing current housing to build new led to gentrification and a decrease of available housing that low-income people could find or afford, especially if their welfare benefits had been cut because they couldn't obtain jobs that met the new criteria of Welfare to Workfare programs (Griffin 2015). The HOPE VI program didn't include enough replacement units for the poorest public housing clients that forced to relocate. Critics have charged that HOPE VI was less about improving public housing for the poor and more about plumping-up real estate values (Raskin 2012). Thus, housing support for homeless families did not advance, and Obama administration support for those with chronic mental illness was not overly effective since his lead agency, the Substance Abuse and Mental Health Services Administration, denied or downplayed the extent to which mental health problems exist (Torrey 2013). The major change to help the homeless under Obama didn't happen.

Now we are in the Trump era. Trump, a real estate mogul, supposedly knows about property but not much about poverty. While history is yet to be written, it is clear that helping the poor and homeless is not his priority. His policies lay the foundation that make the increase of poverty and homeless inevitable (Kimura 2017). The hiring of HUD head Ben Carson, who has no credentials in the housing or poverty fields, exacerbates the problem of Trump's millionaire cabinet that is estranged from everyday reality as the public knows it. HUD official Lynne Patton, who was used as a political prop to illustrate that President Trump isn't really a racist, was picked by Trump to be the New York–New Jersey regional administrator for HUD and has no prior experience in the field; her credentials were an event planner who helped plan Eric Trump's wedding (Murdock 2019).

Looking at the Trump 2018 budget (Rice 2017), his funding decisions made deep cuts in rental assistance for families and other aid for the nation's poorest urban and rural communities, which would shrink the supply of affordable housing and increase homelessness and other hardships across the country. In particular, his request of $40.7 billion for HUD programs in 2018 is $7.4 billion (15%) below what policy makers recently approved for 2017. The budget is designed to eliminate *Housing Choice Vouchers* for more than 250,000 low-income households, $771 million less than policy makers provided for 2017 and $2.3 billion less than what is needed to renew all vouchers in 2018. Because the program mainly helps extremely low-income seniors, people with disabilities, and working families with children, the cuts would hit these groups hardest, increasing *homelessness* and other *hardships* and undermining the stability that children need to *thrive and succeed*. Public housing funding is to be slashed by $1.8 billion, or nearly 29% compared to 2017. Public housing already faces over *$26 billion in repair needs*, such as fixing leaky roofs or replacing outdated heating systems and electrical wiring and new cuts, on top of the *21% cut from 2010 to 2016*. It further jeopardizes the health and safety of public housing's 2.2 million residents and sharply accelerates the loss of affordable units. President Trump has cut $133 million (5.6%) from homeless assistance grants to help communities prevent homelessness, help homeless families move quickly out of shelters and into stable homes, and prevent chronic or episodic homelessness. His budget also eliminates the HOME, Community Development Block Grant, and Choice Neighborhoods programs that give aid to poor rural and urban communities. Altogether, poor communities would lose more than $4.1 billion a year to improve basic infrastructure like streets and water and sewer lines, provide life-enriching services to youth and seniors, build and rehabilitate affordable housing for low-income residents, and promote economic development. It also eliminates the *National Housing Trust Fund*, Fannie Mae and Freddie Mac, which provided $174 million in 2016 toward state and local efforts to develop affordable rental housing for those who struggle most to pay the rent and make ends meet. He has also attempted to gut key portions of the *Dodd–Frank Act*, which would remove some of the rules protecting Americans from another recession (History.com 2018).

Summary

The past reflects a wide array of approaches used to address housing needs of people. It shows how changes in social policies and funding strategies either alleviate or exacerbate homelessness. There have been some times when presidential administrations have shined light on poverty and homelessness and taken clear and decisive policy and fiscal actions to do something about them. There have been many more times when obstacles and other presidential priorities have occurred, laying the foundation for current – and future – homelessness. It is important to note that both Democrats and Republicans have been both protectors of homeless services and funding, and times when they have both been impediments. In this regard, homelessness has been bipartisan.

Note

1 www.fns.usda.gov/snap/able-bodied-adults-without-dependents-abawds.

5   Where We Are Now

Homelessness is no longer a rarity – homeless people can be found in almost every community, large or small, across the nation. Unless we do something drastically different – such as creating an alternative paradigm for addressing homelessness – we predict it is here to stay. How it is being addressed is influenced by the past, by theories, and surely will impact future trajectories.

We live in more bifurcated social and economic systems than in the last 50 years. Racial divisions, hostility toward the poor and immigrants are increasing and polarizing the public as the social safety net is being eroded. An underlying premise of this bifurcation seems to be that the rich deserve keeping large sums of money; unless others are willing to follow rules set by elites, they are viewed to deserve life challenges. Homeless people – not social systems, and not the policies set by elites – are the target for change.

One would hope that preventing poverty and homelessness would be a bipartisan issue, but it's not. Jacob Hacker's book *American Amnesia: How the War on Government Led us to Forget What Made America Prosper* (2016) points out how the nation's quest for equality is dying because of political alignments that promote different economic models, values, and strategies. Clashes between the haves and have-nots are ideological, political, and powerful, impacting everyday operations of society. The quest to success means stepping on the backs of others. Humanity has taken a backseat to money.

Richard Reeve's book *Dream Hoarders: How the American Upper-Middle Class Is Leaving Everyone Else in the Dust* explains that inequality festers when we don't have a strong public commitment to help poor children as much as wealthy ones. Educational apartheid, as witnessed through the growth of private and charter schools while underfunding public ones, is counterproductive for democracy. Intergenerational inheritance of status is interwoven into our social institutions. Children from resourced homes with tutors, coaches, enrichment opportunities, super-nutrition, and lifestyles with discretionary resources, time, assistance, and money start off light-years ahead. When inadequate funding is given to schooling all children, not providing all children with good health care, and skewing opportunities in an unfair playing field, then the deck is dealt in a way that almost automatically ensures challenges will be almost impossible to overcome. The current intolerance festering between people is a product of our lack of commitment to human rights instruction and implementation across America. The disparity we observe is the product of years of under-investment in creating whole and healthy generations of children, who have become adults and spawn new generations. The spread has become so great between these two groups that the gap may never be made up. Not unless we decide to do something about it.

While once owning a home and having a good job was a goal, today the American dream is simply getting by. People tread water financially, and most haven't seen a substantial increase in their incomes in years. Two-parents work, often multiple jobs, to make ends meet. While the rich have savings and no debt, Americans *have more than $1 trillion in credit-card debt*, according to the Federal Reserve, plus another *$1.5 trillion in student loans* among 45 million borrowers. The fact families owe more in student loans than on credit cards is noteworthy. Motor vehicle loans are over $1.1 trillion. People have $15 trillion in mortgage debt. Vacations are spent working, retirements less common, and time of leisure increasingly rare (LaMagna 2018; Robin and Dominquez 2018). Rising income inequality is fueling racial disparities and immigrant oppression (Manduca 2018). Racial tensions are climbing at rates not seen since the 1960s Civil Rights struggle. The dog-eat-dog mentality is a consequence of the stratification system that sees growth of the top skyrocketing while everyone else is struggling to not fall further down the ladder.

While certain groups are more likely to live in poverty, no one is immune to being poor. An Associated Press survey found that four out of five US adults have limited economic security, which can lead to poverty and homelessness. People move in and out of poverty throughout their lives, many from middle-class backgrounds with years of steady employment who fall into poverty and can't recover (Froelich et al. 2018). The housing crisis in America is "a ticking time bomb that's only going to get worse," according to a Harvard University study (2018; Hobbes 2018). Current conditions are inevitably going to lead to more family housing distress.

Yet the nation's paradigm continues to focus on individuals instead of society as the culprit of this mega-distress. The view that poor people deserve to be poor because they are lazy permeates the American mindset. Former House Speaker John Boehner announced that poor people think "I really don't have to work. I don't really want to do this. I think I'd rather just sit around" when in reality, a large and growing share of the nation's poor work full-time – sometimes 60 or more hours a week yet still don't earn enough to lift themselves and their families out of poverty (Reuters 2014). It's also commonly believed that the rich deserve their wealth because they work harder than others, but actually "a large and growing portion of the super-rich have never broken a sweat. Their wealth has been handed to them" (Reich 2010a, 2015), manifestation of privilege.

As discussed earlier, stratification exists because it is beneficial to people at the top. Rise of the working poor and nonworking rich challenges core American assumptions that people are paid what they're worth, and work is justly rewarded. Ranks of working poor are growing because wages at the bottom have dropped, adjusted for inflation, with more people taking low-paying jobs in retail, food, hospitality, and caregiving services, making minimum wages that are lower today than a quarter century ago. Recipients of public assistance must meet qualifications that are extraordinarily difficult to meet, forcing them to do without or finagle in ways rich people can't fathom.

In the meanwhile, a new American aristocracy grows. "Self-made" men and women have shrunk while numbers of nonworking rich heirs are swelling. Becoming wealthy is associated with inheriting money from family and growing up in elite neighborhoods with access to resources and networks that money provides. Six of today's ten wealthiest Americans are heirs to prominent fortune; Walmart heirs have more wealth than the bottom 40% of Americans combined. Elites are transferring wealth to their children and grandchildren – the Boston College Center on Wealth and Philanthropy projects $59 trillion will have been passed down to heirs between 2007 and 2061. Tax code changes encourage this by favoring unearned income over earned income. The tax rate paid on capital gains dropped from 33% in the late 1980s to 20% today, putting it below the top tax rate on ordinary income (36.9%); if owners of capital assets hold them until death, their heirs pay zero capital gains taxes. Such gains account for over half the value of assets held by estates worth $100+ million. Investments of major assets flow into hands of people who have never worked, which endangers our economic stability and democracy as dynastic wealth inevitably and invariably accumulates political influence and power (Reich 2015). Tax changes are a transfer of wealth from the public to rich private individuals, and it's likely to intensify in the coming years as the country borrows to fund the $1.5-trillion tax cut enacted in 2018 that benefits corporations and the ultra-rich. Congress is cutting programs that benefit middle and working classes, like Social Security and Medicare, because the nation "can't afford" them. That would be an even further draining of wealth from lower-income Americans to the 1% (Hiltzik 2018).

Things have never been better for America's mega-wealthy. *Forbes* magazine lists the nation's 400 richest people; in 1982 you had to have a net worth of $80 million to be included, with their average net worth of $230 million – but in 2016, rich Americans net worth was $1.7 billion to enter the *Forbes 400*, with average members holding $6 billion, over ten times the 1982 average after adjusting for inflation (Inequality.org 2018). These Forbes 400 richest people are .00025% of the population yet together they own more than the 150 million adults in the bottom 60% of Americans. At the bottom end of the stratification ladder, the share of the nation's wealth held by the bottom two-thirds of the population dropped from 5.7% in 1987 to 2.1% in 2014 (Papenfuss 2019a, b). Thus, the rich

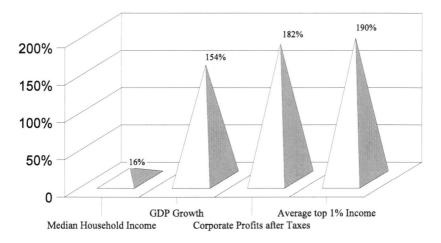

Figure 5.1 Change in Selected Indicators of Inequality Since 1980.
Source: U.S. Census Bureau, Tomas Piketty, Emmanuel Saez, St. Louis Fed.

are getting a lot richer while middle-class and poor people in America are losing ground.

Income inequality in the US has steadily been increasing since the 1980s and has reached levels last seen in years just before the Great Depression (Ebbinghaus 2015). The National Bureau of Economic Research found in 1929, just before the Wall Street Crash that precipitated the Great Depression, the top 0.1% richest adults' wealth was close to 25%. During the Depression and World War II, wealth of the top 0.1% declined until reaching its low watermark in the 1970s, but since the 1980s wealth inequality has increased, with the top 1% wealth at 40% in 2016 versus 25% in the 1980s. Wealth owned by the bottom 90% has collapsed in similar proportions. They found that the only country with similarly high levels of wealth inequality was Russia (Kelleher 2019). As Figure 5.1 shows, the richest 1% of Americans and US corporations have done very well since 1980, but the vast majority of individuals have not seen financial growth, with the disparity between the haves and have-nots growing.

Bifurcation between the rich and poor is staggering. Over the 100 years the income gap between the richest of the rich and everyone else widened dramatically, richest 0.1% claim as much wealth as 90% of the US population (Ehrenfreund 2017). This is not an accident. The results are by design. Income inequality refers to the extent to which income is distributed in an uneven manner among a population. The gap between the rich and everyone else has been growing by every statistical measure for 30 years. The Economic Policy Institute (2018) found that the top 1% of US families made over 25 times what families in the bottom 99% did (Sommeiller and Price 2018). But the biggest divide is seen in the upper 0.01%, which have over 198 times the income of the bottom 90% (Figure 5.2).

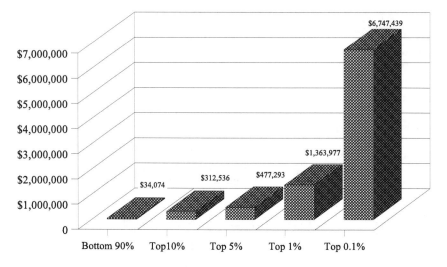

Figure 5.2 Concentration of Income in US, 2015: Mean Income.
Source: Data downloaded from https://c6dl5xiuaua7tk6u-zippykid.netdna-ssl.com/wpcontent/uploads/2017/05/US-Average-Income-2015-1-768x424.png.

Despite a growing population, homeownership rates have fallen for young and nonwhite adults, who experience glaring housing inequality compared to older, white Americans. The average home sold in 2017 cost over four times the median income. Low-cost housing is disappearing from the market and what's available appreciated at twice the rate of high-end homes. Incomes can't keep pace with soaring housing costs – since 1960, renters' median earnings increased only 5% while rents have spiked 61%; homeowners earn 50% more while home prices have gone up 112%. One-third of US households (38.1 million) paid over 30% of their incomes for housing in 2016, over half (20.8 million) are renters, and 80% of renters and 63% of owners making less than $30,000 are housing-cost-burdened. The result is a sharp divergence in housing costs and incomes which have fueled a long-term increase in the cost burden that renters and homeowners face (Harvard University 2018).

The rate of homelessness is higher for nonwhite families, a reflection of racial wage inequality. It also reflects that many people who need housing support can't get it. The homeownership rate between black and white Americans is widening; since 1987, white homeownership rates increased 3.6 % while black homeownership rates fell by 2.7%. Black Americans are 30% less likely than whites to own a home; Hispanic homeownership rates trail by 26.1% (Harvard University 2018).

Often, rents cost as much as mortgages. If people can't find affordable homes to buy or rent, they are at risk of homelessness. If they spend a third of their income on housing, they are at risk of homelessness. It is well documented that US income inequality has risen steadily since the 1980s. Because the wealthy have access to many opportunities for tax avoidance and tax evasion, traditional data sources under-estimate actual inequality (Kelleher 2019).

The Dirty Truth about Taxes

The notion that poor people take more of taxpayer money than the rich is bunk, yet people continue to buy this myth. The notion that tax breaks to the wealth will trickle down and give poor people benefit is also nonsense. Tax breaks, especially under Reagan and Trump, have strategically been designed to enrich the already wealthy and manipulate the poor and middle classes to think that it's somehow fair – perhaps to massage them with the illusion that one day they too could be rich.

The federal government spent $190 billion in 2015 to help Americans with housing, but little of it went to struggling families (Fischer and Sard 2017). Wealthy people get far more government aid, including housing assistance, than do poor people (Badger and Ingraham 2015). The mortgage interest deduction for big houses and second-home tax breaks results in 5 million people making over $200,000 getting more housing financial assistance than the 20 million people who live on less than $20,000 annually. Rental assistance programs are deeply underfunded and reach less than one in four eligible households (Fischer and Sard 2017). Tax breaks for the rich in deductions for mortgages incentivize people with big homes to buy bigger ones, or second homes. This mortgage interest deduction is equivalent to the government offering you money, not your keeping your *own* money (Meni 2018). Interest on second homes or yachts is tax deductible, as are rental property expenses. Capital gains and estate taxes benefit the rich, not the poor, resulting in poor people paying higher tax rates than rich folks. Social Security taxes aren't taken out after incomes reach $118,500, so when people decry that Social Security (which helps poor people the most) is running out of money, the program's long-term deficit could be cut by 86% if there was no income cap.

The 2019 federal budget announced cutting the Supplemental Nutrition Assistance Program by more than $260 billion over ten years, a 40% cut, through radically restructuring how benefits are delivered, cutting eligibility for at least 4 million people, and reducing benefits for many others. The unemployed, elderly, and low-income working families with children would bear the brunt of the cuts. These proposals come on the heels of a tax law the President championed that benefits the wealthy and corporations, adding $1.5 trillion to deficits (Rosenbaum et al. 2018).

The Trump administration claimed corporate tax cuts would lead to wage increases *of up to $9,000 a year* for ordinary workers, but to date workers' wages remain stagnant. Tracking by Americans for Tax Fairness shows that only *about 400* out of America's 5.9 million employers have announced any wage increases or one-time bonuses related to the tax cuts.

That's about 0.007%. Real wages have *actually declined* since after accounting for higher gas prices, prescription drug prices, tariff and other costs. Moreover, services that working families rely on are under attack. After signing the tax-cut package that *added $2 trillion* to the deficit over a decade, Trump's budget proposes to cut $1.3 trillion for Medicare, Medicaid, and the Affordable Cart Act, and House Republicans went even further, proposing *$2.1 trillion* in health-care cuts. Fifty-three Republican members of Congress who voted for the law could claim upward of $280,000 a year each in tax cuts, with some receiving millions (Kitson 2018). This is at a time when the typical 401K holds under $13,000. Eighty percent of tax breaks for 401Ks and individual retirement accounts go to the richest 20% of Americans, with only 7% going to the bottom 60% (Konczal 2014).

Meanwhile, the deficit soared 42% and tops $22 trillion for the first time in US history (Papenfuss 2019a). According to the Institute on Taxation and Economic policy, *Amazon* doubled its profits from $5.6 billion in 2017 to $11.2 billion in 2018, but the company isn't expected to pay a cent in federal taxes – a negative 1% tax rate, compared to the standard 21% corporate tax rate and a far cry from the proposed 70% top tax rate for people making $10 million or more, regarded as a "moderate, evidence-based policy" (Blumberg 2019; Levitz 2019). The Trump Organization, a collection of 500 pass-throughs, *could save over $20 million* annually from that deduction alone and give the real estate industry new loopholes (Kitson 2018).

There is a widespread disparity in income since 1980, with the median household income rising only 16% while the top 1% has seen incomes grow by over 190% (Levitz 2019). Put another way, the top 1% of the richest 1% in the US make 198 times more than those in the bottom 90%. The average income for the top 0.01% grew 322% between 1980 and 2015, while the income for the bottom 90% grew almost not at all at 0.03% (Gilson and Rios 2016).

Racism and Homelessness

The majority of reported homeless individuals are white. But homelessness is regarded as a consequence of institutionalized racism because rates of homelessness by race are significantly higher for African-American and mixed-race individuals (National Low Income Housing Coalition 2018; Olivet 2016; Statista 2018). Systemic racism continues to plague America; while steps forward have been made, minority groups still face discrimination in housing, criminal justice, education, and employment. The average median household income disparities by race are staggering: $56,516 for white households compared to $36,898 for minority households. African-American households are four times more likely to be considered food insecure, which experience unemployment rates double that of the white rate since 1973. Racial discrimination in housing, education employment, health, and criminal justice system increase the risk for homelessness (Janosko 2018). The Urban Institute reports income ratio between whites and blacks at 2:1, while the wealth ratio is 6:1. People of color are shown fewer rental units and denied leases based on credit history more than white renters (Olivet 2016). Latinx individuals, in Los Angeles for example, make up 35% of the homeless population but are only 30% of homeless people who receive outreach services and only 21% of those who receive permanent housing (Qu and Lai 2019).

Socio-emotional Value of Stratification

Homeless and poor people are useful to have around, for they show a visible image of what NOT to be. This is one reason why images of chronically homeless, skid-row-bum, derelict, disheveled people with possessions in garbage bags get promoted, rather than images of clean, hard-working families who try hard at school and love each other. There is no cachet in saying homeless people might be *just like you*.

Stratification is a wealth–prestige–power hierarchy, but also promotes an attitude of what people are like, their goodness, their potential, and their value. Identity is shaped by social class. Our self-concept is shaped through gateway contexts of home, school, and work. Meritocratic values promote the notion people can achieve anything if they have enough talent and work hard. Maybe if you keep trying, you will make the great leap forward. This is an illusion, it's not true because the stratification system is rigged so people at the bottom can almost never make it to the top. If someone from the bottom rungs of society is lucky enough to make it to the top, they receive public acclaim and are used as an example to promote the delusion that if anyone who wants to succeed can (Manstead 2018).

Social placement shapes our minds and how we see the world, ourselves, and other people (Manstead 2018). Lifestyles profoundly influence the way we think. Upper- and middle-class people set standards that reinforce aspirations but design institutions/systems that make it hard for working- and lower-class people to access opportunities that increase social mobility and material circumstances. Lifestyle conditions have lasting impacts on our personal and social identities, which influence ways we think, feel, and act. Working-class people score higher on measures of empathy and helping others in distress but have more prejudice toward immigrants and minorities who they perceive as economic threats to their already precarious position on the stratification ladder. Social class differences in identity, cognition, feelings, and behavior make it less likely that working-class individuals can benefit from educational and occupational opportunities to improve their material circumstances. Changes in our distribution of resources are needed to break the cycle of deprivation that limits opportunities and threatens social cohesion.

People growing up in middle-upper-class environments have more available material and psychological resources and stronger beliefs about their ability to shape their futures. In comparison, individuals growing up in lower-class environments have fewer resources available and have weaker beliefs about their ability to control their outcomes. Prejudice against people of different classes and negative attitudes toward the poor or unemployed occur because people are class-insular, associating with those in their own social class. Research indicates working-class people are more authoritarian in their actions (Adorno et al. 1950). Because they feel disadvantaged by the social systems, instead of questioning and challenging them, those who suffer may be more likely to support them in what is known as the system-justification hypothesis. Feeling their precarious social positions threatened by social benefitting of immigrants, minorities, and those who are poor, even higher socio-economic status people may feel at risk of losing their economic stronghold and resort to discriminating actions and statements designed to be demeaning and keep the downtrodden in their place (Manstead 2018).

Symbolically, it is interesting that homeless people may resort to transporting their meager possessions in garbage bags. Unpacking this, it seems socially acceptable to talk about homeless people as "trash." (Goldberg 2015). The term "poor white trash" is "deft in its ability to demean multiple groups at once: white people *and* people of color, poor people and people who act like poor people, rural folks and religious folks, and anyone without a college degree" (Donnella 2018). The term reduces people to stereotypes like angry, lazy, dirty, overweight, stupid, bigoted, alcoholic, abusive, jobless, tacky, diseased, violent, and uneducated. By accepting the idea that white trash exists, people tacitly accept that there is another, different kind of whiteness. *Normal* white people are all the things white trash aren't – hardworking, educated, classy, kind, and good. Anyone who doesn't conform to those values can't ever really be fully white, hence white trash. There's no "Black trash" or "Hispanic trash," presumably, because for most of American history, those people were relegated to the bottom of the stratification ladder. White trash is an oxymoron, a term with white supremacy baked into it, because it's understood that if you're not white, you're trash (Isenberg 2017; Wray 2006). Isenberg observes that the connection between black populations and poor white people is more than just coincidence. In England's colonization quest they sent outcasts and folks they didn't want; when African slavery occurred, those sent weren't seen as high status. Viewing people as trash to be discarded resulted in our not talking respectfully to, or about, homeless people of any color because they are deemed worthless.

Summary

This arrangement provides a justification for keeping the wealthy and rich in their positions. It employs false-consciousness to entice people with fewer resources to accept what the powerful wish and do their bidding without complaint. It relies upon financial, institutional, and emotional means to justify that arrangement as appropriate. However, other ways to view and address homeless exist that may be more effective - and more humane.

Part II

Homelessness Paradigm Options

6   What's the Current Paradigm?

What are we doing to address homelessness and why are we doing it? The way the nation has approached homelessness reflects a framework, or paradigm, that embodies certain assumptions about homelessness, decisions that are not always transparent. Our interpretation of the dominant paradigm being used is based on what we see, not rhetoric espoused by leaders and beneficiary organizations.

A paradigm is a way to organize thinking about something. It's a lens that filters all the information and tries to make sense of. We see things according to a particular vantage point when other perspectives are available but choose to disregard. When we are attached to viewing the world, a situation, or a person in a particular way, that's all we see. Theories provide explanations, but paradigms are even bigger than theories. Think of a paradigm as an umbrella that surrounds a phenomenon. This umbrella shields us from outside elements and keeps us safe, contained. It can have a hole or two in it, but the umbrella is still functional to keeping a person dry – or in this case, our view of homelessness intact. The holes, or areas that are inconsistent with the paradigm's efficacy, are called anomalies. The more holes or anomalies that occur, the wetter someone will get, the more flawed the paradigm will be regarded, until the umbrella, or paradigm, is deemed to be no good and a new one is sought.

The paradigm we are using now isn't working. We need a new umbrella, a new paradigm to address homelessness. But what will that look like? That's what we are helping you in this book to figure out.

Thomas Kuhn's groundbreaking work on paradigms (2012) suggested when researchers adhere to a deeply entrenched paradigm, it invariably ends up reinforcing that paradigm since anything that contradicts it is ignored or manipulated to conform to already established dogma. This is seen by HUD's approach and data being used time after time. Almost everyone is relying on HUD's definition, methodologies, and numbers to tell us the "truth" about homelessness. But like holes in the umbrella that are getting bigger and more plentiful, it's clear that the current approach our nation is using to address homelessness isn't working well. It "reveals flawed economic logic, a failure to end chronic homelessness today, and (is) a paradigm that might actually sustain chronic homelessness into the future" (Duffield 2016).

Scholars recommend a paradigm shift – a prevention-oriented paradigm to prevent homelessness (Culhane et al. 2011), moving from being heartless to compassionately seeing homeless people as similar to oneself (Zint 2017), creating a feminist female-focused approach (Savage 2016), or countless others. The purpose of this book is to consider other paradigms and what they could offer to the prevention of homelessness.

The current national paradigm is an inadequate way of helping people who are poor or in housing distress. Leaders who have created and are employed by homeless systems have undoubtedly worked hard for something they believe is important and effective. They have vested interest in showing their systems work. The public doesn't have firsthand experience to know if systems work well or not. In the face of unknowing, it's easy to assume they are effective. Things often look good from an outsider's point of view. It's only when you get intimately involved with a system that you learn if it actually works. Through contact with people who use various systems, we have heard firsthand tales of success and failure. Combining the data together, it's clear to us that the existing approach will lead to greater poverty and homelessness unless we do something better.

The way science works, there will always be debate, dialogue, and criticism of paradigms. This is good, because as Kuhn points out, it helps translate knowledge into action. For instance, some scholars regard the Housing First model as a paradigm shift that embraces human dignity and doesn't require homeless people to address all of their problems before they can access housing. It is promoted as a more realistic approach that protects their dignity (Nelson and Prilleltensky 2010). Others see it as a philosophy-based program, but not a paradigm shift (Schiff and Schiff 2014). Others see it is losing focus and needs to be replaced with new and better approaches (Pleace 2012). Other critics allege the Housing First model is a failure, doesn't work, especially for families (Cohen 2015; Eskes 2017; LaMarche 2014).

Kuhn regarded the transition from one paradigm to another as the way science develops. Paradigm shifts are not threats to science but the way science progresses. Reviewing past attempts helps us to learn and create new approaches to homelessness. Paradigm and system changes are usually challenged. People have vested interests and monetary gain to protect. Look at healthcare reform debate as a paradigm shift – what we are doing isn't working well. What direction should we take? Other nations have created smooth and functional systems that keep all their residents healthy. Debates and paradigms are shaped by different views of reality.

Paradigm Options Explaining Homelessness

Part II of this book examines four major approaches to addressing solutions to homelessness. They will be ordered from what we believe are least to most helpful. Briefly, they include:

Let-Others-Fix-It Paradigms

Criminalizing homelessness has become a common method communities and courts use to deal with homeless people, but it may be the worst response to addressing homelessness. It doesn't solve it – but it does get people out of sight, either by putting them in jail or making them so scared that they hide. Relying on volunteers to solve homelessness hasn't solved it either, even though volunteers provide comfort and assistance. Because government abdicated its obligation to prevent poverty and homelessness, churches, NGOs, charitable organizations and philanthropic organizations have stepped up to mind the gap. Business and the private sector have become players in addressing homelessness, often for their own vested interests.

Housing Paradigms

This approach infers that since homelessness is a lack of housing, the solution is to get people housed. The pros and cons of HUD programs will be surveyed. Shelters and the shelter industrial complex will be examined as a solution for addressing homelessness. Considering different types of mortgage strategies will be introduced. The chapter on housing paradigms will conclude with the introduction of other forms of housing for the homeless.

Money Paradigms

Another way to prevent homelessness is through different allocations of money. This view assumes if people had enough money (or resources), then poverty and homelessness would become unlikely. Assistance programs and their cost begin this chapter, followed by examination of minimum wage, negative income tax, and universal basic income or guaranteed income options. It concludes with an introduction of cryptocurrency and blockchain as potential ways to assist homeless people.

Human Dignity Paradigms

The approaches discussed under this paradigm take a starkly different approach to thinking about what people need in order to be healthy, whole, and productive – and not homeless. It explores social responsibility and creation of a new social contract. Trauma as both a cause and a consequence of homelessness will be discussed. This chapter will conclude with a recommendation that a human rights approach be utilized, since it provides a comprehensive framework to address the host of mitigating factors that contribute to homelessness (Figure 6.1).

Most paradigms don't address underlying foundations on which poverty and homelessness are cultivated. Volunteers, police intervention, momentary housing strategies won't fix homelessness. We need more creative,

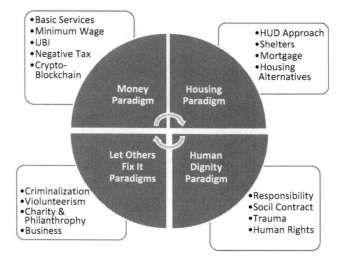

Figure 6.1 A Visual Diagram of the Paradigms and Sub-components that Will be Provided in the Remainder of Part II.

comprehensive, aggressive action plans that include multifaceted partnerships with buy-ins at the grass-roots levels. This requires a shift in mindset about how we work together and think about others.

The Current Paradigm's Underlying Assumptions

The current national model to address homelessness is piece-meal, fragmented, with multiple agendas. Government, philanthropic, NGO, and other agencies aren't transparent about the paradigm they use or the domain assumptions that underlie them. Tension exists between how real and ideal culture intersect. Ideal culture is what we want to see, while real culture tells us the way things actually are. Ideal culture tells us "we are our brother's keeper," but in reality, through intent or benign neglect, people regularly fall through holes of a frayed safety net. Somehow, we manage to straddle those contradictory positions without blinking an eye.

Because no up-front statement about our national paradigm exists, we have identified these trends driving our national approach to homelessness:

1   Homelessness is a product of social construction. Attitudes, beliefs, institutional systems, policies, practices, funding, and laws have increased the amount and severity of homelessness as it exists today. They could be changed to prevent homelessness in the first order and provide comprehensive relief to those currently afflicted so that poverty and homelessness are reduced.

2 National attempts to address homelessness have been piece-meal at best. Instead of endorsing a comprehensive national policy and putting into place the resources to achieve it, we have resorted to a "little of this and a little of that" approach. This patchwork includes government institutions, NGOs, charities, philanthropic organizations, businesses, well-trained professionals, and good-hearted volunteers. Many operate as silos without shared data collection, system monitoring, or supervision to identify best practices or dead-ends.

3 Financial costs to address homelessness have been significant yet not yielded an eradication of homelessness. Massive amounts of money are allocated to programs, contractors, services, and products that could be better apportioned to prevent homelessness and assist those in need. Curtailing manipulation of political/business/economic stakes-holder agendas is necessary. Movement from an expenditure to a social investment model holds promising possibilities for better cost-benefit outcomes.

4 National mind-set about homelessness is not in keeping with reality. There is an assumption that homeless people are defective individuals who have something wrong with them (i.e., mental illness, substance abuse, lazy, uneducated, criminals, unwilling to work, have health or cognitive problems, expect a hand-out). It does not assume that homeless people are "the same as us." It does not assume that homeless people may be well-educated, law-abiding, have jobs, loving families, and contribute to their communities. This model is not realistic or does not embrace their rights or human dignity.

5 The unit of analysis targets fixing homeless individuals. It is not focused on changing social systems, institutions, processes, policies, and funding that underscore the creation of inequality and economic distress. Because the current paradigm assumes something's wrong with homeless people, if we just "fix" them, then maybe they can become "normal." It is not attempting to fix a dysfunctional social structure or infrastructure.

6 The homeless care system prioritizes adult men with chronic problems, not families or children. Because that's where the funding, services, and emphasis have been, other groups experiencing homelessness have become more invisible, out of sight and out of mind.

7 Single mothers who are homeless heads-of-households often suffer from personal trauma, abusive relationships, gender and economic discrimination. Viewed as evidence of the breakdown of the American family, they aren't recognized for their strength and resilience caring for children with whatever resources they can pull together. The pro-marriage, anti-out-of-wedlock babies model to heal "the broken family" is not realistic (Elhage 2014; Filipovic 2018). Trauma as a cause or consequence of homelessness needs better recognition.

8 There is acknowledgment that homelessness may occur from social causes over which people have no control. These include racism, loss of jobs, poor wages, or lack of available, affordable housing. Because homelessness is not just a housing-availability issue, it requires a multifaceted comprehensive system of intervention that addresses underlying classism, racism, and sexism. While much rhetoric around such fixes exists, "isms" continue to thrive and oppress individuals.

9 Depriving homeless people of their rights and stigmatizing them as disposable has become common, making them fair game for ridicule or blame and targets of violence (Almendrala 2014, 2018; Hagle 2019). Things said about and done to homeless people by politicians, comedians, and the general public would be unthinkable/unlawful if said about racial minorities or groups.

10 The public assumes there are social and economic services resources available to help those in need. While some programs exist, they aren't always available and may not provide extensive assistance. For those who qualify (and many don't), there are waiting lists, limitations, exclusions, hoops to jump through, red-tape, documentation issues, and runarounds that make getting aid more difficult than outsiders assume. There is a smoke-and-mirrors approach foisted upon the American public to think that aid exists when it's very hard to get and may not be sustainable.

As a nation, we have calculated ways that make powerful people very rich at the expense of keeping most people poor, we've created assistance systems that look good on paper but actually don't work well for those who need help, we look down on the most beaten-down, vulnerable people of society as the cause of their victimization, and we continue to believe that the economic, legal, and social systems work well – for upstanding members of society. Whether we dare utter the politically and morally nasty truth or not, we have created a system where homeless people are seen as not as good as "us" and should be grateful to us for giving them any leg-up at all, since "beggars can't be choosers." And when poor people complain, our "how dare you?" response is all too common. This is what we see. You are welcome to disagree.

Shorthand Overview of Nation's Homelessness Paradigm

The paradigm assumes that people who are homeless somehow caused it themselves by having something wrong with them, made bad choices, or didn't try hard enough to overcome potential problems. We disagree with this assumption.

The paradigm assumes that there are systems in place that work and could help people out of homelessness and poverty if they just used them responsibly. We disagree with this assumption.

The paradigm assumes that our current stratification system is in the best interest of society and that institutional inequality that results in discrimination of women, poor people, disabled people, and nonwhite people is unfortunate but acceptable. We disagree with this assumption.

The paradigm assumes that poverty and homelessness can never be eliminated and the best that can be done is try to curb it as much as possible. We disagree with this assumption.

The current paradigm assumes that people who are poor have to prove their worthiness to receive help. This means meeting qualification criteria and following rules to maintain assistance. Embedded in this assumption is the idea that wealthy people (who do not have to prove their worthiness to their assets) are better people, and better investments for society, than those who are poor. We disagree with this assumption.

The current paradigm costs the nation, organizations, and individuals a great deal of money. We agree with this assumption and feel there are better ways to arrive at a better cost-benefit outcome.

While rhetoric reports that we want to prevent or eliminate poverty and homelessness, data-driven reality conveys that the current paradigm is designed to maintain poverty and homelessness. We agree with this assumption.

The paradigm stigmatizes and dehumanizes people who are homeless, and their stigmatization serves social benefit. We agree that stigmatization occurs and is not in the best interests of both society and people who are experiencing housing distress and poverty.

The current paradigm handles homelessness and poverty in such ways that cause physical, mental, and social problems that are preventable. Without changing the paradigm, the probability of future individual and intergenerational problems increases. We agree with this assumption.

The current paradigm questions whether poor and homeless people really want to work. We believe that most people want to work and feel useful and be respected for their contributions, as big or small as they may be. However, not everyone is able to work. People experience real and significant physical, emotional, cognitive, and social conditions that make it impossible for them to work. People's human value should not be correlated with their economic production. The difference between can't and won't is huge. Moreover, the way current jobs are configured provides little latitude for the needs of individuals. Childcare, transportation, emotional support, hours one can work, and goodness-of-fit between skills, abilities, and work demands also influence what people can provide.

Assuming that our current paradigm is the best and can adequately address homelessness is something we strongly disagree with. It has not, and will not prevent or eliminate homelessness, and can be predicted to increase poverty and homelessness in the future.

Summary

This chapter has reviewed what paradigms are and why they are useful in conceptualizing how homelessness is addressed. How homelessness is currently addressed in the US is a hodge-podge of components from each of the paradigms.

Every paradigm has an overarching theme with sub-directions. Our use of paradigm with homelessness may be more fluid than in some sciences, but nonetheless it provides a way of understanding and framing what is occurring, and why. In the chapter that follows, each of the aforementioned "paradigms" will be reviewed.

7 The Let-Others-Fix-It Paradigms

American independence embraces an "I will take care of myself" attitude. Daily life is structured around work, family, community, and trying to survive. While believing "being our brother's keeper" is important, people may find they don't have the time, energy, or money to help others. Homelessness is something the public feels needs to be addressed – but who is the one to do it? In this chapter, police, volunteers, charities, philanthropic organizations, and businesses will be examined, since they're often relied upon as the ones to do something about it.

The Criminal Justice Paradigm

Calling police is a common strategy when we need help. Unfortunately, police and courts have gained a reputation of supporting the well-to-do and not advocating for the poor or oppressed (Rikken 2016). An age-old paradigm being revitalized views homelessness as a crime and people who are homeless as criminals. For the poor and homeless, criminal justice communities may not be seen as their friend or protector but someone to avoid and fear. Criminalization of homelessness is counter-productive for individuals who lack housing, police, and judicial systems that spend precious time making victims criminals, and to the community that's given messages that homeless people are dangerous.

Being homeless is now considered a crime in many cities across the country. Peter Edelman's (2017) book *It's Not a Crime to Be Poor* asserts data bely that view. Many systems are predicated upon arresting and prosecuting people for being poor and the problems that poverty brings. Edelman describes how in the 1990s the nation adopted a set of criminal justice strategies that punished poor people in what he describes as government-run loan-shark operations that has put 10 million people owing the government over $50 billion in fines, fees, and other costs associated with misdemeanors that could have been treated in non-criminalized ways. A consequence of the Reagan era tax cuts, communities developed a "broken window" law enforcement policy to reduce deficits. Arrests for offenses that supposedly promote community order and quality of life filled jails and courts with poor people unable to pay bail, fines, or hire attorneys.

Fees poor people have to pay for being "criminals" accrue interest if unpaid, outlive the individual, and may be inherited by their families (Vallas 2014).

The movement away from systems of benevolence to criminalization of homelessness entails a long historical process of public discourse and welfare policies infused with race, class, and gender bias (Neubeck and Cazenave 2001). One of the consequences of having benefits systems being considered as entitlements rather than rights is not qualifying for assistance. Adoption of "suitability" and morality standards for communities, homes, and parents has resulted in ineligibility, denying people aid, accusing them of fraud, or taking away benefits (Gustafson 2009). Giving people a criminal record because they don't comply with arbitrary definitions of suitability is precisely what happens for countless people whose misfortune is that they are so poor they become homeless. Once awarded a criminal record for any reason, including breaking a law that doesn't really have to be considered a crime, poor people may be barred from receiving benefits. If put in jail, poor people don't just lose their liberty, they may lose their jobs, children, right to vote, be deported, and be charged for their jail room and board with no ability to pay it. Debtors are hounded by bill collectors, high interest rates, and new prosecutions until the day they die (Edelman 2017).

Criminalization of poverty motivated Mitch Snyder's homelessness prevention movement. He grew up in New York after his father abandoned the family when he was nine. This triggered behavior that got him in trouble with the police as he tried to find ways to survive. He broke into parking meters to get money, which sent him to a correctional facility. Hitchhiking west, he was found sleeping in a stolen car and convicted of grand theft auto, which led him to two years in federal prison. He participated in hunger strikes and work stoppages over prisoners' rights issues, which were also regarded as criminal violations.

Homelessness as Criminal

The National Coalition for the Homeless documents a national increase in the criminalization of homelessness. Criminal acts now include sleeping, camping, eating, sitting, or asking for money. City ordinances may include criminal penalties for violation, put people in jail, give them fines they cannot pay, destroy their possessions, or justify assaulting them. Many criminalization actions are targeted to make homelessness out of sight, and hopefully out of mind, for the public. Some of the common criminalization measures include:

- Ordering police to tear down shantytowns, forcing residents to flee elsewhere but with nowhere to go. Carrying out sweeps of areas where homeless people live results in destroying or confiscating personal property like tents, bedding, papers, clothing, medications, and documentation. It ensures there is nothing for people to return to afterwards.

- Making camping on public land, parks, or even remote areas illegal.
- Arresting people for being asleep in public, whether on a bench, on the ground, or other locations.
- Arresting people for loitering. People who have huddled over heat vents on the sidewalk to stay warm, go into libraries or stores to be safe, stay too long in restaurants to be in from bad weather, or use the restroom or other facilities may be arrested by authorities, since people don't want to be disturbed by homeless individuals.
- Banning panhandling so people cannot ask for spare change or assistance.
- Making it illegal for groups to share food with homeless persons in public spaces. Religious and other charitable groups have been arrested/fined for giving food, water, or other necessary items to homeless people.
- Enforcing a "quality of life" ordinance relating to public activity and hygiene.
- Making it illegal to sleep in your own vehicle.
- Giving homeless people the option of jail or taking a one-way plane, bus, or train ticket to another town, to become some other community's problem.

The National Law Center on Homelessness and Poverty (2018a) collects statistics that documents criminalization of homeless individuals. Handcuffs instead of housing are often used to penalize people for being poor. These include activities so fundamental to human existence that it defies common sense that they might be treated as crimes – falling asleep, standing still, and even sitting down are treated as criminal acts when performed in public places by people with nowhere else to go. They want local governments to cease police assaults on homeless people and repeal laws that criminalize homelessness. Pursing cost-effective alternatives to criminalization like more affordable housing, emergency services, improved coordination of existing services, and more police training related to homelessness would cost less and help more.

Once a person receives a criminal status, getting help is increasingly difficult, even when the crime committed was victimless or related to trying to survive on the street. Having nowhere to go, 50,000 people enter homeless shelters immediately exiting incarceration. Landowners don't want to rent to them, employers are reluctant to hire ex-cons. Legal restrictions and discriminations exacerbate homelessness. Fines and fees charged when accused of crimes – even for use of the jail cot – escalate because people don't have the money to pay them off (Mitchell 2018).

Violence against Homeless People

Viewing homeless people as criminals and worthless puts them at risk of being victims of murder and hate crimes. The National Coalition for the Homeless (2019) reports thousands of attacks against homeless people occur from coast-to-coast annually. Homeless people have been beaten to death while sleeping, set on fire, pummeled with bats, golf clubs, metal poles, wooden boards with nails protruding. They've been raped, had their meager possessions stolen, and suffer from a host of actions that would be illegal if done to other people. Hate crimes are for immutable qualities such as sexuality, ethnicity, and other innate characteristics, but since homeless people could change their housing status, their assaults may not be covered under Hate Crime laws. The federal government doesn't treat housing status–based crimes as hate crimes and the Justice Department isn't required to collect data on them (Foley-Keene 2017). Data on domestic violence attacks against homeless women (or women who become homeless to escape it) fall between the cracks; while we know it occurs, the numbers are likely numbing. Post-traumatic stress disorder associated from attacks can be significant; most will never receive treatment for it. Homeless people endure humiliations and injuries that cripple their bodies and the dignity of the human spirit. This type of data is never collected. Homeless people are not usually violent and far more likely to be victims of crime and violence than perpetrators of it. Many homeless people have been subject to trauma throughout their lives. This correlation between violence and homeliness is important to remember.

Evictions

Homelessness is a manifestation of an eviction crisis. If people can't pay their rent, they can be evicted. If you're evicted, chances are good that you have no money, no place to go, and have health or social impairments (Stephans 2019). The standard is that any time anyone spends a third to half their income on housing, they're at risk of losing their home. In 2016 over 11 million households spent at least 50% of their income on housing, and another 9.8 million spent more than 30%, not including heat and utilities.

No government data track evictions in America. Desmond, author of *Evicted* (2017), documented over 900,000 court-documented evictions in 2016 and finds it a gross undercount because there aren't systems that collect or aggregate the data on where and how many evictions occur. Eviction calculations include only households involving legal processes, not those where people moved with informal warnings. It's likely that most people who are confronted with eviction notices just pick up and move elsewhere.

Courts support property owners more than tenants fearing eviction. It costs landlords around $3500 to evict someone (Collatz 2018). Courts aren't sympathetic to squatters or renters not paying their bills. Not having money to pay for rent, those evicted don't have money to hire attorneys, and few states will provide a public defender for such cases. Legally there might be rights protections preventing evictions, but it will cost the tenant thousands of dollars for an attorney, court costs, and so on (Cost Helper 2019). States like Virginia lack tenant rights protections, so even if renters went to court to fight the eviction, they may not have a legal leg to stand on (Badger and Bui 2018; Badger and Ingraham 2015; Desmond 2017).

Evictions are higher in some areas than others, and such trends aren't happenstance. Evictions are highest in the Southeast, where poverty rates are high and minimum wage is low. They're higher in nonwhite communities, reflecting both wage and racial disparities. Evictions are also higher in Michigan, Indiana, and pockets of even rural areas across the nation. North Charleston, SC, has the highest evicting filing rate at 35.6% and eviction judgment rate of 16.5%. Other cities with high eviction rates include Richmond, Hampton, Norfolk and Newport News, Virginia, Jackson, Mississippi, and Warren, Michigan (Badger and Bui 2018; Desmond 2017).

If women call 911 and report domestic violence too many times, they can be evicted under "nuisance ordinances," which cover a variety of disturbing the peace issues (Edelman 2017). Because property owners can evict tenants for minor causes, there is a national push for "just cause" evictions. In places like New York, Denver, and Chicago rent control and just-cause eviction protections may offer relief to tenants. Tenant activism support rent controls so landlords cannot arbitrarily hike rents and on short notice. Profit-seeking landlords may evict people when selling their property, eliminating options when there aren't other available, affordable place to live. Forced evictions are supported by economic, political, and legal mechanisms that put tenants at disadvantage (Brickell et al. 2017).

Summary

Increasing laws that criminalize homeless people won't get rid of homelessness. They may, however, hide it from view and allow communities to tout they are doing something about homelessness. Such actions exacerbate poverty and homelessness, not prevent it. As things stand now, unless the nation changes this strategy, homelessness will continue to be a fineable, prosecutable, incarceration response.

Homeless people have enough problems, and adding being a criminal to the list isn't going to help them overcome obstacles. They can't afford lawyers to fight charges. The domino effect results in further criminalization, debt, poverty and homelessness. This may be an increasingly popular approach for dealing with homelessness, but the types of "crimes" that are associated with them would be preventable or handled in less punitive, more humane, and likely productive ways.

Volunteerism, Charity, and Philanthropy

A long-standing approach to helping poor and homeless people is relying upon volunteers, charitable institutions, religious organizations, and philanthropy. This doing-for-others dates back to the Elizabethan age when citizens were encouraged to give alms to the poor; it's part of religious doctrines of being your brother's keeper; it is central to the Bush administration's Thousand Points of Light emphasis on community service. But is this the best way to address homelessness?

There are several ways to look at this. One approach sees helping others to be as good for the giver as for the recipient. Another views helping as a necessary part of human relationships. When people need help and don't have family supports and don't qualify for government assistance, helping others is seen as acts of kindness. If people would fall through the cracks of existing systems, charity could fill the gap. There is the view that volunteers can help educate or motivate people to help themselves. When systems are too complicated to deliver services to all in an accessible manner, charity steps in. Another sees reliance on charity letting governments off the hook to ensure adequate provisions and protections to citizens. As long as others step-up to fill the gap, the government doesn't have to. (Smith 2018b)

Public shouldering responsibility to others can only go so far. Private charitable giving failed to solve challenges faced by public in the Great Depression or the 2008 Great Recession (Konczal 2014). Charity and volunteerism has moved from being an informal activity to being both big business and a government caregiving strategy. Charitable giving is a fund-raising strategy embraced by countless organizations that enables them to provide services as they bolster their assets. Charities and NGOs have become a form of third-party government (Boettke and Prychitko n.d.; Salamon 1987).

Salamon finds the government relies more heavily on nonprofit organizations than on its own programs to deliver human services. Nonprofits receive more of their income from government than from any other single source. Government contracts, and subcontracts, with countless other organizations, businesses, and individuals to provide a wide gamete of goods and services. Without them, the needs of millions of people would be unmet, but is also a money-maker for them. The voluntary sector operates as a shadow partner between government, markets, and consumers. It thrives because government systems failed to deliver needed goods and services to the public or are limited and inefficient.

Critics find reliance on this third-party sector unwise because it is prone to failure under certain inevitable conditions. Consumer demand for help increases while their money doesn't, so donations and compliance with government mandates become essential. Doing what the government wants and will fund becomes essential for NGOs, who cannot risk coloring outside the lines for fear of losing their funding. NGOs cannot be expected to fulfill what governments should be responsible for doing. When profit becomes a motivating factor for philanthropy or business, the caregiving mission may take a backseat.

Volunteerism: An American Value

Volunteering to help the poor and homeless is regarded as a nice thing to do. People pride themselves on working at the soup kitchen over Thanksgiving, delivering Christmas packages to needy children, or making curtains for shelters. Good intentions, kind-heartedness, and compassionate action abound, but we have to be realistic about their place in the big picture of eradicating homelessness. In an article on seven ways you can help the homeless (Fisher 2019), suggestions are (1) make eye contact and smile; (2) be hospitable, show empathy; (3) stop and say hello; (4) listen and respond to them like they were a friend; (5) create a blessing bag in your car and have it filled with items that you can give someone who is homeless; (6) help them to access a shelter; and (7) make a difference by volunteering or donating money. Now, there is nothing wrong with that list, but the suggestions are naïve to eradicating the causes of homelessness. They are perhaps designed to be of more benefit to the helper than the homeless person, who probably knows where the shelter is and may not want to talk with you. Good intentions, whether through volunteerism or charity, do not always result in the desired outcomes.

Volunteerism has roots in morality and politics. Historically it can be seen in Native Americans helping Colonists to survive, volunteer militias like the Minute Men, Ben Franklin's idea of a volunteer fire department, creation of Ladies Aid societies, and organizations like the YMCA, United Way, Rotary Club, Peace Corps, or Habitat for Humanity. Today, service programs are common in schools across the nation to instill the spirit of volunteerism into students. Over 1 in 4 people volunteer, 64 million people give 8 billion hours of time annually helping others (Rosenburg 2013), not counting everyday helping of family/friends. If a dollar amount was associated with their contributions of time, and if the government was responsible for picking up that tab, the amount would be significant – which gives governments huge incentive to promote volunteering.

Volunteerism was encouraged during the Great Depression. President Hoover announced the national response to the economic crisis was to focus on mutual self-help, charity, and voluntary giving. The failure of this approach led to demand for government assistance, which resulted in the creation of Roosevelt's New Deal. President Reagan called for voluntarism to address holes in the Great Society's social safety net that he had cut. Olasky's *The Tragedy of American Compassion* (1994) argument that 19th-century charity did better providing for the common good than the 20th-century welfare state became embraced by conservatives like Paul Ryan, who sought to devolve and shrink the federal government.

This approach views the best alternative to big government as voluntarism to ensure the safety net doesn't turn into a hammock that lulls able-bodied people into lives of dependency (Konczal 2014).

Charity and Philanthropy

While the terms are often used interchangeably, charity is an empathetic, compassionate emotional reaction to a specific situation whereas philanthropy is more of a strategic endeavor that identifies root causes and supports systemic solutions. Charitable actions may address needs unmet by public assistance programs. They may address a specific person (giving money to a beggar or financing a Go Fund Me), issue (like breast cancer victims or sending books to schools in Africa), or place that has suffered a disaster, hurricane, fire, and so on. Charity embodies goodwill toward others and is more micro in focus, where philanthropy focus is macro (Konczal 2014).

Historically, charities consisted of organizations (like churches) feeding and housing the poor and helping the destitute; there was no one else to help. As New Deal, Great Society, and other welfare-type government programs were developed, charities shifted their focus to other efforts, like character-building (Konczal 2014; Morris 2008). Today, agencies provide services that were once under the charity umbrella.

Since economic survival has become the end-game for many organizations, fundraising campaigns that emotionally entice people to open the wallets and hearts are a common strategy. Showing pictures of destitute, dirty, bereft children and homeless people prevails when money is being sought for poverty-related services. Showing homeless people as clean, smart, kind, loving, hardworking, and nice makes "them" seem like "us," and if we are having a hard-enough time making our own ends meet, what then is the motivator to dig deep to help someone who is like us? However, if a charity is seeking funds for middle-class enrichment or character-building experiences, showing faces of children that resonate with the values and lifestyles of potential donors is key. Philanthropic marketing has become big business and relies upon a sophisticated strategy to pick people's pockets and make them feel good about it.

Greek playwright Aeschylus coined the term philanthropy in the 5th century BCE. It meant love of humanity. While it's associated with people who donate large sums of money, a philanthropist can theoretically be anyone who donates time, money, experience, skills, or talent to help create a better world.

Philanthropy today is a form of public relations and advertising. The Chronicle of Philanthropy provides assistance and information to philanthropists. Giving – and making sure others know about it – promotes a company's image or brand through cause-related marketing or other high-profile sponsorships. US corporate spending on cause-related marketing costs billions of dollars annually. While charitable campaigns contribute to the public good and worthy causes, they are designed to increase company visibility, improve employee morale, and create social impact, as shown in Figure 7.1. Tobacco giant Philip Morris spent $75 million on charitable contributions in 1999 and then launched a $100 million advertising campaign to publicize them (Porter and Kramer 2002).

Who does charitable giving help the most? This is a question that one has to consider if assuming that philanthropy, charity, and volunteerism are the cure of homelessness. And does it matter that businesses and organizations make money if some is given to the poor that they would not otherwise have? These questions plague charitable giving.

Charity Choices (2018) report that individuals, not corporations, give 70% of all charitable giving ($287 billion). Individual donations account for four of every five dollars given to charity in the US. Foundations are the second-largest donor at 16% of charitable contributions at $67 billion in 2017. They report over 76,500 US foundations, increasing because wealthy people set up their own family foundations. Corporations, with their big tax breaks, gave only 1% ($20.8 billion) in 2017. This amounts to 0.8% of their profits, compared to 2.1% of individual's disposable income. Giving USA estimated in its 2017 report that charitable donations totaled $410 billion, which is 2.1% of the US GDP and a $20 billion increase from 2016. However, it noted that contributions from middle-class people have declined, and they expect them to continue to go down since the government took away the charitable tax deduction away from millions of taxpayers (Osili and Zarins 2018).

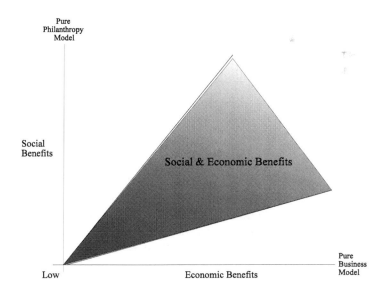

Figure 7.1 A Theory of the Convergence of Interests.
Source: Adapted from Harvard Business Review. https://hbr.org/resources/images/article_assets/hbr/0212/R0212D_A.gif, adapted by C. G. Hudson.

Who gets the charitable money? Not usually homeless or poor individuals, although contributions to food pantries have increased (Konczal 2014). Religious organizations receive one in three dollars, or $123 billion in 2016. Education receives the second-largest amount ($60 billion), with three of four education dollars going to colleges and universities. Human services received $47 billion, health organizations got $33 billion (8% of the total), followed by organizations like United Ways and Jewish Federations, international programs, arts and culture, and at the bottom environment and animal organizations (Charity Choices 2019).

Most giving goes to large organizations with big endowments that can spend more in advertising. Though charities direct some monies to address poverty, it can be difficult to gauge their value. Charitable donations are dependent upon showing effectiveness, and it is to a charity's advantage to put forth information that "proves" they are making a positive contribution. Yet not all charities do as much good as donors likely believe they do; their research and data may not be available, transparent, or accurately portrayed. The charity world is dominated by private organizations that don't disclose all of their activities, so it's hard for donors to know which groups have the most impact.

Philanthropic insufficiency occurs when they can't generate enough resources to provide everything to everyone who needs them. Philanthropic particularism occurs when charities focus on specific groups regarded as more deserving than others. This results in some people being unserved. Philanthropic paternalism results in the people in control of the finances channeling resources to groups and issues that leaders prefer rather than those most needed. The result is that charitable foundations are regarded as a "completely irresponsible institution, answerable to nobody that closely resembles a hierarchy monarchy. Why would we put our entire society's ability to manage …risks…in the hands of such a creature?" (Konczal 2014).

There are many charitable scam organizations that appear to be genuine but aren't. They appeal to our emotions and say they're going to help those in need. Youth assistance, cancer victims, veterans, and police aid are common themes of scam charities (Addressi 2018). Even charitable organizations that have been around for years may engage in funny-money practices that don't deliver much of the donation to the person intended. Take March of Dimes, for instance. Making sure babies are born healthy is a laudable goal. But for every dollar donated, eighty-five cents go to administering the organization and their fundraising efforts; fifteen cents go to grants and program assistance (Paddock 2015). They're not unique; most charitable organizations have administrative costs that are essential to operating their programs. The question is, what is a fair amount for them to keep?

Would giving money directly to those in need ultimately be better spent? We don't know. People are reluctant to give money to beggars because they don't know if it's for food or drugs, even though data indicate most donations to individuals go for legitimate purchases. Group or professional panhandlers make people confused about whether or not to donate. Panhandlers can be found across the country, looking like teams, often holding signs at intersections saying "Homeless – Hungry. Will you help? God Bless" (Keye 2013; Laughlin 2018; Severance 2017).

Charitable and philanthropic approaches to helping homeless people have benefits, but they are not a panacea. But increasingly, there is more pressure to count on them to provide solutions. Turn now to one that is receiving considerable attention.

Business Approach

Lines have become blurred between charity, government, private, and nonprofit businesses that help the needy. The fuzziness between when an organization is helping the needy person or themselves is fine indeed. We question how much profit or operating expenses a business "ought" to have. There are no clear-cut answers to today's relationship between running a business and helping others.

Some businesses are designed to bilk the poor out of billions of dollars, such as bank over-draft fees, check-cashing companies, pawn shops, debt collectors, payday loans, car title loans, but the shadow bilkers are perhaps the largest violators, who use their social capital and positive reputation to mask exploitation of vulnerable peoples (Quigley 2016). Hatcher (2016) finds the private sector partners with government to create a complex, multifaceted "poverty industry." Companies extract billions of dollars in federal aid earmarked for poor families, children, and the elderly. For example, Insurance Business (2016) reports "shelters are a nonprofit segment that reaps big revenue for (insurance) agents." Shelters are encouraged to have a variety of insurance coverages for protecting the organization's financial assets from negligence, resident care and supervision, abuse, molestation, personal injury, transportation, and umbrella coverage.

Because poor and homeless people have more health problems, emergency rooms, mental health, detox and substance abuse facilities are but a few businesses that have seen booming caseloads of homeless people rise as their conditions exacerbate. Poverty and homelessness may not be good for individuals, but they are money-makers for countless businesses. As the saying goes, we came to do good, and we have done very well indeed (Gusfield 1984). The balance between an organization's ability to do good things for society, and to financially do very well for themselves, is worth pondering.

Case Study: Amazon's Solution to Homelessness

Americans are losing faith in government to solve social problems and are turning to businesses who announce that entrepreneurship can solve anything (Stewart 2018a). But not all social problems can be solved by business (Janus 2013). Corporations gain social capital, and tax deductions, through their philanthropic donations. Amazon is now the largest public company in the world with a market value of $797 billion (Feiner 2019). Now the richest man in the world with over $150 billion, Amazon's CEO Jeff Bezos decided to address homelessness. He named 24 organizations to receive $97.5 million in grants for them to work with the homeless population (Feiner 2019). These organizations are in 16 states and the District of Columbia and at least half come from a faith-based history or current orientation. On the surface, this offer of help to the homeless is great news.

The focus of this philanthropic approach is using nonprofit volunteers, especially those from the faith community who are "equipped with special qualities of care that can heal the homeless from the inside out" using trust and patience (Christian Science Monitor 2018). Bezo's views are undoubtedly influenced by what he sees in Seattle, which has a large homeless population of which two-thirds are sheltered by organizations affiliated with communities of faith. His one-billion-dollar bet is hedging on faith workers looking "into the heart of the homeless." This program assumes that people don't become homeless when they run out of money – they become homeless when they run out of relationships. His program believes volunteers can provide stabile relationships based on selfless, unconditional assistance that can give homeless people mental and moral strength to then accept living in a supportive, permanent home and move toward self-sufficiency.

> To truly end homelessness rather than merely "manage" it will require investments in people dedicated to expressing the kind of compassion that will heal a homeless person's life. Wealthy philanthropists can support such qualities of care. But first those types of volunteers must step up.
>
> (Christian Science Monitor 2018)

Lots of questions arise about how the money will be spent or if the end-goal is really to prevent homelessness. Bezos has funded a variety of programs, including creating space programs like Blue Origin and Blue Moon to colonize space as well as preschools to support better lives for children (O'Kane 2019). But Bezo's plan has little chance of addressing root causes of homelessness – shortage of affordable housing, economic inequality, and viewing homeless people as inherently defective. It assumes that homelessness can be cured by people being nice to one another and giving hope to the hopeless. It assumes a privileged-knows-best approach. It assumes that good, faith-endorsing volunteers could fix defective folks. It assumes that by giving money to heavily faith-oriented organizations that greater humanity will ensue. These assumptions might not be true.

Critics question if Bezos truly understands, or cares, about the issue. The National Low Income Housing Coalition found that a worker in

Seattle would need to make $36.12 an hour to afford a two-bedroom unit in the city. The minimum wage Amazon pays is $15. While Amazon announced it would raise its minimum wage to $15 an hour, it *then elim-inated several financial perks* apparently as a way to fund the hourly raise (Papenfuss 2018). Announcement of his homelessness initiative came three months after Amazon helped *overturn* a proposed tax on large employers in its hometown of Seattle that would have raised $50 million per year to fight homelessness and create more affordable housing. Amazon fought hard against Seattle's proposed per-employee tax for homeless services and affordable housing. The e-commerce giant accused the city of wasting money and threatened to slow hiring there if the tax went through. There have been similar tensions in San Francisco between those benefiting from the tech boom and people fighting to survive in the wake of skyrocketing rents (Berman 2019).

As backdrop to this decision, the Seattle City Council was set to vote on an employee-hour tax (EHT) that would raise $75 million a year to help the city battle its housing and homelessness crisis. The city had no long-term solution and relied on policing using "sweeps" to move homeless people out of public areas.

The EHT would require businesses grossing $20+ million year to pay 26 cents per hour for every employee. Amazon kept this bill from passing by announcing it would halt construction on a new tower in the city and move 7,000 jobs outside the city to avoid paying the tax. The EHT would cost Amazon $24 million per year for the next two years, about one-hundredth of 1% of its 2017 revenues of $178 billion. After two years, the EHT would be replaced with a progressive payroll tax and Amazon's bill would go up two-hundredths of 1% of 2017 revenues (Peoples and Montgomery 2018).

As Amazon seeks to expand its operations into new communities, housing advocates in both Crystal City and New York City complained that while the cities would appreciate new jobs, Amazon's presence would push rents and home prices upward and lead to more homelessness, just as it did in Seattle (Paul 2019).

> If people making decisions at the local level don't have some sense of making sure that they have housing available to accommodate that growth, the natural effect of that is going to be that rents are going to go up and people at the bottom of the rental market, people with the lowest incomes, are going to be pushed out the bottom.

Bezo's move to help the homeless is criticized as a hypocritical manipulation. More than a cost-saving effort, it was seen as the company's desire to control local public policy, even if causing communities of color to bear more of the costs so Bezos could accumulate more wealth (Peoples and Montgomery 2018). Seattle City Council woman Kshama Sawant, an advocate for the tax, criticized Bezos's charitable pledge as an effort to "mitigate his image" after "threatening" to pull people and resources from Seattle over the tax. How much of Bezos' attention to homelessness as a publicity stunt for a potential presidential run is unclear (Freed 2017).

Summary

Volunteering and charitable donations are useful but are not a solution to addressing deep-seeded social problems generations in the making. Data indicate the majority of charitable contributions come from individuals, and if the economy sours for middle-America, they aren't going to have discretionary income to give away. Corporations, despite the big tax breaks and revenues they receive, are by and large not paying back to society.

The philanthropic framework often provides more benefit to the giver than to the receiver. Many organizations use donations as a smokescreen to increase their reputations and incomes. They may contribute some individual or social benefits, but in the cost-benefit analysis at the end of the day, donors and recipients have the right to ask – is this the best way to address homelessness?

8   The Housing Paradigm

A major paradigm views homelessness as caused by a lack of available, affordable housing and proposes that the best solution to prevent homelessness is to get people housed (Rosser 2017). But the housing-only solution has failed when it doesn't incorporate other factors that contribute to homelessness. Let's take a look at HUD's programs, shelters, and other housing options.

HUD Approach

The Department of Housing and Urban Development (HUD) is the nation's agency for providing housing assistance, especially for poor people. It is a governmental hydra, an entity with many programs, heads, affiliate agencies, partnerships, and consultant organizations – so many it's hard for an outsider to comprehend. It would be no surprise that someone who is homeless, without a phone or computer, would find it hard to identify who does what and who to contact for help. Add into not knowing how to negotiate complex systems, being sick, frustrated, angry, confused, or having limited time to access needed, important, complicated information fast. This section will briefly simplify HUD's programs and explain why some people think the organization is providing great service to homeless individuals, why others think HUD fails to adequately help those who are homeless, or if HUD's programs actually keep homelessness alive.

HUD's priority's is on chronic homelessness in single adults. Its programs have not focused on homeless youth or families until recently, and even now it's debatable how much of a priority they are. In 2010 HUD's decision to make chronic homelessness their primary concern seems made for financial and political reasons. They report the costs for individuals are much lower ($1,634 to $2,308) than those for families ($3,184 to $20,031), due to more services and longer stays. Individual, overnight emergency shelter has the lowest daily cost, providing fewest services and more limited hours. Transitional housing is more expensive than permanent supportive housing; transitional housing services are usually offered directly by the homeless system rather than by outside providers. Family emergency shelters are expensive because families might have private rooms or apartments. Emergency shelters for families are also likely to be open

24 hours, provide supportive services, have fewer units and higher fixed costs. Costs associated with providing housing and services for homeless people reportedly exceed the Fair Market Rent cost of providing rental assistance without supportive services (Spellman et al. 2010).

Getting skid-row homeless adults sheltered gets them out of the public eye at less cost that pleases Congress and taxpayers. Reducing visible chronically homeless adults would be more likely than reducing family poverty, so HUD's approach is designed to demonstrate greater agency and program effectiveness. Greater "success" could lead to more agency funding. As a result, focus on single chronically homeless adults became the target.

HUD's Point-in-Time (PIT) count of homeless people is the standard used by almost every organization and for funding decisions of how much money goes to what programs in which communities. They influence what the public and government officials think they know about homelessness. HUD's definition and methodology have been refined and considered state-of-the-art. But the method counts only the homeless people that they can identify one night a year and focuses on visibly homeless people in shelters and on the street. It misses those couch-surfing, hiding, or doubled-up with others – which tend to be families and youth. When HUD asks Congress for funding, the need that they can document tends to be the need of single, chronically homeless adults.

Make no mistake, hundreds of thousands of people have been helped by HUD programs. But the degree to which HUD is effective depends upon the program, funding, target client, eligibility criteria, and the way data are collected. HUD's Notices of Funding Availability (HUD 2018; National Alliance to End Homelessness 2019) reflect HUD's existing programs and their priorities. The following list showcases different budgetary streams HUD operates and the many organizations and players manipulating large amounts of funding for various services, programs, and populations. Their programs include:

Capacity Building for Community Development and Affordable Housing Grants
Veterans Housing Grants
Family Unification Program
Choice Neighborhoods Planning and Implementation Grants
Jobs Plus Initiative Grants
Lead and Healthy Homes Technical Studies Grant Program
Community Compass Technical Assistance & Capacity Building Program
Lead-Based Paint Capital Fund Program
Community Development Block Grant Programs for Indian Tribes/ Alaska Natives
Lead-Based Paint Hazard Reduction Grant Program
Continuum of Care Program

Resident Opportunity & Self-Sufficiency Service Coordinator Program
Family Self-Sufficiency Program
Veterans Housing Rehabilitation and Modification Pilot Program
Housing Counseling Training
Homelessness Assistance Grants
Rapid-Rehousing Grants (Domestic Violence, Youth, Unsheltered)
United States Interagency Council on Homelessness (USICH)
Tenant-Based Rental Assistance (Section 8 Vouchers)
Project-Based Rental Assistance
Community Development Block Grants
Healthcare for the Homeless Grants
SAMHSA Homeless Programs
Runaway and Homeless Youth Act
Projects for Assistance in Transition from Homelessness (PATH)
Education for Homeless Children and Youth (ED)

What kinds of data are collected about what populations and about what issues highlight the importance of the role researchers can play in preventing homelessness. The National Alliance to End Homelessness (2018) announced that "Congress should invest in proven solutions to homelessness by providing at least $2.8 billion for Homeless Assistance Grants in FY2019. This represents a $287 million increase over the FY19 level and would end homelessness for 25,000 households." Supposedly, this increase is for homeless domestic violence victims and youth. It is also to increase Section 8 housing, build or rehabilitate housing in the private sector, including the HOME Investment Partnership Program ($400 million), Community Development Block Grant program ($300 million), and Low Income Housing Tax Credits. Over 90% of federal 2019 homelessness funding is earmarked for the Continuum of Care (CoC) organizations (Data Lab 2018), which provides fund for permanent supportive housing, raid re-housing, transitional housing, coordinated entry, and pilot programs. Emergency Solutions Grants fund street outreach, homelessness prevention and diversion, emergency shelters, and rapid re-housing. All this sounds promising, but whether the funding is sufficient, obtainable, and implementable complicate whether rhetoric will become reality.

Their website goes on to state:

> Consider the results: Since 2007, homelessness has decreased by 15%. Meanwhile, communities and states across the country have announced that they have ended veteran and chronic homelessness. That progress is only possible through bipartisan Congressional investments in the program (HUD).

HUD and its affiliates are quick to claim success for how they are addressing homelessness in the US, but we beg to differ.

HUD's proposed budget is not designed to make helping homeless families, children, and youth a priority. It's asking for increases in funding at the same time it's announcing a decrease of homelessness in recent years – even though other data don't confirm that. There are those who feel HUD manipulates its research design and numbers to downplay actual homelessness figures so it can appear to be more successful than it is. There are concerns about how shelters are run, the funding they receive for providing services to the chronic homeless with the exclusion of families, youth, and children, how definitions of homelessness are made, and how organizational policies are set.

HUD's favoring of chronic homelessness sapped valuable resources away from the prevention of homelessness and poverty, especially for families and youth. People in dire conditions need a safety net able to catch them before they hit bottom. HUD considers someone chronically homeless only if they meet the definition of a "homeless individual with a disability," has been living in a place not meant for human habitation, in emergency shelters, or in safe havens for the last 12 months continuously or on at least four occasions in the last three years where those occasions cumulatively total at least 12 months. The definition excludes many people. Neither HUD nor the United States Interagency Council on Homelessness (USICH) has freed up resources that substantially benefit the needs of children and families who are in housing distress. Programs for homeless families have not seen an increase in resources as a result of the supposed decrease in chronic homelessness; many of them lost funding as a result of HUD's emphasis on chronic homelessness. This loss is compounded since other programs chose to focus on chronically homeless singe adults, thus supporting what Kuhn warned against – "...agencies continue to fight efforts to allow local communities to prioritize other populations with HUD homeless assistance, even when those communities repeatedly identify other, more urgent needs" (Duffield 2016).

Over the years HUD has shifted its funding and priorities to serve chronically homeless people differently. HUD programs were designed to get homeless individuals "ready" for housing by guiding them through drug rehabilitation programs or mental-health counseling, or both. If and when they stopped drinking or doing drugs or acting inappropriately, they might be given subsidized housing on the condition that they stay clean and acted relatively normal. This linear residential treatment model is based on people demonstrating their worthiness and commitment to playing by the rules. If they would "straightened up and fly right," they could be rewarded with permanent housing; if they didn't, they wouldn't (Figure 8.1).

Street Shelter Transitional housing Permanent supported housing Real & stable housing

Figure 8.1 Linear Residential Treatment Model.

It assumes people go through a series of steps in order to transition from being homeless to having a home like other typical people enjoy. Someone has to succeed at the shelter to get into short-term, transitional housing, which they have to have before they can obtain more long-term housing, and only if they are seen to be successful there, they might earn the "prize" of long-term stable like an apartment, condo, or house. Inserted into this linear model are recovery, therapy, education, and vocational programs that people are supposed to attend and comply successfully with. Success at one opens the door to opportunities to obtain others.

This linear model isn't necessarily what people need or want. People may have other agendas for their lives. Just because they have economic or housing problems doesn't take away their right to want to craft their own lives in a way that they think is most fitting for themselves. The "being good enough" model is a concern because the definition and criteria for what constitutes "being good enough" is subjective. It speaks back to a time when morality was the standard for judging who would be allowed to go to Heaven or Hell. For instance, is drinking alcohol a sin or sign of moral ineptitude? Many shelters have refused to allow alcohol on the premises, and if someone staying at the shelter has alcohol on their breath, it can be used as a reason for dismissal. A different view may regard alcohol use in the US as a normative behavior and that the sober-house model doesn't fit the times or people's lifestyles. To toss them on the street because they have consumed alcohol, used a nonprescription drug, had sex, or broke a law enhances the person's "moral failures" and does nothing to protect them from the problems associated from homelessness. It doesn't help enhance their strengths, since it is likely that everyone strengths as well as socially defined deficits. Looking at situations realistically and using a best-practices for the best-benefit approach to best-helping someone is different than the old model of providing no services if you weren't on a high moral path to be good enough.

Continuum of Care (CoC) groups were designed by HUD to bring together local stakeholders such as realtors, shelters, churches, and agencies to be decision-makers. They are supposed to decide collectively what they want to do for their communities with HUD dollars. Because there are insufficient HUD dollars to go around to all agencies and for all needed services to be delivered, there is reported in-fighting at local CoC meetings where stakeholders disagree on whose needs are highest. Some agencies reportedly engage in strategies that undercut the chances other agencies will get monies in order to secure their own funding base. HUD requires a scorecard with point values for what they will fund, so if communities don't come in within their point schemas, they aren't going to get funded. This means that programs advocating for youth, families, and those at-risk have lower chances of getting funded than shelters for chronically homeless adults.

It's hard to live a stable life when you have to keep moving to different types of housing in different locations. The Housing First approach tried to change that and moved stable long-term housing to the front of HUD's operations. "Real" housing was no longer a prize to be won by complying with performance steps and program goals. When it first emerged, Housing First was seen as a radical, paradigm shift. Instead of forcing people to jump through hoops to prove that they were worthy, such as succeeding in different recovery programs, not violating curfew or sobriety rules, not being late coming home, the Housing First model said "give people a permanent home first so they don't have to worry about where they're going to be long run, and then they can work on these other things." This was seen as a very positive step because many programs gave only transitional housing to people who came for help, and they weren't given the stability or resources that would allow them to be successful.

The funding that went into Housing First had to come from somewhere, and that somewhere was other housing programs. Shifting how HUD money was distributed negatively impacted shelters and other programs. While Housing First may have short-term success helping a segment of homeless people to get help, the successful application of this program to other groups of people is questioned. This "robbing Peter to pay Paul" approach has been met with sharp criticism from programs that were downsized or eliminated to pay for Housing First. Many safety-net organizations must now scramble for alternative funding or contemplate closing altogether. Some changed their mission to adhere with HUD's funding priorities.

Housing First supports people into stable housing for perhaps two years. The idea is that during that time they can get help to become independent in paying for their own housing. After that they have to figure out how to manage their expenses on their own. While some people can, many aren't able to do so. This underscores insufficient income dynamics that got many people into housing distress in the first place. Having financial support to live so they can live in one place for a long time may enable them to work, care for families, and rebuild successful lives. But housing isn't the only issue that got people into homelessness; they may have other economic, work, health, family, or personal issues that need to be addressed. If they can get help for them while in Housing First, they have a better chance of creating stronger futures. But if they aren't given supports while in Housing First and then afterwards, the steps forward may result into back-slides into homelessness. They may return to the shelter, increasing shelter need and expense, but without sufficient levels of funding since many of shelter/service funds were cut for the Housing First program.

Housing First was appealing and many communities jumped onto that bandwagon, only to find that it wasn't as much of a panacea as they'd hoped. Many communities have touted the benefits of the Housing First model, with some proclaiming that they even "eliminated homelessness."

They didn't. The term "Housing First" and what it entails has become overused and its optimistic claims of success have been politically motivated, at least in part. New York City (Carrier 2015) and Utah (Boone 2019) are two such areas. For instance, both declared they had eliminated chronic homelessness a few years ago because they achieved "functional zero" levels of homelessness but now admit they still have a homelessness crisis.

While Housing First gets people housed in the short run, in the long run it may create homelessness when the aid that got them stable ends. Thus, Housing First is not regarded by all housing experts as a panacea and may actually increase homelessness, not diminish it. As Ralph da Costa Nunez (2017a) observes, it is fair to say that HUD – in the name of housing the homeless – has paradoxically adopted a policy that could stimulate homelessness. By withdrawing the very funding that supports this nation's homeless safety net, HUD is leading the nation down a perilous path.

Expansion of permanent housing subsidies, especially for longer duration, is unlikely. Public housing and Section 8 vouchers have been funded at flat levels for some time, so it is unrealistic to expect more housing money coming that way. Unless the housing affordability and wage ability are addressed, potential future homelessness remains real.

Hidden Life of HUD

HUD (2013, 2016) runs over 100 programs and subprograms, and for one of the largest agencies in Washington, it's also one of the least transparent. Its reports aren't necessarily data driven and its lack of public scrutiny has contributed to HUD being able to distribute billions of dollars with little examination into actual program effectiveness (Mercatus Center 2018; Millsap 2016). On the surface, HUD programs, numbers, and budget look like they are doing a lot of great things to help people who are homeless or in housing distress. To some degree, they are. But underneath the glitz is another story, one that critics are scared to utter. It's hard to know really understand HUD agendas, the backroom machinations, what they actually do, who all the internal and external players are and how successful HUD programs are – and in what ways success is defined. The lack of transparency for the public to know how much money is being provided to whom and for what is noteworthy.

Through our investigation, people working directly and indirectly for HUD, and those who receive HUD funds, are reticent to say what they really think about HUD's leadership, funding priorities, PIT counts, or services. Their primary concern? If they complain or disagree, they're afraid their programs will lose their funding. Because HUD is the primary financer of programs, if you don't play their game their way, you won't get to play at all. HUD can cut or eliminate your funding, so programs won't be viable unless securing external funding, which has become increasingly difficult to get since many programs vie for the same money. Concerns exist about the lack of qualifications of HUD's director Ben Carson, and economic goings-on that seem to provide financial benefit to his family and hand-picked insiders (Dooley 2018; Riley 2018; Stewart 2018b; Wallace and Marsh 2018), like New Jersey's housing director who had no experience except being a wedding planner for the Trump family (Louis 2017).

Under the Trump administration, there have been major financial benefits for those ostensibly serving the homeless. HUD director Ben Carson, who has no housing credentials, made over $213,000 annually and has an estimated worth of over $26 million (CBS 2018; Paywizard 2018). A *Washington Post* analysis of HUD political hires (Booker 2018) revealed annual salaries between $98,000 and $155,000 for the five appointees, all of whom had worked on Donald Trump's or Ben Carson's presidential campaigns. Three of them did not list bachelor's degrees on their résumés. They include a former event manager-turned-senior HUD adviser making $131,767 after a 23% raise. The political hires were among at least 24 people without housing policy experience appointed to the best-paying political positions at HUD, an agency charged with serving the poorest Americans. They account for a third of the 70 HUD appointees at the upper ranks of the federal government.

How effective has HUD been? "No one knows" (Millsap 2016). Under Carson's tenure, HUD "has steadily devolved into a do-nothing department" (Jones 2018). Under Carson's leadership HUD has slowed or ceased many existing initiatives, especially those protecting rights of LGBT people. He reportedly "doesn't want to make housing for the poor too cozy" (New York Times 2017). Carson, who reportedly wanted to spend $31,561 on a new dining room table he could dine on when at HUD (Marsh and Wallace 2018), is reported barely to be seen according to employees (Jones 2018) and is unfamiliar with basic HUD programs (Sink 2019). HUD has rolled back efforts to enforce fair housing policy and advanced housing proposals that would triple rents for the poorest residents in public housing (Booker 2018).

Politicians have the ability to move legislation and funding forward to help people who are poor and homeless – or set up roadblocks that prevent it. Many say they will do something to help them in order to get elected, and then their promises disappear from sight (McSwain 2017; Roberts 2011; Salam 2019; Walker 2018). As history shows, separating politicians from their rhetoric, funding and policies, is challenging indeed.

Earning a living is a necessity. Some workers benefit handsomely from serving the homeless, like Ben Carson and some of his appointees at HUD, yet most people working for homeless organizations don't earn much money. They may make enough to get by, but aren't getting rich, as many directors of homeless organizations tell us. Agencies are often staffed by people who volunteer or are making minimum wage. Many take such jobs because they were once destitute and want to help others, or these were jobs that were available for them with limited skill levels. Most workers may see the flaws of the way homeless business operate, but they aren't in positions to challenge or change policies and practices without being at-risk of getting fired.

Summary

Having a federal housing authority to ensure that everyone has access to a home is vitally important. Making sure to have resources and supports available for those who are in distressed situations is essential. Without a housing agency, people would be a terrible risk. But the definition they have chosen, methodologies for their counts, service priorities, co-dependent relationships with other vendors that sap money away from giving direct aid to those who need help to afford housing reflect that HUD change is necessary if homelessness is to diminish.

HUD needs to focus on shifting trends of homelessness. In 2018, a homeless person may have a bachelor's degree, a 9–5 job, and health benefits but unable to find available, affordable housing. If people had the supports they need to prevent them from getting into financial problems in the first place, or having resources available to help them as soon as they showed signs of unraveling financially, homelessness would not be inevitable, and shelters would not be necessary.

Shelters

Shelters are a necessary resource for some people in distress, but shelters aren't a solution for homelessness. Shelters are not homes for the homeless. A roof over one's head does not constitute it being a home. When a community creates a shelter, it means that they haven't created other safety-net systems to catch people before they fall.

Shelters are popping up everywhere – over-emphasis on them can actually prolong the homeless crisis. To make up for the lack of available, affordable units, cities may rely on shelters to pick up the slack instead of creating more affordable housing and housing assistance.

Shelters vary in type, design, structure, services, professionalism, and quality of care. This variability is important to consider. Some are run by caring, well-trained staff who provide good accommodations and care at a reasonable cost, while others don't. Many are mom-and-pop shelters created by altruistic individuals, faith-communities or organizations, while others are part of multifaceted big business. Some are supportive, some are punitive, some are respectful, some are demeaning. All shelters are not the same.

Once a shelter is built, they are there to stay. Increasing numbers of them are built to meet this new demand. They expand their structural, administrative, and service components. They develop affiliates. And somewhere in all of this is the tired, weary, dispirited person who has lost all options and has to resort to asking the shelter for help.

Shelters Emotional Costs

No one wants to live in a shelter, but homeless people don't plan on being destitute, sick, mentally unstable, substance users, or poor. When their lives fall apart for whatever reason, they need help. Shelters are a way to give people a place to sleep, eat, get clean, obtain services and resources to overcome future challenges. But there is a self-fulfilling prophecy that once labeled "homeless," one gets embroiled into further despair. Avoiding the label, stigma, and association with homeless lifestyles are reasons why families try to avoid going into the shelter system. If they can scrape together resources or housing alternatives, homeless families may never set foot in a shelter or ask for help. They have a fighting chance of making it out alive for themselves and their children to live normal lives if they figure out ways to get help.

Getting into a shelter can be more than challenging for an individual or family: There may not be one nearby; many people don't meet qualification requirements; there are long waiting lists; and not all shelters serve all kinds of people. Maintaining the ability to stay at a shelter is hard, since many have arbitrary rules that make chances high that people can't adhere to them (Fuller 2011). Shelters are full of regulations designed to promote safety and reduce conflict. Rules may include no smoking, no sexual activity, designated times to be out in the morning, and set times when they can return. Cooking, bathing, warehousing possessions may be regulated. Curfew violations may result in eviction, and once you lose your spot, it's back to the end of the line.

From a resident perspective, there can be shelters that are acceptable, but many are so inhospitable that people avoid staying there in the first order. Their efficacy is questionable, challenging to live in, and may not fulfill their mission to get people into housing and prevent future housing distress. Shelters have different entry and residential requirements, depending on where one goes. Domestic violence victims leaving their homes are different than runaway and accompanied youth, who have different needs than homeless veterans or those who have addiction or illness, who have different needs than those who lost their jobs. Goodness-of-fit between people's needs and services is a huge factor in outcome of the sheltering experience. Many shelters aren't pleasant places to be, especially with single adults who have chronic behavioral issues due to mental illness, substance abuse, or challenging lifestyle patterns.

Many shelters overly and covertly demean people. Staff dwell on deficiencies. There are daily ritual degradation rituals. There is a "what's wrong with you" approach as opposed to a "what's right with you" model. Shelters are an entry to service gatekeepers. But some require people become destitute and troubled before providers can/will do anything. If people are couch-surfing with acquaintances, they aren't considered homeless by HUD and have to be on the street or living in their car before they can officially qualify for services. This is analogous to child abuse, where a child has to be badly, visibly hurt before the system will step in. If a child is hurt "just a little bit," their pain and suffering can be ignored until it is so blatant that no one can ignore it – or the child is dead.

In an example of how systems operate from a deficit rather than a strengths model, one single father of three sons and a disabled brother, hovering back-and-forth on homelessness, asked us, why is it that social workers always come into his home and talk about the things he doesn't have as compared to all the things he's doing right? Why is it that they are focusing on his deficits rather than his strengths, even though a few things in their lives could be improved? They had shelter, food, watchful concern, and unconditional love. Social services indicated they could not help the family much until the father lost his job; once they became homeless they could help him more. This, the father felt, was "just plain stupid. Why would they wait until I lost everything to help us?"

Depending on the shelter, who is taken in when there isn't enough room for all? There may be a triage approach where people who might have the possibility of making it on their own aren't helped whereas the folks who may die on the street if they don't receive care are taken in. Some take the "worst first in" where people having the biggest problems are given beds, where others take a "worst first out" approach where residents are selected (creamed) that may be easiest and have greatest chances of success to make the program look good.

Shelters Financial Costs

A lot of money is being spent on homelessness but with questionable results. Whether we are spending too much on homelessness or not enough is a topic of debate. Many estimates are that we are not spending near enough to actually dent the problem, while others suggest that if we handled economic issues differently that poverty and homelessness could be largely eradicated.

Reports of how much it costs to help homeless people ranges from $10K to $50K. It's not that there aren't numbers – there are. How numbers get constructed and what they include varies. A Central Florida Commission on Homelessness study found that the region spends $31,000 a year per homeless person, largely because of medical and nonviolent offenses like sleeping in parks. Their study found a cost of $50 million each year to let 1577 homeless individuals in three counties languish on the streets. Targeting resources at core causes – providing permanent housing and services like job training and healthcare – would only cost $10,000 per person. This permanent housing approach could save Florida taxpayers over $350 million over the next decade. A shelter in Fort Lyon, Colorado, costs $17,000 per person to put someone in housing, compared to $43,240 to leave them remain homeless. Another study found taxpayers saved $1.8 million in the first year after a new apartment complex oriented toward homeless people was created in Charlotte (Keys 2014; Yglesias 2015, 2019). New York City's shelter system reportedly serves all but a few thousand of its 77,000 homeless people and spends *over $2 billion a year on shelters.* Los Angeles has conducted financial calculations to determine how much it would cost to shelter every homeless person, but their estimates are on single, adult, chronic homeless people visible on the street – not families and youth. They use a figure of 23,000 adults and estimate that annually it would cost over $354 million to run the shelters, plus they would need to build 197 more to meet this need since there are only 10,200 shelter beds in the city (Palta 2018).

Knight (2018) examined the sheltered person costs in San Francisco and found in 2017 the city spent $305 million on homelessness on 74,999 homeless people, or $40,000 per homeless person per year. The average monthly rent for a one-bedroom apartment in San Francisco is $3,300. The $305 million was composed mostly of $250 million spent by the city's Department of Homelessness and Supportive Housing. Of the $250 million, two-thirds went to people who aren't homeless at all – that's the amount spent on rental subsidies, eviction prevention, and permanent supportive housing. Subtract 11% for administrative costs and one-time capital spending, and what is left is only 17.6% spent on temporary shelters, 3.2% on street outreach, and 2.2% on health services. That means $57 million was spent on the visible homeless population. But that number shouldn't be divided by 7,499, the city's homeless population on one random PIT count night. Over the course of a year, 20,000 people will be homeless in San Francisco, but an estimated 5,000 won't use city services because they figure out their own housing arrangements. Divide $57 million by 15,000 homeless people who need city help each year, and the city spends $3,800 per person per year, or $10.41 a day. This is a very different picture for the public and government to consider, compared to the $40,000 per year. There is no question that the money is being spent, but much of it is not going to the homeless. It's going to a lot of other people.

Housing a person and providing caseworker to see to their needs costs about $10,000 a year, some estimate. That means for less than a billion dollars a year, chronic homelessness could be ended in the US. If momentarily homeless people were housed in temporary housing, and if each temporary residence were occupied half the time, homelessness of all kinds could be eliminated for about $10 billion a year. That's less than a seventh of what the government spends on *food stamps* (Smith 2018a). HUD estimated it would cost the government *$20 billion to eliminate homelessness* in the US (Lowrey 2017). While that sounds like a lot of money, let's put it in perspective:

- It is about the same amount that Americans spend on Christmas decorations (Kavoussi 2012).
- Taxpayer subsidies to the oil and energy corporations cost over $20.5 billion annually in the form corporate welfare (Roberts 2018).

- American consumers spent $50.3 billion in 2018 on social media (Cooper 2018).
- Americans spent $72 billion on their pets last year (Woiem 2018).
- Americans spend over $465 billion annually on Christmas gifts (ABC 2018).
- Investment taxes at lower rates than salaries and wages lose $1.3 trillion in a decade (Americans for Tax Fairness 2014).
- Corporate capital gains cost taxpayers $3 trillion over a decade (Wamhoff 2018).

While numbers vary, these examples indicate it's possible to reduce both homelessness and its costs simultaneously, while not impeding the quality of life for most individuals. A 2014 Think Progress article (Covert 2014) provided a variety of financial solutions to "end homelessness forever." These included recommendations by the Bipartisan Policy Center to give rental assistance to everyone whose income is at/below 30% of area median income (AMI) through a reformed voucher program. At a cost of $22.5 billion, homelessness could end for the majority of those experiencing it. Another plan recommended funding a National Housing Trust Fund, which government proposed but never adequately funded, which could create a million affordable homes over ten years. The United for Homes campaign proposed modifying the mortgage interest deduction by cutting off eligible mortgages at $500,000 and converting the deduction to a 15% nonrefundable tax credit that could free up $200 billion in revenue over ten years to create affordable housing through the trust fund. While the cost of solving homelessness is in the billions, those without shelter, need emergency medical services, or get put in jail end up costing taxpayers more.

How money is provided for homeless services has been perhaps most apparent in reports about New York City. It has become a barometer for understanding how money gets spent on housing. The 1996 play, Rent, brought the issue of housing distress to the public's awareness. In 2018, New York City spent 1 billion dollars on sheltering the homelessness (Picture the Homeless 2019). Sheltering a homeless person can run up to $7,500/month, which is more than the cost of a luxury apartment for shelters that provide restrictive, austere, and inhumane conditions. In the Picture the Homeless (2019) report "The Business of Homelessness," the authors ask "if the system is bad for the budget, bad for homeless people, and bad for neighborhoods, who exactly is profiting?"

Shelter-Industrial Complex

While it sounds humane to build a shelter to help the homeless, it's also naïve to assume that is the raison d'etre of why people do it. There is substantial money to be made from keeping people homeless. Shelters have become big business. As businesses, they not only seek to help others but also seek to survive by building alliances, partnerships, contracts, and a convoluted system of associations from which all benefit only if homelessness is allowed to survive. The homeless shelter business in the US has been growing and in 2018 was a $12 billion industry with over 12,750 related businesses (IBISWorld 2018). The costs to run this business are high – Cincinnati, Ohio, found it was going to cost the city over $40 million to build three shelters (May 2012).

While homelessness is a growing crisis in America (Bachega 2018), it has provided significant financial benefits for certain segments of the population. While poverty may be dysfunctional for society and poor people, it can be quite lucrative for those who serve them or beneficiaries of "welfare for the rich" tax breaks and financial incentives (Gans 1971). The shelter-industrial complex thrives because some people have a vested interest in it growing (Kowalchuk 2018). Homelessness could be seen as quite useful, quite functional, providing attitudinal, individual, organizational, financial, political, and social benefits. It hires a variety of workers who would be hurt if poverty and homelessness were eliminated (Harrington 1962).

Many see families in poverty and seek to help while others see opportunities for profit. The poor as a group provide a juicy target for anyone "depraved enough to make a business of stealing from them" (Ehrenreich 2011). There is a long history of financial exploitation of people who are poor. It is common practice for the poor to pay more for the same things than rich people (Caplovitz 1967; Ehrenfreund 2016, 2017; Ellen 2017; White 2015). People with incomes below $35,000 and nonwhites are three times more likely to be targeted for financial exploitation (Quigley 2016).

Shelters, like private prisons, have to fill their beds and meet quotas in order to receive and maintain funding. It's to their advantage to have people homeless, otherwise they succeed themselves right out of business. Because there aren't enough shelters to meet the demand, shelters don't have to vie for customers by promoting why one shelter is superior to another. Desperate people are glad to get any help. It isn't like homeless people have the option of shopping around for the best shelter, like one would do when picking a hotel on Trivago.

The poverty industry, introduced in the charity paradigm chapter, turns America's most vulnerable populations into sources of revenue, bilks billions in federal aid designated for vulnerable people. Hatcher (2016) exposes how the poor and needy have become "revenue generating mechanisms" for private companies and government agencies that "do nothing but generate profits" from misery. The business of sheltering has become so big, complex, and lucrative that it is known as the shelter-industrial complex. It's associated with the welfare-industrial complex, the poverty-industrial complex, the nonprofit industrial complex and the criminal justice–industrial complex. All of these multifaceted businesses make huge profits off poor people.

While policy experts debate how to structure government assistance programs, a massive siphoning of the safety net is occurring behind the scenes. People in positions of authority use illusory budget shell-games that divert funds from needy people so that state governments and private organizations profit. Sophisticated algorithms are used by analysts and contractors who put forward self-serving budgetary recommendations that justify exploiting innocent people in order to reap huge financial revenues (Hatcher 2016; O'Hara 2019). This is done without transparency and with the intent to keep exploited people from realizing that they have been financially taken advantage; the trick is to rob people in ways that are systematic, impersonal, and almost impossible to trace to individual perpetrators (Ehrenreich 2011). Homelessness exists because we actually don't want to get rid of it. The extent to which the poor have become prey for profit predator is enormous – but that's a topic for another book.

Shelters have to hire staff to work at the shelter, including administrators, admissions personnel, cooks, custodians, and providers of whatever services they have. They have on-site personnel and contract with other organizations to have social workers, case managers, therapists and counselors, employment specialists, and so on. They have contracts to provide food, laundry, cleaning supplies, cots, bedding, transportation, education, insurance and a multiplicity of other goods and services (New York Times 2018).

As the corporate sector has identified shelters as a growing industry, and instead of investing in affordable housing, there is a concentrated move to build more shelters. In New York City there are over 60,000 people living in homeless shelters. Many are employed, holding down low-paying, minimum-wage jobs trying to pay for housing in a soaring market. Rent has surged nearly 20% in real dollars from 2000 to 2017, while household income decreased by only 6.3%. The average apartment goes for $2,000. When renters can't afford the rent and can't afford to quit their jobs, shelters become the option. Rather than addressing the root cause of homelessness by building long-term housing that all can afford, the city's approach prioritizes for-profit development and building homeless shelters (Picture the Homeless 2019).

Instead of helping communities find ways to avoid citizens falling into homelessness in the first place, the shelter-industrial complex has swooped in to make cities feel that shelters are a necessary evil to care for the destitute. Rather than trying to solve homelessness, shelter and poverty-reliant businesses rely upon poverty and homelessness existing in the first place. Shelter staff, administrators, partner agencies, and contractors only receive funding if there is continued use of shelters and the services they provide. Agencies are only kept in operation if there is a renewable, rotating population of clients. Eradicating homelessness means that one would eradicate their job or funding stream, so there is a built-in disincentive to actually getting rid of homelessness.

A woman in a rural Midwest area that one of the authors ran into on a bus, who had no idea that she was talking to a homeless researcher, chatted freely that she was building a shelter because it was a quick and reliable way to make money. She had scoped out the situation and felt there were all kinds of corners she could cut that would enable her to enhance her profit margin. This included hiring volunteers and less-qualified staff that she didn't have to pay high wages to (she cited high rates of local unemployment as a way for her to tap a needy, eager job pool), she didn't have to use "real" orange juice but could substitute much cheaper products to give people "since they can't really complain about what they get," and a variety of other mechanisms to cut corners and still comply with the regulations. The idea that anyone can run a shelter if they know what to do speaks of both the exploitative nature of the shelter-industrial complex and the perceived worth-less-ness of homeless individuals.

Creating homeless shelter is so lucrative that a quick Google search will show you a Wiki with steps and pictures of how anyone can make one (https://www.wikihow.com/Start-a-Nonprofit-Homeless-Shelter). So will the How Stuff Works site (https://money.howstuffworks.com/how-to-start-homeless-shelter.htm), Pocket Sense (https://pocketsense.com/start-homeless-shelter-10847.html), and Bizfluent (https://bizfluent.com/how-5530676-start-nonprofit-homeless-shelter.html). The OGS Capital will help anyone to write a homeless shelter strategic business plan (https://www.ogscapital.com/article/homeless-shelter-business-plan) or you could modify Land for the Homeless one here (http://www.landforthehomeless.org/wp-content/uploads/2015/04/NonProfitPlan2.pdf).

Appendix, Business Plan for Building a Shelter, of this book is a lengthy and easily obtainable document from Profitableventure.com found online that shows anyone how to start a shelter. The website is a guide designed to show anyone how to set up a homeless shelter with the use of government funds. Refer to the Appendix of this book and look at how extensive this entrepreneurial site is so that anyone, with no knowledge of the housing industry at all, and no real concern about the well-being of homeless people, can make money by sheltering people who are homeless.

Community Resource Center Approach

How might shelters work better? They can be transformed into Community Residential Resource Centers, intensive educational, employment and social service facilities that prepare families for stable independent living prior to a housing placement. Advocates believe shelters should be more than places to sleep, eat, and shower. Traditionally residents must bounce from agency to agency, filling out applications, attending appointments, and doing tasks in order to obtain assistance. It can be a full-time job to do this. Community Residential Resource Centers can be one-stop-shop facilities where all the resources one needs are in one place. This includes medical facilities, counseling, trainings, meetings with agency personnel, libraries, computer access, and other supports. Moreover, having one case-file that all agencies can access improves case management, reduces time-delays, and improves coordination of services.

Bergen County, NJ, has received acclaim for having moved toward this direction. Their facility provides housing and employment services; collaboration between government, NGOs and faith partners uses the same philosophy and goals, an open qualification application system, and a county Homeless Trust Fund. They use a Housing First model that they feel is helping to reduce their chronically homeless population (Hobson and McMahon 2019).

The Right-Way Approach

Another approach is to provide the right services for the right person at the right time delivered in the right way. Joseph Finn (2019), head of the Massachusetts Housing and Shelter Alliance, advocates for a tiered response of the right resource for the right person at the right time. A low threshold approach refers to accepting the person where they are, instead of where providers might want them to be. A model used by many shelters is one of a moral and behavioral hierarchy where residents have to act in particular ways and espouse certain beliefs in order for providers to move them forward in the system and reward them with better resources, supports, and types of housing. Instead of forcing the person to adjust to program rules, a better approach may be for programs to adjust to a person's needs.

Pay for Success

Pay-for-success programs have been lauded as silver bullets for intractable policy issues. They emerged in 2010 with a criminal justice project in the United Kingdom under another name – social impact bonds (Wogan 2018). The Pay-for-Success (PFS) model, or the Social Impact Bonds model, is a way to finance improvements in persistent social problems. PFS brings together investors and local, state, and federal government agencies to fund and improve education, health, and social services. This approach is being implemented in many communities around the country.

For example, a local company or community investor might fund programs to reduce homelessness or strengthen literacy among young children. Connecting funding to specific program outcomes requires independent evaluators to determine whether the outcomes have been met. If these services deliver their intended results (e.g., reduced homelessness, improved student literacy), the government then reimburses investors for the cost of the service, along with a modest return on their investment (typically 1%–2% of the overall investment). In this design, the investors bear the initial cost of services and take the risk of not being reimbursed should the service not produce the intended outcomes as measured by the evaluators (American Institutes for Research 2017).

Intermediary organizations may provide technical assistance to agencies and providers to strengthen their capacity to deliver evidence-based programs and achieve outcomes. For instance, greater literacy in pre-kindergarten through third grade may have important effects on broader social and public sectors through increased earnings, greater consumer buying power, less homelessness, and decreased reliance on government safety nets.

The PFS model has been used in the US since 2012, with more than 12 projects underway and about 50 projects under development. The typical stakeholders include investors, service providers, a public agency or success payer, and an evaluator. These four team units work together to provide risk capital to finance the program and pay for implementation of activities to achieve desired outcomes.

Pay For Success was piloted in Santa Clara County, California; its recipients have stayed housed for at least two years and now contribute a third of their income to rent. In Denver, similar findings are reported. At least six PFS projects focused on housing the homeless have come online since 2014. These include Santa Clara County, California, Salt Lake County, Utah, Denver, Colorado, Cuyahoga County, Ohio and Boston, Massachusetts.

Perhaps the most successful model for using this approach to address homelessness is run by the Massachusetts Shelter and Housing Alliance. Its PFS program is a model for consideration. It is a social innovation of performance-based contracting between government and organizations responsible for implementing a given intervention. Instead of trying to demonstrate efficacy, the project focuses on issues of scale and cost. Under this model, impact is measured rigorously and government makes "success payments" based on results, not activities. Paying for positive social impact, rather than paying for services performed, helps ensure that incentives are properly aligned to achieve social impact and provides a mechanism for government to pay only for what works. Social Impact Financing in Massachusetts is backed by the Commonwealth and allows nonprofit organizations to access up-front working capital required to implement intervention proven to save money over time. Its upfront capital investments are provided by philanthropic sources as well as institutional investors, who receive a modest return on investment attained through success payments tied to the intervention's performance.

Its partners include the Massachusetts Shelter and Housing Alliance, United Way of Massachusetts Bay and Merrimack Valley, Corporation for Supportive Housing, Third Sector Capital, and Santander Bank, as well as the Department of Housing and Community Development, Mass Health (Massachusetts Medicaid program), Boston Healthcare for the Homeless and Health and Human Services. Together they created the Massachusetts Alliance for Supportive Housing (MASH). With MASH, private capital was used to leverage the capacity of a network of housing and service providers to help people move from the streets and shelters into affordable housing with services to build stability and independence. Its focus was on the chronically homeless, not families or youth. The program aligned public resources to adhere with the Commonwealth's plan to end homelessness. Supportive housing reduces inappropriate use of emergency rooms, inpatient hospitalization, and behavioral and correctional services. This saves public resources and creates returns on investment tied to achieving the impact of transitioning the most vulnerable homeless into stable, supported housing.

The program performance model for the MASH PFS was rooted in Housing First. Its objective was to house homeless persons and targeted people most likely to be "high utilizers" of costly emergency and acute medical services, assuming that targeting a scarce resource to those most in need would result in greater savings and efficiencies. Such savings, if appropriately recaptured, could help to pay private investors. PFS uses program and self-report data to guide its action. Data are collected at four points: Triage, Entry, Monthly follow-up, Quarterly follow-up, and Exit. Outcome performance metrics include housing retention rate, hospitalization nights, medical respite, days in a detox facility, number of days in detention, emergency shelter, incarceration, and emergency room visits. Providers enter data into Clienttrack, the PFS online database with real-time updating capabilities, that includes demographics, homelessness history, income sources, health insurance, quality of life, disability, and health history and service usage six months before housing. Survival analysis is used to compute housing retention in a pre-post study design where service utilization six months before and after program enrollment and up to a year after enrollment is used to measure impact.

The PFS leaders (Finn 2018) report that savings were made on each service. Total use of services amounted to $11.8 million prior to housing entry and $3.7 million after, a cost-saving of $8 million. This translates to about $6,000 per person for six months, a potential saving of $12,000 per person per year. In terms of the breakdown, emergency shelter use was reduced by about $1.4 million. The cost of hospitalization dropped by $5 million. The cost of detox use, medical respite, and emergency department visits was reduced by $300,000, $390,000, and $645,000, respectively. A saving of $230,000 was made based on reduced ambulance use.

PFS in Massachusetts provides an example of how one state created a housing initiative and collected critical data to see if costs could be reduced while quality care and reduced homelessness occurred. The program reduced number of nights spent in emergency shelters, inpatient hospitalizations, and days spent in detox. It brought needed services to clients who could not otherwise have accessed them. It foreshadows a new way of financing services and a new way for public entities to promote social change. Finn finds the greatest achievement of the PFS program was the break-down of siloes that brought multiple agencies together to work successfully on what had previously been thought an intractable problem. It both added financial resources and became a way of re-directing existing resources to more effectively address the problem in a new way for public agencies and private nonprofits to work in collaboration on reducing chronic homelessness, utilize metrics to gauge success, and engage private capital to leverage resources to scale for appropriate evaluation.

PFS touts three main merits. First, PFS shifts the focus of government service provision from inputs to outputs. By focusing on payment for delivery of results, the focus of government funding becomes output-based. Second, PFS transfers risk for failure of programs from the government to private investors and providers. If the program does not produce results, government can refuse to pay the investors and service providers as agreed in the contract. Third, PFS has potential to increase accountability and evidence-based decision-making in government.

Like all potential paradigms, critics remind us to ask questions and consider the hidden loopholes (Wogan 2018). These include questions about what the goal of a PFS project ought to be – help the homeless, reduce public spending, raise social impact, provide financial benefits to investors, use data for decision-making, or be a society's moral conscious. Providers have voiced concerns that the program's redistribution of funds away from emergency services toward prevention may hurt their ability to sustain their organization. The impact on service contractors could be significant, but the impact, positively or negatively, is unclear at this point. The PFS model shifts the conversation about delivery and funding with the ultimate question – what is the outcome for vulnerable populations.

The People's Policy Project (3P)

The 3P is a think-tank founded by Matt Bruenig. Their report, "Social Housing in the United States," argues that the country's market-oriented approach to affordable housing development is woefully inadequate. Section 8 vouchers, low-income housing tax credits, and inclusionary zoning use a variety of incentives and subsidies to encourage private developers to build or maintain affordable housing across the nation. While these are important, they are too small, too timid, and rely too heavily on private interests to truly meet the needs of desperate renters. The result is that this model hasn't provided enough affordable housing. Therefore, 3P offers a solution of mass social housing.

Social housing is defined by a mix of public projects led by city authorities, philanthropic approaches led by charities, and collective schemes led by residents. Common to them all is the idea that there are alternatives to a purely market-oriented system of housing provision. With this concept as context, the People's Policy Project put forward a proposal for how the American people should endeavor to develop 10 million units of large-scale municipal housing, built and owned by the state over the next 10 years. This is in response to a projected national shortfall of 7 million affordable units. Such a program exists in Sweden and Vienna. Both middle- and lower-class people benefit from this housing model, which avoids the stigma of being either vertical ghettos or housing-of-last-resort. Social housing is based on universalist principles, with the aim of moving toward a housing model with no means-testing. They should be mixed-income, served by public transportation, and have easy access to amenities and shops. They should be regulated in a manner that prohibits discrimination and provides for the disabled and other marginalized populations, and should be largely self-financing, with tenants paying rents on a sliding scale (Tobias 2018).

Social housing is different from the creation of intentional communities as they are traditionally conceived, but there is significant overlap between their philosophies. The idea for both is that the community is designed to ensure that the residents will have affordable places where they can live long term, where there are libraries, stores, transportation, internet, and resources that will enable them to live safe, good, and productive lives.

The 3P program proposes its funding through repeal of the Republican tax plan, which could generate enough revenue to build 10 million houses, at an average cost of $150,000 to $220,000 per unit. They call upon the federal government to institute a revenue-neutral low-interest loan program to fund urban housing authorities across the country. Federal capital-grant programs could provide financing to municipal housing authorities equal in value to what the private sector receives under the low-income housing tax credit. This type of social housing could generate a powerful constituency capable of resisting political attacks that have plagued public housing for decades. It would also create an enormous number of jobs. To do this will require a movement that can reshape popular narratives about housing, collectivity, and overcoming a huge real estate lobby that has spent untold sums to secure their control of the housing market (Tobias 2018).

Institute for Children, Poverty, and Homelessness Three-Tier Approach

In 2012, the Institute for Children, Poverty, and Homelessness suggested a three-tier shelter approach as an improvement over the existing model used by most shelters. Their domain assumptions are that parents want to get a job and maintain a household but may be in situations where they cannot. It recognizes that current systems of services are often designed to meet the needs of families as identified by the system, rather than those identified by the family itself. They promote a strengths-based, family-focused, trauma-informed system. Systems that don't end up providing services are deemed unfair, ineffective, and expensive. Without an education, job and a stable, healthy family, their future is at risk for them and society.

This program creams a subset of clients who they think will be successful with more intense and supportive services. Clients have rules and goals they are to comply with, but the program is designed to help them do that, rather than punish them for missteps along the way. They recommend:

Tier I: Emergency Shelter Stays: This tier looks similar to the current system of services for families who enter Prevention Assistance and Temporary Housing (PATH) programs. Sheltering for families in crisis usually is for a short period of time (30 days). But some families return and need more care. During Tier I stays, case managers work with families to identify needs and services to prevent future homelessness.

Tier II: Transitional Shelter Stays: This tier also looks almost identical to the current system where families stay between 2 and 12 months. The parents use this time to find work, go to school, locate secure housing, and be able to get on their feet and become independent.

Tier III: Specialized Shelter Programs: Families who have more complex needs and higher barriers to maintaining permanent housing would be eligible for a Community Residential Resource Center (CRRC). Tier III CRRC programs would focus intensively on education and employment, as well as domestic violence and child abuse/neglect prevention, and substance abuse treatment.

Other Housing Options

Under the housing paradigm, we have explored the HUD approach with its evolution toward First Housing, we have examined shelters as a strategy to address homelessness, and, in this section, we will look at other strategies. The United Kingdom, which has also struggled with homelessness, alleges that homelessness could be "a thing of the past" there within ten years (BBC 2018). The charity Crisis and their report, *Everybody In: How To End Homelessness In Great Britain*, asserts that if 100,500 homes were built each year for 15 years, then everyone would have decent and affordable housing, instead of living in unsuitable temporary accommodations. They advocate that people be provided a package of specialized support and protection of their housing rights. Hospitals, prisons, care systems are other residential programs that would be legally required to find homes for people leaving their care. They regard housing as a human right and see the building of new units as the way to address that right. Others see long-term rent subsidies to be effective in reducing homelessness.

Renters Insurance

What if homeowners or renters could purchase insurance that could assist them to pay for housing if they lost their job, became ill, or couldn't pay their rent or mortgage? Christopher G. Hudson proposes this solution to the eviction problem. Low-cost rental insurance could be paid for by the property owner or tenant. Because most people have only a few months savings put aside in case of emergency, a rental insurance policy could provide a six-month (or longer) buffer that renters could use if they fell upon hard times. This solution would ensure that the landlords would get their monthly rent and would themselves not be adversely impacted by the tenant's financial problems. It would give security to individuals so they did not have to fear immediate eviction. Knowing that you have 6 or 12 months housing security that you could fall back on would give people enough time to put other financial housing arrangements in order.

Longer Mortgages

When financing a home, banks traditionally give buyers a choice between getting a 15- or a 30-year mortgage. This is the period of time that it would take to pay off a house. Taking a 15-year mortgage means higher monthly payments but the house is paid off faster; 30-year mortgages mean lower monthly payments but ultimately the house costs you more because interest is stretched over a longer period of time (Ramsey 2019). Forty-year mortgages exist, but they are harder to find. They can have fixed or variable interest rates that stretch out payments for an additional decade (Johnson 2019).

A premise for 15- or 30-year mortgages was that if a family bought a house when they were in their thirties, at the time of their retirement their house would be paid off, leaving them more discretion on how to manage their money. But today the average (median) homeownership is 13 years; a few years ago it was six (Moon and Miller 2018). People are more transient and it is less likely that they will stay in "the family home" for the duration it would take to pay a house off. Therefore, if people have no intention of staying in a house for 15 or 30 years, but they would like to have the security of owning a house that they can fix up and build equity into, longer-term mortgages – even 50 years or more – could be a way for people to get into affordable homes, become part of communities, and build more socially and financially secure lives.

Young families automatically have heavy expenses with childcare, health care, buying cars, and having incomes that are often at lower or modest wages. Having the opportunity to use the same amount of money that they would be spending on rent that would enable them to own a home would be welcomed relief for millions of families.

Peru's De-Bureaucratization Model

The traditional model of addressing homelessness in the US has been to give assistance to those deemed truly needy through complex regulatory

government organizations and systems. The application systems are usually time-consuming, as paperwork needs to be filled-out and documents
secured and provided to authorities; it may take days, weeks, or months to
process applications before one ever gets any assistance. Those who don't
qualify for whatever reasons may have waited a long time only to find that
they won't receive any help.

This type of system is frustrating for the person applying for assistance,
and it's probably frustrating for the workers in charge of the processing of
materials, especially when there are rejections or resubmissions required.
The allegation of "red tape" killing people, literally and figuratively, is
commonplace.

An alternative approach to this model has been proposed by Peruvian
economist Hernando de Soto. He believes his model could help pull people out of poverty; evidently others do too, as he was awarded the 2017
Global Award for Entrepreneurial Research in Sweden. Essentially, he
proposes a "de-bureaucratization" model that permits those of the lower
classes to advance while maintaining authority among government and
corporations.

He alleges that a society may benefit more when requirements are second to overarching compliance with the law. When a nation decides how
to deal with people who are poor, a common technique is to require additional regulation. We see this when poor and homeless people apply for
aid, whether for food stamps, housing, medical care, disability services, or
countless others. The regulations may be so extensive and exhaustive that
few people who need the services may actually be able to qualify for them.

Too much red tape, de Soto alleges, can do more harm than good for
people and societies. Being unable to access needed help, people may turn
toward illegal activities in order to survive. When society's poor cannot
turn to official authorities for help or assistance to grow businesses or find
legitimate ways to use their skills, it is reasonable to assume that they could
turn toward illegal or illegitimate players. Alienated from mainstream
supports, minor criminals, major terrorists, or those who exploit others
for their personal gain may flourish. In some ways, his argument reinforces Robert Merton's (1968) explanation of ritualism as a contributor to
deviant behavior, when a society focuses more on the means of achieving
a goal than the goal itself. If the goal is to provide housing, health care, or
aid to prevent poverty, over-the-top compliance with application requirements may interfere with people actually getting help.

As Monica, a single mother of three children, found when she lost her
benefits because she took a part-time job that didn't pay enough for her
to afford the services she lost (like health coverage, food stamps, housing
and fuel support), she had to find another way to make ends meet. Because
legitimate options were now closed to her because she no longer "qual-
ified," she was embarrassed to admit that she started dealing drugs. She
did not use them but knew that it was an under-the-table way for her to

earn money that would keep her children fed and housed. She was scared all the time that she could get caught and put in jail as a drug dealer, have her children removed, and lose her ability to live a normal life and be a productive member of society.

As de Soto notes, engaging in crime and creating inequality can become a hefty price to pay for not following "the rules." Because de Soto found this traditional method to be counterproductive, he realized that we can change the rules or the way we address those rules. De Soto concludes that by "simplifying" bureaucracy, lessening "certain requirements," and permitting individuals to grow under a broader umbrella of "complying with the law," the poor may prosper more fluidly and yet still legitimately. He was able to identify the big picture benefit of the populations of multiple socioeconomic classes. He finds that access to affordable, safe housing is key.

As background, he is author of "The Other Path" and "The Mystery of Capital" and founder of the Institute of Liberty and Democracy in Peru. His notion of de-bureaucratization focuses on replacing rules which specify how to fulfill certain requirements by rules stating the ends to be achieved. This could lighten the burden on those who must obey the laws in question, because instead of having to meet certain requirements before they can do something, they will be monitored afterwards to see whether they are complying with the law. Instead of automatically assuming people are going to take advantage of systems and be law-breakers, one could assume that when people ask for help they genuinely need it. The benefits they receive may set them up toward paths of greater success and end up contributing to society economically, not costing taxpayers anything.

In some ways, his trust in the goodness of people to make good on assistance is similar to that of Nobel Peace Prize winner Muhammad Yunus. Yunus founded the Grameen Bank, which gave loans to entrepreneurs too poor to qualify for traditional bank loans. His efforts were credited with creating economic and social development from below because lasting peace cannot be achieved unless large population groups find ways in which to break out of poverty. His work demonstrates that even the poorest of the poor can work to bring about their own development.

De Soto's model emphasizes ex-post de facto monitoring rather than prior paperwork, reduces red tape without abandoning necessary controls, but also provides more efficient means of enforcement. The elimination of red tape does not mean no tape, but the model's advocates allege it provides opportunities for liberty for all levels of society to grow, and thus benefit all. DeSoto reports his model shows the free market (not to be confused with mercantilism) does not chase away productive citizens as socialism does but encourages big picture productivity. It gives a chance to bring millions from informal economies to legitimate ones (Navarez 2017).

He has developed a relationship with Overstock.com's Patrick Byrne to advance cryptocurrency and blockchain into the Peru's housing arena. They are developing a global property registry system utilizing decentralized blockchain technology. Their approach is by making property rights and claims of individuals publicly recorded and globally verified, they can enable the poor to safely unlock the value of their land; mollify disputes by clearly stating who claims what property; and empower local land ownership (Nelson 2018). Their assumption is that blockchain can bring wealth not just to people of Peru but to poor people everywhere, including perhaps the US (Consorte 2018). Blockchain will be described more in the next chapter.

Different Housing Structures

When homelessness is viewed as a housing-caused problem, this approach assumes that if you get people into affordable housing, homelessness should disappear. But what kind of structure makes a home? Is it a single-family house? An apartment? Shared space? Is a trailer or RV a home? What about tents, yurts, campers, shipping containers, solar cube refuges, sleeping pods, tiny houses (portable or stationary), or cardborigami shelters? (Williams 2013).

Fifteen-year-old Mikki's father is a cross-country truck driver who lives in the extended cab of his semi; he has a post office box in one city to get mail; he has a cell phone so he can make calls, but no permanent residence. He has an income that enables him to pay bills, but is he homeless? One can argue that people like him are, or aren't. Housing styles, what is deemed as appropriate, fashionable, and functional, have changed over time and place. People benefit from having a stable place to stay, where they can keep possessions, sleep, cook, keep clean, and decide who can come in and who must stay out.

Architects are stepping up to meet the demand for low-income stable housing. The varieties are extensive. A decade ago, Sears, Roebuck & Company sold over 400 different types of houses and buildings. From 1908 to 1940, Sears sold 75,000 affordable homes that people could construct on their own – homes that are standing sturdy today. They were delivered by train from Alaska to Florida, and anyone could buy them, avoiding Jim Crow housing discrimination. Prices varied according to housing style, but people could send blueprints and have Sears construct materials, and most houses could be built by novices in 90 days. Sears even sold mortgages until the Great Depression forced them to stop. They provided homes for single families, making multigenerational housing less desirable, thus changing housing and family configurations for the nation. Amazon is building on this theme, selling tiny, container, prefab cabins and homes of various sizes they will deliver to your door.

The University of Southern California's Homes for Hope was created by a class of architecture students. Their prototypes of tiny housing pods can be produced for $25,000 (or less). By involving the Skid Row Housing Trust and city officials, they've created an efficient, simple model that can be easily assembled and moved around. Although sturdy, these prefabricated housing units are designed to be transported on the back of an 18-wheeler truck. That means they can be re-sited in the face of potential zoning challenges (or neighborhood pushback). Each unit comes in 92 square feet, with a rounded, protruding wall on one side designed to reduce space taken up by the foundation, while increasing usable area (Wolfe 2017).

In Seattle, the Compass Crossing pilot project proposes modular steel buildings that are cheaper to buy and faster to build than many housing alternatives and comply with the city's code. In San Francisco, project MicroPADS uses pods about 160 square feet, built in China and shipped to the US. Another San Francisco development is Mission Bay South Block 9, which built 120 350–400 square feet studio units for homeless people. In Orange County, American Family Housing converted shipping containers into housing pods for homeless veterans; units are 400 square feet, and the whole 16-unit project took less than five months to complete (Wolfe 2017). The Sanctuary in Los Angeles Palo Verde Apartments is a bright, stylish facility with 60 units, community rooms, a computer lab, patios, and a beautiful tree-lined courtyard (Fessler 2015).

The 51 acres Community First! Village (2019) in Austin Texas is built by Mobile Loaves & Fishes and has 100 RVs and 125 micro homes, with plans to build 310 more units to provide permanent homes for 40% of Austin's chronically homeless population. The philosophy behind it is that housing will never solve homelessness, but the creation of community can. Small homes are designed to provide privacy and comfort with residents sharing kitchens, laundry and washrooms, meeting halls, playgrounds, markets, medical facilities, dog parks, art studio, car repair shop, music areas, counselors, job placement facilities, mentors, along with other common areas and micro-enterprises run by the residents (Dawson 2019).

The tiny-house movement is a viable alternative to affordable housing. Some tiny homes are on wheels, legally considered a recreational vehicle. They have to be registered as an RV and have a license plate. Someone can travel with it and not deal with building or zoning codes. While they can be parked in backyards or locations with the permission of owners, most states prohibit them as full-time homes. Others are built on foundations, legally considered an accessory dwelling unit (ADU). Building a tiny house on a foundation requires zoning and building regulations. Some states prohibit buying land and building a tiny house on it and may require another residential property be on the same property (Nonko 2016). Accessory Dwelling Units can be mother-in-law apartments, granny flats, backyard cottages, and called by other names. They are regarded as alternative housing solutions for low-income because they tend to be affordable. They provide people with their own living space while being near to others, which can provide both privacy and support. ADUs are home-owned and operated, which means money goes into the hands of an individual homeowner instead of to a corporation or government agency (Dain 2018). While they may increase the housing availability, most are small and may be better designed to accommodate single people or families of two or three individuals.

Other housing alternatives are stackable homes, pod housing, and units hooked onto the sides of existing buildings (Rascon 2015). Converting vacant buildings into affordable apartments is a strategy being used nationwide. There are a variety of jump-start programs around the country which have emerged to transform vacant buildings of all sizes into housing units. Such efforts demonstrate that this can be done, but it often takes partnerships, a charismatic leader pushing forward the initiative, and, of course, money (Voice 2019). Allowing some tent cities to stand is another, but less desirable, option that keeps popping up. Transportation centers, which often become pseudo-homes for the homeless, could be creatively transformed to provide more supportive housing options for them (Badger 2013).

The development of 3D printing to make homes is surfacing as an interesting alternative to the shelter dilemma. New Story, a charity dedicated to providing shelter for impoverished and distressed communities, and printing company ICON collaborated to design a 700 square feet house which can be built with a 3D printer in under a day for about $4,000 (Kaser 2018). New Story reports that its first projects will be in rural areas of Central America. San Francisco–based company Apis Cor printed a house in a day using materials that cost $10,000. The company boasted the world's first mobile 3D printer, capable of being easily moved. ICON co-founder Jason Ballard reports that his 3D house's energy and comfort level will exceed traditional building standards because of its materials and design.

Framlab in New York has proposed a new type of single room occupancy architecture for housing New York City's homeless population. Its Homed proposal finds the city has an abundance of vertical land – blank sidewalls of buildings. Using scaffolding to anchor the homes on the sidewalls, Homed has hexagon-shaped housing modules that could form temporary micro-neighborhoods and a type of private and attractive housing that are unlike shelters. Units are comprised partly by 3D-printed hexagonal pods that use scaffolding to attach to the sides of unused, windowless building facades that could be customized for different uses and transported to where they are needed (Wang 2017). As innovative as they are, 3D homes at this point are not considered to be long-term solutions for long-term housing solutions for individuals or families.

Summary

This chapter explored different ways to address homelessness, either by the creation of new forms of housing or adapting the customary models. Many of them require brain adjustments for governments and public as new ideas of doing things are explored. In the Sociology of Knowledge, it is always a struggle to get people to think differently about things that they have habituated views about. What we are doing to address homelessness isn't working, so some of these new approaches hold positive potential.

Homelessness is not just a housing issue. It is related to income, health, childcare, education, skills, transportation, and a bunch of other things for which people may need help. Da Costa Nunez (2016 and 2017c), Finn (2019), and others remind us that a one-size-fits-all housing approach doesn't fit everyone's needs. It doesn't take a genius to see that there is a lot of money being spent on homelessness but the problem isn't going away using a shelter-based approach.

Homelessness is a political issue as well as an economic one. Housing the homeless makes politicians seem warm, not cold-hearted, and generates votes. Politicians can institute laws, zoning ordinances, police enforcements to help everyone get housing, or hide homeless people from sight (Kowalchuk 2018; Picture the Homeless 2019). With the amount being spent on homelessness today, it seems as though there are other housing options worth a try. Time will tell if vested interest groups will purse viable housing options for low-income people – or themselves.

9 The Money Paradigms

Homelessness cannot be separated from money, wealth, expenditures, and investments. This chapter explores them from a variety of different angles, starting with the purpose of wealth, money, and its application for basic services; income, taxation, cryptocurrency, and blockchain.

Meaning of Money and Wealth

What is the purpose of money? This question is fundamental to the creation or eradication of poverty and homelessness. Historically, people bartered for goods and services and exchanged different aspects of caregiving, but over time a flat-money approach predominated. This system focused on money as a medium that replaced bartering, a standard of worth or value, a way to pay debts, and something that can be accumulated, retrieved, and used over time. The Federal Reserve was created to create money, the banking industry to control it, and its distribution and accumulation became essential to both macro and micro elements of social functioning. As bartering decreased and needs for assistance increased, governments were called upon to provide more goods and services, which required more money be expended. Outcomes and recipients of investments were determined by leaders as definitions of what constituted wealth in societies were debated. Capitalism and meritocracy have reigned, with hard-work and self-promotion vital. Competition and success, usually defined by monetary income as well as social power to control its distribution, have become normative.

What is money really good for? Investing in people's well-being can result in investments to make society stronger; therefore, money spent at the individual level will have benefits at the social level. Therefore, investments in the care of children's well-being should result in healthier and more productive adults. Preventing problems ultimately costs less than trying to fix problems.

One of the most respected frameworks for meeting needs of society – and individuals – comes from Maslow's work, which scaffolds needs from the most fundamental to how they relate to productivity and higher-level social functioning, as shown in Figure 9.1 (McLeod 2018).

The Needs

1. **TRANSCENDENCE:** This entails developing a relationship with a larger reality than the limited ego, and helping others do the same as well as developing their potentials.

2. **SELF-ACTUALIZATION:** This involves developing the range of potentials of the individual, both those of a personal and occupational or professional type.

3. **AESTHETIC:** Symmetry, order, and beauty.

4. **COGNITIVE:** The need for knowledge and understanding.

5. **ESTEEM NEEDS:** The need for social recognition and approval as well as self-respect.

6. **BELONGINGNESS / LOVE:** Relational needs, both to be part of a larger social whole as well as having individual loving relationships.

7. **SAFETY / SECURITY:** Protection of harm and other longer term physical deficiencies, such as the lack of a home.

8. **PHYSIOLOGICAL:** Primary or immediate needs for food, air, water, warmth, and other requirements of life

The Principle of Prepotency of Needs

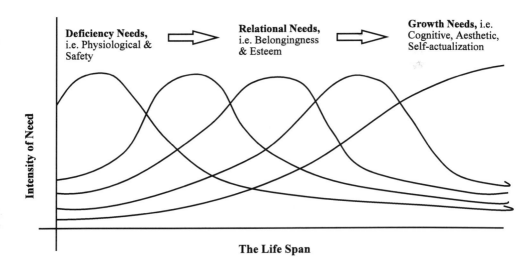

Figure 9.1 Abraham Maslow's Theory of Prepotency of Human Needs.
Source: Adapted from Hudson, C.G., 2009, based on Maslow, 1954; Maslow & Lowery, 1998.

At the bottom of the model's pyramid, basic physical and safety needs are deemed fundamental to a person's well-being. These include food, housing, clothes, healthcare, education, employment, property, and resources. Without these basic needs being met, people are unable to develop the types of personal and social relationships that are essential to higher levels of functioning and satisfaction.

A similar model for addressing human needs has been promoted by Chilean economist Max-Neef (Democracy Now 2010; Khandelwal 2016). He defined a taxonomy of human needs and a process by which communities can identify their "wealths" and "poverties" according to how these needs are satisfied. He describes needs as being constant through all cultures and across historical time periods. The thing that changes with time and across cultures is the way that these needs are satisfied. According to this model, human needs are to be understood as an interrelated and interactive system that includes subsistence, protection, affection, understanding, participation, leisure, creation, identity, and freedom.

Societies have a choice on how money is invested in people and society. Money and wealth aren't the same thing. Expenditures don't necessarily equal investments. Wealth includes property, labor, knowledge, physical infrastructures, and things that cannot be bought – such as good health, happy children, loving families, caring communities, healthy environments and elements of artistic, spiritual, or utilitarian value that may not have a market price. "For most purposes, real wealth is living wealth, and living wealth is real wealth. Money is neither" (Korten 2019).

Investing more in people and their well-being will produce more positive social, economic, and quality-of-life outcomes than investing in the traditional economic ventures, from a societal (not necessarily individual) perspective (Wilson 2018). Investments in wages, time, and energy could invigorate productivity, as happy workers who feel well cared for are more likely to give more and require less government economic intervention. Human capital, not financial capital, is one of the scarcest resources taped, and reinvesting in it could unlock new levels of labor productivity for the economies and companies around the world (Garton 2017).

Homeless people have a money problem – they don't have enough money to pay for the housing available. Sometimes this is due to housing costs being very expensive; by the time one adds together rent/mortgage, insurance, taxes, heat, electric, phone, utilities, and what it costs to keep a household operating effectively and efficiently, it can easily take half of an average income.

They also have a wealth problem – people are valued by their economic productivity and merits, so people who are poor and homeless are seen as worthless according to the traditional monetary framework employed. They are not regarded as good financial investments. The government's entitlement emphasis refuses to pay for housing, health care, education, food, and other life-essentials unless people prove they are worthy or qualify within a set of arbitrary merit-based criteria.

Yet psychologist Maslow and economist Max-Neef come down on the same side of the equation – wealth of a society is reflected in how it cares for and supports its citizens. Providing foundational resources that everyone, everywhere, anytime need in order to become healthy reflects how we value people in general, and the degree to which we wish to invest in building a strong and healthy society. Given the current financial allocation system described in Chapter 5, it should be no surprise that homelessness and poverty are rising and that our nation's social climate has become fraught with division, conflict, and competition as the rich get richer and more people fall to the bottom of the stratification ladder.

Fundamental Services

The Four Horsemen of the Apocalypse that ride roughshod over lives and fortunes of people are identified as accident, illness, old age, and loss of a job (Rubinow 1934). These are the ills that Social Security, Medicaid, Medicare, Supplemental Nutrition Assistance Program (SNAP), and other assistance programs have sought to address. These safety nets are social insurance that aren't just programs but a reflection of who we are as a nation and how we intend to help our citizens to navigate the risks of life (Konczal 2014).

Governments are designed to meet the needs of its citizens. Everyone benefits from help for life's fundamental home, food, health, and security challenges. The social welfare system in the US is structured in ways that impact homelessness. As one national expert in sheltering observed, high-income people need lower benefits because they can afford to pay for things themselves; low-income people need high benefits to help them survive (Finn 2019). Katz (1996) observes that there is tension between what is considered public assistance and what is social insurance. Public assistance is a means-test program that includes aid to dependent children, food assistance, housing assistance, health care, in what is typically regarded as welfare. People have to qualify for assistance in order to receive it. Social insurance, on the other hand, is not means-tested – anyone who is eligible, according to a predetermined set of objective criteria such as age, disability, or unemployment, can receive it. Programs like Medicare or Social Security are available for everyone and are not social class related, the way public assistance is. Public assistance has become synonymous with welfare, and those who apply for it are often stigmatized and treated rudely, despite the fact that most public assistance programs only stop the bleeding and are not designed to lift one out of poverty.

While writing the book *Out of Sight, Out of Mind: Homeless Children and Families in Small-Town America* (Vissing 1997), President Clinton announced he was going to eradicate homelessness, thus the author thought the book may be unnecessary. Clinton did what politicians do – announce a "we will help the poor" policy and then not help them, instead creating social policies that hurt them. His policy helped set up our nation's current economic diabolical (Ehrenfreund 2016; Lichtenstein 2018). Politicians before and since announce they are going to "fix" the existing system of services. But obviously, homelessness is thriving and shows no sign of abating. One must ask the question: Is the current system effective?

According to the US Census Bureau[1]-[2] between 21% and 35% of Americans receive some form of means-based government income assistance, like unemployment insurance, SNAP, Medicaid, Temporary Assistance for Needy Families (TANF), and Supplemental Security Income. Based on US Census data released in September 2018, Social Security continues to be the most important social assistance program – it helped move 27 million individuals out of poverty in 2017. Over 15% receive food assistance from the SNAP, 26% receive Medicaid, and a quarter of women receive welfare assistance. About a third of people receive assistance for a year or less, 43% for three to four years, and almost all the money received is for basic necessities like housing, food, and transportation.

Government assistance programs have helped keep people out of poverty, from being homeless, and have improved the quality of life for millions. This is a fact. It is also a fact that many more people need government assistance than get it. It is a fact that the programs are often clumsy, hard to apply for, hard to maintain as people scramble to get and keep aid. In many ways, systems seem designed to keep people out rather than allow people in. As good as the existing systems may be, they could be improved and expanded to help people from becoming homeless in the first place. Past public programs have reduced poverty and could today if we adequately invested in them. Instead, many programs are designed to look good on the surface so the government or public can point to them and say, "see, there are programs that work," and if they don't, homeless people get blamed for what is essentially a system failure. Thinking that poverty and homeless can be solved by tweaking the delivery of basic services is a nice but unrealistic thought. This is a variation of the same Band–Aid approach that we've been using for years that hasn't worked yet. There are those who believe that if we just invested enough into tried and true programs, then we could turn the tide away from homelessness.

If homelessness is seen as essentially a housing problem, then creating an increased availability of affordable housing units, and the homelessness problem solved from this perspective. But this is not necessarily the case. Families and homeless individuals need more than housing in order to make it. There are other resources that one must have. These include health care, education, food, jobs, childcare, transportation, a phone, and discretionary money. These are not optional — they are essential resources that everyone needs in order to live a sustainable lifestyle. But many of them are regarded to be privileges that someone must earn to be entitled to, as compared to universal life preservers for which people have a right.

Food Benefits: SNAP and WIC

Foodways scholars indicate that hunger is becoming the new normal in America. More people are hungry, eating less food, less often, and consuming less healthy (but more affordable) foods to stretch money (Coleman-Jensen et al. 2011). The traditional systems for hungry people to get food are insufficient in meeting the needs of most people. Over 72% of households live at or below 100% of the federal poverty line, which makes it hard for them to purchase necessary nutritious food. The US Census Bureau finds that without entitlement programs like food stamps, the rate of poverty would be even higher than it is (DeNavas-Walt et al. 2011; World Hunger.Org 2011). The number of households receiving nutrition assistance from the federal government's SNAP has increased 50% since 2009. Over 47 million people receive food stamps or some other form of public aid, according to US Department of Agriculture statistics (Delaney and Scheller 2015). Even with this increase in people accessing SNAP, the food stamp system barely fills the bellies of hungry families. A survey of 29 cities conducted by the US Conference of Mayors (2014) found one in four people needing emergency food assistance unable to receive it. This makes the assistance provided by food pantries of increasing importance.

More food stamp recipients are employed, middle-class people. Poverty and hunger are no longer relegated to the lower socioeconomic strata but are now regularly found in middle-class America, working families, and even among graduate students and those with PhDs. Of the 22 million Americans with master's degrees or higher in 2010, about 360,000 were receiving some kind of public assistance. The rolls of people on public assistance may be dominated by people with less education but the percentage of middle-class people and those who hold graduate degrees more than doubled between since 2007 (Patton 2012).

In short, who is hungry in America has changed dramatically (Feeding America 2014a, b). It is no longer just the poor and destitute. It is now the middle class; the working class; the elderly, children, and youth; and middle-aged Americans. This multidimensional spiral of poverty requires that food pantry and soup kitchen workers be sensitive to the patron's embarrassment and frustration surrounding their request for food assistance.

Food programs are essential for everyone, but especially for children's development, health, and well-being. SNAP, Women, Infant, and Child (WIC) nutrition, and school lunch services keep millions of children from starving. A 2018 Urban Institute analysis estimated SNAP lifted 8.4 million people out of poverty in 2015 and reduced child poverty by 28%. Yet these government food programs aren't enough. According to statistics by food pantry network and nonprofit group Feeding America, about 73% of food-insecure individuals are eligible for at least one of the major federal food assistance programs. This leaves 27% of food-insecure individuals who do not qualify for federal assistance, many of whom must turn to charitable organizations.

Children often get their only meal of the day at school, and yet many schools refuse to allow children to eat if they don't have money, in a process non-affectionately referred to as "school lunch shaming" (Murphy 2018; Nasheed 2019). Over a half-million children are only able to eat during weekends, because many schools send students home with backpacks of food to sustain them until they return on Monday (Feeding America 2014b, 2019).

Because growing hunger needs aren't being adequately addressed by governmental assistance programs, the US Department of Agriculture (2014) has encouraged people to utilize food pantries as a way to supplement their food needs. This places demands on community-based food assistance programs to provide more food to increasing numbers of people. This requires that they address a wide array of dietary requirements, have facilities that are open at convenient hours, and have sufficient food at a convenient location and operated by a trained staff. This is costly, complex, and has turned them into businesses.

Nationally, food pantries are receiving more requests for food assistance from middle-class people, students, and others who are going hungry because they can't meet financial needs (Vissing et al. 2017). Hunger in America (2014) found that of people who use food banks, most are white (43%), 26% are black, 20% are Hispanic, a third have at least one family member with diabetes, and two-thirds (65%) of households have a child under 18 or someone 60 or older. More middle-class and working families now seek food assistance for their families not to go hungry (Delaney and Scheller 2015). Over 5.6 million households use food pantries (Abel 2003; Bhattrai et al. 2005; Bosman 2009; Feeding America 2014; Gotsis 2012; PR Newswire 2011; Mabli et al. 2010; Tiehen 2002) and estimates predict this pattern will increase in the future (Feeding America 2014b).

Despite increased need for food assistance, the government has responded with cuts to the SNAP program (Rosenbaum et al. 2018). President Trump's 2019 budget proposes to cut SNAP by more than $260 billion over the next ten years, a 40% cut, through radically restructuring how benefits are delivered, cutting eligibility for at least 4 million people, and reducing benefits for 34 million people in 16 million households. The unemployed, elderly, and low-income working families with children would bear the brunt of the cuts.

Changes would impact 90% of SNAP users who would no longer get meager food benefits that amount to only $1.40 per meal or $4.60 per day per person.

Currently SNAP recipients can use EBT cards to purchase whatever foods they want from whatever stores they choose. This gives people freedom to manage dietary needs and preferences at stores that are convenient for them to use. But Trump's proposed changes would drastically reduce those options. Instead, SNAP qualifying households would receive a box of government purchased non-perishable food. Items would include canned food, peanut butter, cereal, beans, dried milk, and not have fresh produce, dairy products, eggs, or meats. Participants would have no choice in what food they receive. For people who are trying to manage sodium, sugar, fats, gluten intake or food allergies, this option could be disastrous. Currently they can go to the store of their choosing to shop, and this box-approach would hurt thousands of grocery stores and businesses who would no longer have EBT patrons. Over 260,000 large and small retail stores around the country who sell food to SNAP users would be hurt as this program would cut at least $26 billion in revenue to food stores. The economic loss to businesses would be enormous (Barnes 2018).

This shift assumes that SNAP recipients are unable to make wise purchases with government money. Companies that the government contracts with for products would thrive. Government surplus foods would be included, foods that were earmarked to help certain farmers or corporations, and foods that weren't necessarily of highest quality that the government could unload onto the poor while increasing the finances of big businesses. Families would likely have a reduction in the monthly amount of food and not have the ability to get certain food items when they needed them, which could disrupt not just menu construction but health.

Workers would have to be hired to pack up and distribute these food boxes to 16 million families each month. An entire new network of government-subsidized contractors would emerge as individual's choices of what to eat are curtailed. This is an unnecessary expansion of government bureaucracy to build a redundant food program. Administrative costs of distributing $13 billion worth of commodities to 16 individual households each month would run over $250 million, compared to about $50 million now for the Emergency Food Assistance program.

The SNAP changes are designed to make it more difficult for people to qualify for food assistance. Must-work-for-food rules, imposing time and age limitations, and making exemptions from rules harder are predicted to put at least 2 million people into food distress. Other harmful effects of the SNAP provisions include creating the box distribution system that will cost more and give less nutrition and no choice; institute a benefit cliff that would cause working families to lose benefits as their earnings rise; cutting benefits for people with disabilities and for the elderly; and penalizing large families by capping benefits for big households and other services people have come to rely on.[3]

The budget proposes to terminate funding for SNAP nutrition education (SNAP-Ed) grants, a cut of $4.7 billion over ten years. SNAP-Ed is an evidence-based program aimed at helping SNAP households eat well and live healthier lives on a limited budget and is a long-term investment in the well-being of low-income individuals, designed to curb obesity and improve health.

Hunger in America is growing and increasing numbers of people need assistance so they can eat. Cutting programs like SNAP and WIC are not in the public's best interest, neither is the insane boxed-food delivery proposal. Forcing people to rely on charity, backpack food programs, and food pantries are not sustainable methods to address hunger. The entire method of how we are addressing food needs to be re-envisioned.

Health care

Whether access to health care is a right or privilege underscores the health-care reform debate in the US. While other nations have universal comprehensive health care coverage for all residents, America views health care as a privilege to which not everyone is entitled (Teitelbaum and Wilinsky 2017). The US is the only developed nation that does not have universal health-care coverage (Amadeo 2018b). It relies upon an employer-based private insurance system. According to the Census, employer-based health-care coverage has declined in recent years (Konczal 2014). Medicaid is available only to those who qualify; even Medicare doesn't cover all health care unless people buy additional policies. People on Medicaid have to be reauthorized annually and if they do not qualify for some reason (including something as simple as forgetting to check a box), they can lose that benefit. The Affordable Care Act (ACA) was to provide affordable care to those who didn't have other means of getting insurance, but since 2017 cuts the number of uninsured has gone up by at least 700,000 people, with over 44 million Americans having no health insurance and another 38 million having inadequate health insurance. The biggest reason people report for not having health insurance is cost. Even if people have insurance, it may not cover every procedure, there are co-pays and other health care –related services and materials to be purchased that make care unaffordable (Kaiser Family Foundation 2018). A requirement that people work at least part-time in order to receive health-care benefits is part of the Trump administration's plan, which has resulted in countless people losing health insurance (Ludwig 2018).

The public may assume that all children have health insurance coverage, but this is not true. According to US Census data, there are over 4.3 million children without health insurance in 2018, and that number has risen to 5.5% in the last year due to cuts in public healthcare coverage

(Berchick 2019). Uninsured rates for children were triple in states that didn't expand Medicaid under the ACA. According to Joan Alker, director of Georgetown's Center for Children and Families, the nation is going backwards on insuring children, and she predicts it's going to get worse. Congress let the Children's Health Insurance Program (CHIP) lapse for several months in 2017, putting states in a position of having to warn families that enrollment would be frozen. Congress restored federal funding in 2018. In the last two years Congress has threatened to repeal the healthcare law that gave coverage to millions, and the Trump administration has slashed funding for Obamacare navigators who help people sign up for coverage. Its public charge rule makes it harder for legal immigrants to obtain a variety of benefits, including health care (Rhodan 2018).

When people are poor, sick, not well-educated, can't work, don't have good (or any) insurance, and limited support services, it's fertile ground for the growth of illness that can be exacerbated by homelessness (Tran et al. 2017). Homelessness is associated with a range of health, developmental, cognitive, physical, and psychological risks. Good health is easier to maintain when one has a home, stability, adequate sleep, a bathroom, kitchen, regular routine, low stress, enough money, and support. Children are at greater risk when they are poor and homeless. Chronic disorders like cardiovascular disease, cancer, respiratory ailments, diabetes, and autoimmune problems will get worse due to homelessness. Communicable diseases like colds, the flu, STDs, tuberculosis, and skin problems are common. Substance use, especially as a coping mechanism to deal with untreated problems, may get out of hand. They are more likely to miss vaccinations, use emergency rather than preventative care, develop asthma, obesity, malnutrition and hunger, accidents, chronic and acute diseases, hyperactivity, behavior problems, and have less access to medical, mental health, and dental care. Youth are more likely to experience emotional distress and be suicidal than housed peers (Child Trends 2019a, b; National Health Care for the Homeless Council 2018; Wetsman 2018).

Health problems of poor and homeless women suffer badly, and many have preventable conditions that are exacerbated by stress, lack of housing, food, shelter, regular sleep, and ability to attend to hygiene issues. It is essential to undertake efforts to prevent homelessness, expand community-based services for the homeless, and provide adequate health care for this underserved population. Health-care providers can help address the needs of homeless individuals by identifying their own patients who may be homeless or at risk of becoming homeless, educating these patients about available resources in the community, treating their health problems, and offering preventive care (ACOG 2013).

If insurance is inadequate, necessary care may be denied. Procedures and services are rejected unless providers are paid out-of-pocket ahead of time, which most poor people cannot do. As example, one suicidal youth was denied care because his inexpensive insurance policy didn't cover residential mental health care, even in life-threatening situations like his. He was sent on his way with only a Xerox copy of stress-reduction strategies.

The private insurance model is designed for insurance companies to make money. Medical for-profit managed care companies often oversee services for sheltered homeless people and get money if an organization performs to meet a goal. Generally, the more services provided, the more money the organization makes, so pushing potentially unnecessary services isn't unusual. Reimbursement models may pay for a particular service, an hourly rate for providing care, or it can reimburse multiple services on a daily rate. Many reimbursement models now charge by the day, but whether they include food, shelter, counseling, vocational assistance, and so on can vary. Individual, family, or group treatments are separate services and could have different hourly reimbursement rates. What is for certain is that different reimbursement models create different funding costs and savings for individuals, organizations or communities.

Health-care reform debates splinter along partisan lines. Some advocate for universal health care, single-payer, Medicare for All approach that would emphasize preventive care, mental health, physical care, treatments, rehabilitation, eliminate all co-pays and deductibles, and include costly services like long-term care, which Medicare doesn't cover. Universal health care lowers health-care costs for an economy because the government controls the prices of medications and services through negotiation and regulation. Even when using the same term – like universal health care – policy makers may have different definitions of it and what will/will not be covered.

Currently doctors have to deal with many different insurance agencies, each with their own regulations, so a single system would eliminate administrative costs of working with different private insurers since there would only be one. All doctors, hospitals, and health facilities could provide the same standard of service at a lower cost, with a greater emphasis on prevention to reduce need for as much emergency care. As children have access to more comprehensive and preventive care when they are young, later health problems will reduce, culminating in a significant decrease in health-care costs and improvement of well-being over time.

Those who oppose it complain about the short-term costs, the danger to the free-market, and government control and regulation. They do not want to pay for other people's care. People with chronic diseases use more resources than the general population. It's estimated that 5% of the population are responsible for 50% of health-care costs while the healthiest 50% are responsible for 3% of costs. Critics allege that poor people will exploit care and have no incentive to keep down costs and seek unnecessary care (Amadeo 2018a).

While we appreciate that there may be no perfect system, a movement to universal, comprehensive health care will improve the health and quality of life for virtually everyone – especially our youngest citizens who will inherit the future and be parents to our next generations. From our analysis, the benefits of moving towards a single payer system far outweigh both the financial costs and the unnecessary human suffering that people now experience – problems that often thrust them into homelessness.

Education

Education is the primary vehicle for success for children. Homeless children weren't allowed to enroll in school if parents couldn't provide birth certificates, vaccination records, home addresses, phone numbers, and other documents. If parents moved to areas with a different school district, students were shuffled from school to school and had difficulty gaining skills and credits that enabled them to graduate on schedule. Trying to catch-up on studies, do homework, come up with money for school essentials, and trying to fit in and make friends were challenging for children (School House Connection 2018a, b, c).

In 1986, education and homeless advocates introduced the Homeless Persons' Survival Act in Congress. But only small pieces were enacted into law. PL 100–77 was renamed for its chief Republican sponsor Stewart B. McKinney in 1987 under President Reagan. This act was to ensure that states gave homeless children the same right to a free and appropriate education as non-homeless students. It appropriated funds for states to create a coordinator for education of homeless children and youth, who developed a statewide implementation plan. Coordinators found homeless students encountered significant obstacles in obtaining education, so the McKinney Act was amended in 1990 to require states review all policies, practices and laws that might act as barriers to their enrollment, attendance or academic success. These included before- and after-school programs, tutoring, referrals for medical and mental health services, preschool programs, parent education, counseling, transportation, and other services. In 2001 Congress reauthorized it to be the McKinney–Vento Homeless Education Assistance Improvements Act in the No Child Left Behind Act (PL 107–110) in response to awareness that over 1 million students annually were likely to experience homelessness and poverty placed them at great risk for educational challenges. More support was given for local liaisons to ensure student needs were met, as was prohibiting segregation of homeless students in schools and programs. It was reauthorized in 2015 by Title IX, Part A of the Every Student Succeeds Act. Details can be found at School House Connection (2018a).

Education advocates have significantly improved educational opportunities for homeless children and youth. School House Connection, headed by Barbara Duffield (2016), is a national organization working to overcome homelessness through education and provide advocacy and practical assistance in partnership with early childhood programs, schools, institutions of higher education, service providers, families, and youth. The National Association for the Education of Homeless Children and Youth has been influential in helping raise awareness about the educational obstacles homeless young people face. Chapin Hall's research documents how child and youth homelessness is the primary pathway into adult homelessness; homelessness often starts early in life, with the majority of homeless young adults having experienced homelessness in childhood or adolescence. With one in three homeless young women are pregnant or parenting, their babies start lives homeless, leading to poor health and education outcomes that place them at greater risk of homelessness later in life. Education is one of the most effective ways to break this trajectory.

Education is in crisis as our national commitment to building and preserving public education is eroded by private, charter, online, and for-profit schools. The foundation of providing all students with a free and equal education is the basis for building democracy. Allowing schools in poor neighborhoods to deteriorate and accept buildings, resources, and teacher quality for students who are inferior because they are poor is a national insult. National reinvestment into the public schools across the nation will shore up our economy, create greater equality and opportunities for all. Public education must be our new frontier (Gentzel 2017): "I cannot think of an important issue facing America where public education doesn't have a role in providing the solution. Perhaps, most importantly, public education is essential to ensuring an educated electorate that can protect our treasured democracy." We are watching the public narrative demeaning public schools in favor of other forms of education is moving away from our historic commitment to public education. The push away from public education is just another part of the paradigm that is allowing homeless to thrive.

Childcare

Childcare is a necessity for any parent. Making sure children are well-cared for is a parental priority; infants and toddlers require intense care, and this is the time period when their bodies and brains are under critical development. When students are in school, before- and after-school care is essential for their well-being. Homeless parents, who are often female and single, need childcare perhaps even more than other parents if they are to avoid poverty and afford a stable home for their children. Imagine toting a baby, toddler, and other children to appointments that are do-or-die for receiving aid – the logistics are overwhelming. Childcare in general is often hard to find, of questionable quality, and annually can cost as much as college tuition, and these challenges are even greater for homeless parents (Zillman 2018).

Government-run childcare was available during World War II. Women went to work in factories and childcare was considered a national priority by President Franklin D. Roosevelt. A nationwide network of public childcare centers was open 12 hours a day, year-round, costing about $10 a day in today's dollars for everyone. Every state but New Mexico had them and they were deemed very successful. Data found subsequent long-term increases in their employment rates, education level, and earnings. Despite pleas from parents and advocates, President Truman closed them when the war ended. A similar childcare program was considered under the Nixon administration, but he considered it a form of communism that would destroy families. Barack Obama floated the idea of universal preschool, but it was opposed in Congress by legislators who adhered to an antiquated model of a working father and stay-at-home mother.

Childcare is a human right for children. According to Census data, paid childcare is used by 8 million American households – not counting family care and under-the-table childcare. Social networks, daycare centers availability and accessibility, and geography impact availability of care, with childcare unavailable in what is known as childcare deserts (Covert 2018). Safe and stable child care allows parents to look for and maintain work and participate in the job training, education, and other programs essential to resolving their homelessness.

In the 2018 Care.com Cost of Care Survey, the average weekly cost for an infant child is $211 for a day-care center, $195 for a family care center, and $580 for a nanny – and these prices are rising. A third of all families spend 20% or more of their annual household income on childcare. That survey was conducted on over 1000 typical families. They found the cost of childcare, along with the quality and availability of that care, varies dramatically depending on where you live, with North Dakota, Utah, Wyoming and South Dakota being the most affordable states and Washington DC, California, Utah, New Mexico and Massachusetts being most expensive. Families with means can budget for childcare; poor families have no money to budget with. They rely on family, friends, older children, or resort to using unlicensed, more affordable care options. Working moms try to devise schedules that will enable them to care for their children, but the decisions they are forced to make usually result in curtailing their career options.

Homeless families face many barriers to accessing child care; homeless mothers are less likely to receive child care subsidies than poor housed mothers. With the annual cost of center-based care for a four-year-old averaging $7,817, nearly half the federal poverty line for a family of three, the cost of care is impossible. Finding providers who can accommodate homeless families' often irregular, unpredictable schedules can be challenging. Restrictive documentation and eligibility requirements can prevent homeless families from getting subsidized care (Institute for Children, Poverty and Homelessness 2018a, b).

Current childcare systems are expensive and don't work well for most people, and especially for homeless families. Only six states include homeless families in the definition of those with protective-services needs allowing them to qualify for care without meeting traditional eligibility requirements. Forty-one states don't include homeless children as a priority population, and 24 states require families applying for childcare to provide birth certificates which can be challenging for homeless families to locate (Institute for Children, Poverty and Homelessness 2017).

Universal childcare would provide relief to every parent and even the playing field for all parents and children to succeed. Homeless children are vulnerable and deserve a safe place to learn and grow while their parents work or engage in activities that will help them move their lives forward. Efforts in the past to provide homeless parents with more access to childcare have not been very successful (Institute for Children, Poverty and Homelessness 2014). The Better Deal agenda for childcare was proposed but failed – in order to qualify, parents had to look up her state's median income and calculate 150% of that number. People who fell below the threshold would pay part of the cost. For instance, in Maryland, a single mother qualifying for help would still pay over $5,500 a year – and if her income was above the cutoff, she'd get nothing at all. A universal childcare approach could make high-quality child care available to all families, for the entire working day, at a price that they could actually afford because the care was subsidized for all. This occurs in many counties like France where government-run daycare with providers who have degrees in early childhood education are available at charges based on a sliding scale that corresponds to parental income. France pays about 1.3% of its GDP for childcare; the US spends less on early childcare than all other developed countries except Turkey, Latvia, and Croatia (Covert 2018). A universal childcare program is a smart investment for the nation, as well as children, families and providers (Covert 2018). Not providing it ensures that parents won't be able to work, and it locks people into poverty and homelessness that they are desperately trying to escape.

Transportation

Homelessness and transportation availability are closely related (Badger 2013; Eden 2018). Public transportation is a huge concern for people who have limited incomes. Many people cannot afford their own car, plus insurance, registration, maintenance, repairs, and petro. Sharing cars often doesn't work; schedules conflict and it's difficult to coordinate getting to work or home, especially if there is childcare. Walking can be too far and too dangerous especially in places with no sidewalks or where they aren't cleared of snow and debris, and crime-prone areas. Having access to buses, subways, trains, or taxis is essential for successful daily survival, which are often unavailable in rural areas. Achieving the American Dream for many depends on access to public transportation. Public transportation is now a civil rights issue, and its access remains unequal and those who rely on public transit the most — often the poor and people of color — face the greatest hurdles in finding it (Deppen 2018). Transportation is also a human rights issue, especially when unwanted homeless people are bussed to other communities (Gee et al 2017).

As carbon emissions and climate change become everyone's concern, reducing cars on the road and having more available, efficient use of public transportation is sensible and timely. It is something that would benefit everyone. Increased government investment into public transportation, including buses, subways, trains, taxis, bicycles, and other transportation systems would help people of all income streams. Increase of private transportation systems that are affordable, including jitneys, Ubers, Lyft, rickshaws, and ride-sharing programs could be good for people and good for small business people. Helping to figure out how to invest in people so they can earn livings that they can then plow back into the economy, whether by buying cars and petro or paying bus-fare, business people is a worthwhile consideration.

A Harvard University study (Bouchard 2015) found that commute time is the single biggest indicator of whether a household can pull itself out of poverty. Poor people and cheaper housing areas often have little or no transportation nearby. Rural areas may not have any buses or trains, and even getting a cab to come may be both expensive and time-consuming. The reality that there are transit-deserts is now a part of the transit-justice movement. There is increased recognition that the affordable housing crisis is also a transit crisis. Low-income and non-white families are more likely to be plagued by a lack of affordable housing where they will find themselves displaced into transit deserts (Deppen 2018).

Viewing the transportation-homelessness relationship from another angle, many street people live amid transportation infrastructures, like at rest areas, underneath highway bridges or underpasses, train and bus stations, in cars. They may sleep on trains or busses because it's a place where they can warm and hopefully safe for a few hours. In a study of state transportation employees and rest area managers in 25 U.S. states and British Columbia, 70% said they had encountered homeless people and encampments; most did not know what to do, not wanting to be punitive but understanding that they probably weren't supposed to be there (Badger 2013). Having reliable transportation impacts not just physical mobility but social mobility as well. Andree Tremoulet at Portland State University asks the provocative question – What if transportation engineers started designing bridges, for instance, to accommodate the needs of homeless people instead of chasing them away? (Badger 2013). There are indeed many ways transportation systems could become more beneficial to those with, as well as those without.

Cell Phones

We are in an era where communication is immediate, pervasive, and essential. If you are homeless, you don't have an address where you can get mail, unless you pay for a post office box. If you had an address and moved, and moved again, mail may be forwarded but likely not for long and you may never receive important mail to which you have to respond or find that your benefits are cut. Snail-mail is not a realistic method of communication for people who are without housing. Neither is a land-line telephone. Those are on their way out. Pay-phones are virtually nonexistent.

If you have an email account, you can receive and send information. Public libraries are a god-send for homeless people to access computers, but libraries may have rules that make them inaccessible or limit the amount of time one can use them. Trying to find a service is almost impossible if you don't have a computer since Yellow Pages are a thing of the past. Cell phones allow people to make and receive calls, and if they have internet capabilities they can apply for services online, find the status of their job applications, find needed information and seek help. If you apply for a job online (which most employers prefer these days), you can give employers your cellphone and email and this increases chances of getting hired. Employers don't know where you sleep at night, so cellphones provide privacy and security. Phones allow us to make doctor appointments and find how to get there. Students can look up information and do homework online. In short – cellphones are lifelines for homeless people. Apps are being created to help homeless people to find the assistance they need or services near where they are, thanks to GPS technology. For example, in San Francisco, Zendesk partnered with St. Anthony's Foundation to build Link-SF which helps people find medical, housing, or other services (Murphy 2018).

Phones don't have to be fancy but they do need to be functional and affordable. Many carriers provide phones to domestic violence victims to keep them safe. Giving homeless people a phone line isn't a luxury – it is a lifeline. If they don't have one, how are they going to get a job, get care, and build a sustainable life? The cost is small, the benefit large.

Summary

There are fundamental resources that all people need. Systems exist to deliver them – but they are not universally or comprehensively available to all. Excuses that they cost too much reflect expenditures that don't embrace a social investment model. Societies that do end up with happier, healthier citizens and societies; the US comes in #37, behind Canada, Iceland, the Netherlands. "Economies of the future may end up being judged on three levels….traditional measures of the whole economy, such as GDP and employment rates; indicators that point to how equitable and fair a country is; and a new layer including measures of health, happiness and well-being (Blenford 2019). The costs are great – as are benefits to moving towards the kind of wealth-based focus that Max-Neef and Maslow suggest. But the main model remains one of money, not social wealth.

The Work Argument

"If only they'd get a job" is a common public lament about a proposed solution to homelessness. This view assumes (a) homeless people don't have jobs; (b) that there are plenty of jobs they could get that are available; and (c) these illusory jobs pay a living wage. These assumptions are not necessarily correct. First, many homeless people do have jobs – one or more part-time jobs, full-time jobs, or even full-time plus part-time jobs. Two, jobs may not be available that fit people's skill level, childcare or transportation realities. Three, jobs may pay un-livable wages, not provide benefits, and not give people enough to live on, but too much to meet benefit guidelines, which may actually put them in worse straits than they were before they took employment. Therefore, this common argument is not a sufficient way to currently address poverty and homelessness in the USA.

Minimum Wage

When the minimum wage was first established it was supposed to cover a decent place to stay, a way to buy food, take care of families, and provide a minimum existence – but not destitution. Back in the 1940s and 50s families survived on one income, where today it takes two – at least. The first state minimum wage occurred in Massachusetts in 1912 and the federal minimum wage occurred under President Franklin Delano Roosevelt in 1938 as part of the Fair Labor Standards Act. At that time, minimum wage was set at 25 cents an hour, which works out to about $4 per hour in today's money. It has been raised 22 times by 12 different presidents, last to $7.25/hour by Obama in 2009. Since 1989, minimum wage as a percentage of the poverty level has averaged around 60%, and one can work 40 hours a week and still be in poverty Five southern states have no minimum wage laws (Louisiana, Mississippi, Alabama, Tennessee, and South Carolina), four states have a state minimum wage lower than the federal minimum wage (Wyoming, Minnesota, Arkansas, and Georgia), and 21 states and the District of Columbia set their rates higher than the federal minimum wage (BeBusinessEd 2018; Van Buren 2016). Other occupations, such as tipped restaurant servers or young people, can be paid at a lower rate than minimum wage (Doyle 2018a, b; Roberts 2018). As shown in Figure 9.2 people cannot afford housing, and all other basic necessities, on a minimum wage.

Adding housing costs, childcare, health care, and other necessities, the minimum wage today doesn't come close to meeting those needs. Housing costs vary widely, as does what one can earn at a job, or what one can cobble together for child care. Living in New York, New England, the DC area, California or the Pacific Northwest costs considerably more than if one lives in states like Iowa, Oklahoma, Ohio, Kentucky, Tennessee, and other mid-western states (Carrier 2015; Martin 2018).

New York Minimum Wage	Per month
$8.75	$1,400
Median Cost of One Bedroom Apartment	$3,100
	~ **220%** of Minimum Wage (at 40 hours/week)

Figure 9.2 Comparison of Minimum Wage Income and Housing Cost in New York City, 2014.
Source: New York Department of Labor, Zumper.

Living Wage

Many people advocate for a Living Wage rather than a minimum wage. A living wage is the amount it takes to afford basic essentials. The wage debate is over ability to survive economically but is also a moral question on how much is an hour of our lives worth – and who should decide what that value is. President Roosevelt valued work in one way, and President Reagan another – which was the move to a free-market where employers could pay workers whatever they were willing to accept, even if it was low, with the view that any work income stream was better than none. The minimum wage, Reagan argued, led to unemployment by pricing poor people out of the job market. The only good minimum wage, he argued, was no minimum wage, or a wage of $0 (Baker 2018).

Policy wonks have debated about moving the minimum wage upwards, to $15 or more. Whether $15 is sufficient is a debatable point. Some business leaders feel that $15 would cost them too much and that the work employees give isn't worth that amount (Saltsman 2017), while other critics feel that $15 is still too low to pull people out of poverty (Spielberg 2017). Estimates of a $30/hour minimum wage may be more realistic for avoiding poverty, but as a business owner we know said, "That ain't ever gonna happen." The debate over the pros and cons of raising the amount an employer has to pay in order to give employees a living wage is nothing short of controversial (Doyle 2018). Scholars, pundits, and analysts line up their arguments on what's best for employers and the nation, and their research findings are contradictory and feed the frenzy over whether to raise the wages of the lowest-paid workers, and if so to what amount. Many share the assumption that the only important measure of the success of a minimum wage is whether economic studies show that it has increased the total earnings of low-wage workers – without this increase being outweighed by a cost in jobs or hours (Baker 2018). This seems ridiculous to the Fight For $15 Movement, who advocate for a minimum wage of at least $15, and more to make it livable, depending geographically where one lives (Baker 2018). Longitudinal and national data consistently show that when the minimum wage is raised to at least $15/hour that physical health increases, mental health improves, child abuse and neglect goes down, and there are other quantitative and qualitative benefits (Desmond 2019). For single moms who work part-time to avoid poverty and homelessness, raising the minimum wage may help a little, but it doesn't stop the bleeding. Even a living wage may not be enough.…

Universal Basic Income

What if people had a guaranteed income that they could use for housing? The premise of the Universal Basic Income (UBI) is that every citizen would receive regular, no-strings-attached payments from the government that, when paired with living or minimum-wage work, could yield a livable income and decent, stable housing. The UBI would be a fixed income that every adult—rich or poor, working or idle—would automatically receive from government. Unlike means-tested or earned benefits, payments would be the same size and arrive without request. Depending on who designs a given system or the amount of income, a UBI, might replace all existing governmental assistance programs or complement them as a wider safety net. A UBI ideal is that a society, as a first priority, should look out for its people's survival.

To many, the idea of a basic income for all Americans is as "unthinkable" as "women's suffrage and equal rights for racial minorities" was in the past. It's difficult to imagine that we'll ever be able to shake off the dogma that if you want money, you have to work for it (Bregman 2016). The UBI has been hotly debated, with proponents charging it will level out economic inequality and buffer against automation-related job losses, and detractors arguing it will be too costly and encourage laziness. It is a concept that is being piloted in several countries as well as in some US communities. Interestingly, it is both advocated and opposed by all sides of the political spectrum (Heller 2018). A Universal Basic Income of $12,000 a year given to every American citizen would cost taxpayers $3.8 trillion, according to a study by investment management firm Bridgewater Associates (Jaeger 2018). This figure is opposed by those who feel it's too expensive and would be a burden on taxpayers (Santens 2017).

Deindustrialization and servicetization, and the impact of technological developments, including robotics, AI and IT, will continue to eliminate traditional jobs. This will be most acutely felt by people with less education and fewer skills. We are just at the beginning of this trend, and the impact on employment as these trends continue will be even greater. For these reasons, it will be critical for us to think about guaranteed income as well as educational supports. These will also have impacts on family lifestyles, transportation, health, and other factors that impact our social and personal well-being.

There are many examples emerging of UBI. A full-time worker in New York who earned a minimum wage of $13.50 an hour and also received $12,000 in UBI would have a before-tax gross yearly income of $40,080, which could make housing more affordable (Santens 2017). Finland helped people in a study testing UBI by giving 2000 randomly selected unemployed Finns a monthly sum of €560 ($640) from the Finnish government, no strings attached, for two years. There was no paper work or qualifications. Everyone was equal, everyone got the same amount. It cost the government $22.7 million, administered through the country's social insurance agency, Kela. The experiment aimed to help the country assess how to respond to the changing nature of work and how to get people back into the labor market. The 2,000 participants were surveyed, along with a control group of 5,000. Compared with the control group, those taking part had clearly fewer problems related to health, stress, mood and concentration and people had more trust in their future and their ability to influence it. They identified constant financial stress for the long term to be unbearable and the small amount of money gave people security. Sweden has attempted to separate income from work, and seeks to get people jobs that they will enjoy, that they are good at. Having a UBI takes away stigma of doing lower-level jobs and worker competition for more success; people in Sweden report being among the happiest in the world. In another UBI example in Ontario, Canada, 4,000 people on low incomes received $13,000 a year for individuals and was thought to be successful but was axed following the election of right-wing politician Doug Ford, who thought it cost too much. In Kenya, unconditional money has been distributed since 2016 to *more than 21,000 people* in villages across the country in a trial set to last 12 years. Initial results show a boost to the well-being of participants. Stockton, California is giving *$500 a month to 100 low-income families;* Oakland, is giving $1,000 a month with no strings attached to *1,000 people across two US states* for three years. In India, the main opposition party is *running on a pledge to introduce a guaranteed minimum income* for the country's poor (Paddlson 2019).

Earned Income Tax Credit

Instead of focusing on income, some experts argue that reducing taxes is a way to reduce poverty and provide assistance. The IRS allows for people with low income to apply for an Earned Income Tax Credit (EITC). In 2018, the maximum credit for families with one child was $3,461 and $6,431 with more than three children. Childless workers age 25–64 might receive a maximum tax credit of $519. It would reduce tax owed by that amount, or in some cases people could get a refund. Requirements include residents' birth dates, Social Security information, tax returns W2 and 1099, income, unemployment statements, pensions, stocks, details of dependents. While the EITC may lessen taxes, it doesn't provide much disposable income to poor people to pull themselves out of poverty.

Negative Income Tax

A negative income tax is an ideal that has not been instituted as a way to provide people below a certain income level with money. People earning a certain level would owe no taxes, those earning above the level would pay a proportion in taxes, and those earning less would receive a payment equal to the shortfall. It is seen as an incentivization-to-work system that would keep people from being destitute. In contrast to a standard income tax, where people pay money to the government, people with low incomes would receive money back from the government. This would be done by providing people a percentage of the difference between their income and the level at which they start paying income tax; if an official income level was set at $40,000 and the negative income tax percentage at 50%, someone earning $20,000 would receive $10,000 from the government or if someone $35,000, they would receive $2,500.

The idea is that in insuring a minimum income level, aid for housing, Social Security, food, health care, welfare, and administrative costs could be cut as programs were reduced or eliminated. This would save the government money, according to its advocates. It would eliminate a minimum wage, thus allowing businesses to hire workers at any wage and therefore increase availability of cheap labor.

Economist Milton Friedman (1962) advanced this tax, arguing it would give people cash instead of welfare. It would reduce government bureaucracy while giving people money to spend as they choose. The downside is that it would reduce most benefits programs and not necessarily provide people with the difference financially to pay for what they could have received from existing assistance programs. Some argue that a true flat-tax where everyone pays the same rate with no deductions would be useful, while others advocate for a marginal flat tax with progressive rates and excluding some types of income being defined as taxable, while others encourage limited deductions. The negative income tax is sometimes regarded as a flat tax with personal deductions.

This model has not been deemed political feasible. It might be more designed to help the system than the individual, and its viability in reducing poverty and homelessness is highly questionable.

Block Chain and Cryptocurrency

One provocative approach to addressing humanitarian crises, poverty and homelessness comes out of the world of cryptocurrency and the blockchain. Cryptocurrencies are electronic/computational/mathematical monetary units not issued by governments. Blockchains are distributed ledgers. Blockchain cryptography technology is digital transfer of ownership of "money" that can also be used for things other than money — for example, tracking supply chains — quickly in a transparent and public way that provides a clear record of transactions. Essentially anyone could create a blockchain and cryptocurrency.

William Blair and Brian Singer announced in 2015 that Bitcoin and blockchain encryption had the ability to bring the world's population out of poverty. It was highlighted by Steve Forbes in his magazine of economic projections (Forbes 2015). Bitcoin was the first but is only one form of cryptocurrency. There are many more. It's the blockchain that's the key. It is an approach hailed by some as a new, better economic system; it has been criticized as a fad that will fail over time, and it is regarded as a model with huge potential by the majority of "wait-and-see-ers."

JPMorgan Chase is the nation's largest bank and must believe that cryptocurrency is here to stay because they've created their own cryptocurrency, JPM Coin. The logic behind this move is that the entire banking industry is headed this way, and it's considered essential for banking of the future. It is thought to reduce clients' costs and risks and makes money transfers instantaneous by reducing the amount of capital they need to hold onto. JPMorgan moves trillions of dollars around the world every day on behalf of customers. While once considered a fad, it's clearly here to stay (Isidore 2019).

Blockchain is, or could be, regarded as a technology for social change. It is an affordable, fast, and transparent means of transacting that holds much promise to benefit the poor. It is seen as a way for poor people to gain wealth, or at least the ability to engage in routine commercial exchanges to meet their needs. What excites many people is the idea that blockchain can influence several factors influencing both wealth and poverty. For instance, the NutriCoin platform could be an alternative to the food stamp/EBT card system. It has the potential of increasing food accessibility, tracking what is purchased from what vendor, and reducing concerns about mismanagement or fraud, as well as improving access to high-quality foods (chiefmappster 2017; Radocchia 2018).

Blockchain is pregnant with possibilities. Over 134 million people around the world are in direct need of humanitarian aid (Taylor 2018). Data from World Bank indicate that 11% of the world's population, or 750 million people, lives on less than $1.90 a day. Many are without access to essential services like food, health care, or housing. Over 2 billion people have no access to banks. Over a billion lack government-issued identification cards (Kuznetsov 2017; Taylor 2018). Many more don't have access to paper records that service providers require in order to give assistance. But the blockchain could fix those structural obstacles.

Blockchain technology has emerged as a way to help people who are in need to access goods and services, and create new housing and financial options that may shrink homeless as we know it. The technology is new, it hasn't yet solved poverty and homelessness, but it is certainly something that has potential and worth exploring. Blockchain and mobile money provide needed alternatives since no physical branch presence is needed for information to be transferred. It operates on a distributed network that doesn't require a complex and expensive private infrastructure to run, although "expensive" is relative, since not everyone can afford a laptop or phone to run a cryptocurrency wallet when using bank accounts or performing mobile transactions. It is thought to provide unprecedented transparency and be almost immune to corruption. It's not just good for banking but can be used for data-gathering, record-keeping, asset certifications and other important documents. It enables a convenient way to store identity, financial, and reputational information on a decentralized ledger, giving communities in even the most rural parts of the world the ability to build credit, receive federal funding, or obtain services. Information from birth certificates, property ownership, loan or banking can be put on the blockchain and obtained from anywhere in the world. People can download a cryptocurrency wallet without providing a photo ID. One doesn't need a bank account.

Since cryptocurrency isn't like regular money created by governments Treasury Department, it's unknown how the government or banks will attempt to regulate them because they're decentralized. Bitcoin has more than 10,000 nodes around the world and it would be hard to destroy them without causing significant disruptions to the system. It's the decentralization that's the issue. In the US, the SEC has started some regulatory activity that creates new monetary platforms that could even the playing field between entrepreneurs and those who are economically disadvantaged or homeless.

It is already being used globally. Sweden is currently testing the use of blockchain for *land registry*, Japan is trialing it on government contracts, and developing nations are using it to protect people's property rights. ThaneCoin (TPI) is being touted in the UK as a way for people to engage in a rent-to-buy program that they hope will prevent homelessness. Venezuela's economic woes have resulted in many homeless people needing help through non-traditional means (Berman 2018). The Venezuelan Minister of Habitat and Housing Ildemaro Villarroel announced his government is planning to fund construction of houses for the homeless with the national oil-based cryptocurrency, Petro. This Great Mission for Venezuela Housing (GMVV), aims to make quality housing more accessible to the homeless. According to the GMVV website, the government has finished more than 2 million houses and 33 companies so far have started technical, financial, and logistics tests to start the construction process (cryptocurrencyclarified 2019).

It hasn't taken long to figure out that blockchain can be used not just to address global poverty, but problems like homelessness in the US. Consider how a few communities have already instituted blockchain technology to help people who are homeless:

In Berkeley, California, the city launched an ICO, initial coin offering, which generates revenue that the city uses to increase community services, housing, and outreach to people who would benefit from help. Berkeley has over 1000 people identified as homeless, funds to help them are drying up, so Ben Bartlett began working with Neighborly, the University of California at Berkeley's Blockchain lab, and financial tech startup to create the ICO. The idea is that investors would buy tokens linked to municipal bonds that could then be spent in local stores and with service providers or dedicated directly to a community improvement project. Bonds aren't commonly used but could be very helpful to the community. The city of Berkeley's attempt at creating their own cryptocurrency came as a response to President Trump's December signing of the Republican tax bill, which discourages private contractors from constructing affordable housing by undercutting existing incentives. Berkeley's ICO will be less volatile than tokens like Bitcoin because it is linked to the value of municipal bonds, which cannot fluctuate in price the way cryptocurrency can on the open market (James 2018a; McMahon 2018). San Francisco is using Propy, a real estate blockchain developed by Natalia Karayaneva, a Bulgarian-American with a master's degree in urban sustainable development from the University of Oxford, to bring together homeless people in communes where they will be housed and allowed to engage in money-earning ventures primarily agriculture (Rae 2018). New York City has been working with Blockchain for Change since 2017. They have passed out over 3000 smartphones with the app Fummi to homeless people. Digital identities are created for the recipients. They can also access digital Chain Coins that they can use to buy services or earn more coins through different activities (Rothrie 2018). Austin, Texas, is piloting a new blockchain platform, MyPass, to improve identity services for its homeless population of 2000 as part of a pilot grant awarded by *the Mayor's Challenge program* sponsored by Bloomberg Philanthropies.

Identity is a thorny challenge in serving homeless people because paper documents could be lost, damaged or stolen, making it hard for them to qualify for aid. The goal of the Austin's blockchain program is to consolidate the identity and vital records of each homeless person in a safe and confidential way while providing a means for service providers to access that information. By using blockchain, the city hopes to replace paper records with electronic encrypted records that would be more reliable and secure. Additionally, blockchain could create a decentralized authentication mechanism to verify a particular person's identity or information. Because vital records on the blockchain could build over time, providers would know what services a person had used previously. Using a health care example, when a homeless person seeks care, the blockchain could provide the entire patient history of that individual to the provider, which would enable better care to be delivered faster. Austin is partnering with the Dell Medical School at the University of Texas to work out how best to implement the blockchain for medical professionals (Crichton 2018).

Toronto records over homeless 5000 people who lack adequate food and clothes, as well as shelter. A local 28-year-old, Hamza Sibai, decided in 2017 that he wanted to start a Bitcoin Cash related project to offer Bitcoin cash to people as a reward for donating slightly worn clothes to keep people warm. He teaches people how to download a cryptocurrency wallet, educates them on the benefits and shows them where to spend it, transforming his Coins4Clothes into a homeless clothing, bitcoin cash-educating machine (James 2018b).

In Rockland, Maine, Nate Davis and Jim DeFrancesa are using blockchain in a couple of different ways to serve the homeless (O'Brien 2018). One is through their smart phone DoGood platform. This was piloted at Christmas party held for families served by Knox County Homeless Coalition (KCHC). Here's how it works: First, the DoGood team authorizes a charitable organization like KCHC to issue an allotment of DoGood currency to its volunteers. Volunteers download the DoGood app on their phones that allows them to sign up and get cryptocurrency credits for doing certain charitable work that they spend for goods and services in the community, save, or do with whatever they want. Anyone who volunteers to "do good" for others can earn the currency and then transfer it into tangible benefits. The other way DeFrancesa and Davis are developing blockchain is to a design allows for individuals to donate to a homeless individual who has a designated code or skew on their phone or on a card that they can carry in their pocket. While some people are hesitant to donate to homeless people because they're not sure how the money will be used, this blockchain strategy avoids mismanagement. Part of the donated money would go directly into that individual's designated cryptocurrency account for them to spend or save while the other amount could go to an agency that serves that individual so that they have more resources they can provide people in need. The idea behind this system is that there would be oversight of donations and greater accountability of how donations are being spent. They have ambitions of creating a circular, self-sufficient economy that mitigates some of the weaknesses of American-style capitalism. They hope to develop a system that rewards people for types of labor that increase social capital, like caring for an elderly relative currently doesn't pay much (or any) money. They are building in mechanisms to discourage the hoarding of wealth; what blockchain can do is not just relevant to specific projects in specific locations, it's a response to things like income inequality and general concerns about fairness in the American economy and other market economies.

In Ohio, POINTS, an innovative cross-platform cryptocurrency joined the fight against homelessness by partnering with DeveloPods and non-profit Housing Humanity. DeveloPods is a housing solution that allegedly puts traditional building to shame. They promote cutting-edge designs that are stronger, adaptable, transportable, eco-friendly, and safe, take less time to build and are less expensive (chiefmappster 2017).

Tech innovators are mushrooming to figure out how to help home-less people through the use of blockchain. One innovator put forth the idea to create a CryptoCurrency system that would give homeless people assistance through a system that cannot be cheated. The goal is to have homeless people break out of homelessness through accumulated wealth. It is recommended that a group of CryptoCurrency financial, experts work with volunteers at homeless shelters to help manage Crypto for local homeless people. Some of the Crypto might be dedicated to individuals to use how they want, while the rest is only available to the Crypto/financial experts. Part of the Crypto will be diversified and traded in a way to accumulate more value. Wallets can be assigned to each local group or maybe even to each homeless family or person, looking for housing. In either case, more and more Crypto will, if all goes well, accumulate for individual volunteer groups or homeless people depending on the strategy. Workshops to teach people about what Crypto is and how you can manage it would be given (chiefmappster 2017).

Blockchain's decentralization and immutability holds tremendous promise in allowing philanthropic organizations to accurately assess the exact size and the scale of the current global humanitarian effort so that services and solutions can be generated (Taylor 2018). Smartphones are essential to this approach. It is estimated that by 2020 90% of the world will have one. People around the world have Facebook accounts or use social media to connect with each other on a daily basis, so it's logical to assume that the underlying technologies for a successful blockchain attack on poverty is possible. However, it's still a reach to claim that blockchain end poverty, since poverty is a multifaceted problem that needs a broad-based solution.

How blockchain will develop isn't yet clear. Decentralized freelanc-ing platforms like Blocklancer or Openbazaar are emerging. Discover-ing the many ways blockchain will allow for things to happen in a way that wouldn't otherwise happen is yet to be determined. In the case of DoGood, the answer is they want to establish a system that people trust without reliance on a single centralized authority. But dissemination of information about cryptocurrency is still largely informal and people who are homeless may not know how to establish themselves on a freelancing platform. Some platforms want users to have a Paypal account or other storage system for the receiving and distribution of cryptocurrency. As with other economic systems, knowledge of them and use of cryptocurrency exchanges are central to their success (Hecht 2017).

Summary

If money rules the system, systems need to consider how their expenditures will achieve greater social investments. Attempts to tweak wages or taxes are not going to prevent poverty and homelessness unless much more comprehensive approaches are undertaken. Shifting a national mind-set to support wealth towards human justice and development frame merits consideration. Investing in people so they have the physical, emotional, educational, and attitudinal opportunities to become their best selves, to build the best nation possible, is possible if we expend more than lip-service to this goal.

Cryptocurrency and blockchain are emerging not just as a different economic exchange system, but as a different human relations currency as well. Red-tape and regulations diminished, cryptocurrency and blockchains have the potential for helping people who are homeless to give them resources and help them avoid traps that thrust them into poverty. Cryptocurrency holds potential for helping homeless people who have lost traditional resources and signs of monetary "success" because it affords them a new economic exchange system to help them get their lives back on track.

Notes

1 www.census.gov/newsroom/press-releases/2015/cb15-97.html.
2 www.creditdonkey.com/welfare-statistics.html.
3 The estimates of the size of the cuts throughout this paper are based on the Fiscal Year 2019 Budget of the U.S. Government at www.whitehouse.gov/omb/budget/ and the "Explanatory Notes" the Department of Agriculture (USDA) provides to Congress, available at www.obpa.usda.gov/32fns2019notes.pdf.

10 The Human Dignity Paradigm

The paradigms and approaches previously described in this book have not prevented homelessness. Some have provided momentary relief; none have gone the distance to eradicate underlying causes of poverty and homelessness. We have mentioned some that have potential for helping, and undoubtedly, there are more innovative and creative possibilities being cultivated.

How we think about homelessness and poor people is at the crux of the issue. How we think shapes what we do. What we value determines our decisions. Our decisions determine social realities. Homelessness is totally preventable, as is hunger. Poverty may be as well. If we don't change how we are looking at it, and how we are treating those who suffer, more suffering for all of us is predictable and inevitable. There is a saying that doing the same thing over and over and expecting a different result is insanity. False consciousness is believing what others tell us and going along with it, even when we ourselves are exploited. We are all being hurt by the way homelessness is being addressed, but especially those of us who are living on the edge – which is most of us at one time or another. It's time to change this trajectory (Ratson 2016).

Early in this book we explored how different theoretical assumptions have driven political, economic, and service decisions over the years. Theory and history are important guideposts to where we are now. There have been times our nation has taken comprehensive action to help each other. There have been more times when we leaders and public have turned a blind eye. Whether due to self-interest advancement or weariness that makes us unable to fight the good fight, most of us have money concerns and are scared of losing what we have. We badmouth underdogs because we don't want to become them; and while we resent the fat cats who are in charge, many of us secretly, unconsciously want to be like them since having enough is more comfortable than doing without. Having choices and power is better than being victims who are powerless. Poor people seem easier to blame for homelessness than the rich, but this is ill-focused. In many ways, we are the homeless problem. People in authority who espouse insensitivity and callousness to the destitute go unchallenged – we are allowing it to happen, we accept disparity and are not holding our business and government leaders accountable.

It's time to look at homelessness from a different perspective, one that is respectful of ourselves and others, one that is compassionate instead of competitive, one that gives dignity and integrity instead of promoting worthlessness and despair. Rich people are no better than poor people; everyone has gifts and talents to bring forward. This chapter explores ways to shift the trajectory. Creating new paradigms to prevent homelessness must start in our heads and in our hearts.

Social Responsibility Approach

The "every man for himself" approach is counter-productive to creating humane societies. A social responsibility approach is a framework of mind that suggests people and organizations have obligations to act in ways that promote a balanced well-being relationship with others and the world in which we live. As an ethical theory, individuals are accountable for acting in ways that benefit the whole of society; this is seen as one's civic duty and organizational responsibility. This moves a society away from an economic-profit focus to one in which there must be balance between business profit, welfare of society, and care for the environment.

Organizations can design themselves to not only make profit but also be socially responsible. Social responsibility in business became popularized by Carroll (1991), who designed a pyramid of corporate social responsibility that included economic, legal, ethical, and philanthropic components. This was done largely as a response to a social backlash of corporations caring more about profits than about people and the environment. Socially responsible companies ideally create a climate that fosters ethical actions. Ethical conduct refers to intentionally responsible action and honoring social contracts (which will be discussed next). These include ethics of justice and ethics of caring for others. Unethical conduct refers to intentional actions that evade responsibility, violates social contracts, and harms others directly or indirectly. Often, actions that are not socially responsible are subtle, "background noise" that eats away at one's ethical fiber where people act irresponsibly or unethically without even realizing it. Often, ethical implications of a decision or action are overlooked for personal gain and material benefits. A triple-bottom-line framework recommends that companies commit to focus on social and environmental concerns just as they do on profits. Socially responsible investments are needed to protect the safety and integrity of the whole of society.

Social responsibility becomes active by creating structures and practices that advance well-being, or it can be passive by avoiding engaging in harmful actions. Sandra Bloom (2019) created the Sanctuary Model, which finds that making the commitment to social responsibility means that we are committed to promoting *physical, psychological, social, and moral safety* of others. These four domains are interdependent; any violation of a person's sense of these safeties will elicit a desire for vengeance. It means as individuals and organizations we must take seriously the mission to help others.

Social responsibility, social contracts, and human rights are intrinsically intertwined. Paolo Friere (1968) reminds us that no one can be authentically human while preventing others from doing so. Full humanization for anyone is possible only in a context in which the oppressor/oppressed contradiction has been overcome, people are not dehumanized, and all peoples are treated with respect (Bloom 2019).

Social Contract Model

It's time for a new social contract. In order to consider what it could look like, a quick overview of the term is necessary.

An ancient premise, the term "social contract" was discussed by Thomas Hobbes (1652) and stems from a 1762 book of the same name by Jean-Jacques Rousseau. The idea is that individuals surrender some of their rights to authorities in exchange for protection of other rights. Operationalization of what a social contract entails has changed across time and place. For instance, the New Deal era of the 1930s through the 1970s was shaped by high wages, pushed up by strong unions, limited global competition, low energy and commodity prices, stringent regulations on businesses, and low consumer good prices (Freedman and Lind 2013).

Focusing on the social contract of the 20th century, corporations and governments developed a symbiotic relationship that resulted with 3C behavior from individuals – compliance, conformity, and acceptance of being controlled (Robb 2009). "Good" employees were powerless; they were compliant and behaved exactly as the company expected them to behave. They conformed and suppressed aspects of their individual identity that differed from the corporate culture. If you were a good employee, you might get rewarded with more pay or a job where you could tell others what to do. The company could take care of you for life. But if you made waves and defied those rules, you could be fired and without any income or respected status. Market stability, benevolent bosses, and wise political leaders were assumed to be ongoing.

But in the 1980s economic downturn, rotating corporate leadership and political leaders that don't always seem to have the public's best interests at heart has changed those assumptions and worker complacency (Robb 2009). Seeds for a new social contract were planted and have been growing ever since. People seem to be working longer hours, multiple jobs, under sometimes inept leadership, with no assurance of employment longevity, yet they dare not speak out for fear of losing what benefits they have. Staff turnovers have increased as workers feel less dedication to business that seems less dedicated to their well-being. People want to work and use their skills, but more on their terms instead of the corporations.

The need for a new social contract is seen in other areas too. The public is weary of government programs that don't work, where they are disqualified for bogus reasons, and entitlements seem to go mostly to the rich as the poor are to be grateful for crumbs. The view that poor people are inherently defective, unproductive, noncreative, lazy, stupid, and undeserving is increasingly rejected. While some paint poverty as something that only happens to flawed people, in reality poverty is a mainstream event experienced by a majority of Americans. Four out of five Americans will experience at least one year of significant economic insecurity, living in poverty or near-poverty, or needing to turn to unemployment insurance or another form of public assistance at some point during their working years, and this economic insecurity will last for three or more years (Vallas 2014).

It is possible for a new social contract to put people before profits. As the field of social responsibility points out, profits are important but there must be a balance between the well-being of the business (or business person) and the well-being of individuals and societies. Homelessness is the obvious sign of a failed social contract between the state and the society (Rhule 2017). Tensions between people of different groups have been rising. The Trump administration aims to change how the government defines national poverty threshold, which could result in millions of fewer Americans qualifying for a wide range of benefits (Delaney 2019). Recent and projected cuts to healthcare, food, housing, education, and transportation, with no relief for student loan debt or childcare, eradicate the safety net. Things for middle-income and poor people are going to get much worse if a new social contract isn't created soon.

Chances of it happening aren't good unless the public steps forth to demand it. Social blindness to how rough things are for millions of Americans prevents us from seeing the depth and breadth of it. Denial of our own vulnerability, willingness to stereotype and scapegoat people who are unfortunate, and unwillingness to hold leaders accountable contribute to the continuation of a social contract that has outlived its relevance in a humane society. When a school in Tennessee resorts to sending home toothpaste and tampons because SNAP won't cover them and there is no discretionary money to purchase them, it's a sign that in one of the world's richest nations that this should be considered immoral (Ramrayka 2019). Until we ask why our community thinks that having a shelter or police intervention to deal with the homeless "problem" occurs, we are going to keep relying upon a social contract that has failed the majority of Americans.

A new social contract is needed not just for the US, but for the world as well. The World Bank's report, "Toward a New Social Contract, the International Panel on Social Progress," "Rethinking Society for the 21st Century" report (Bussolo 2019), and Michael Freedman's *New Magna Carta for Children* (2019) showcase the necessity for a new way of living and caring for each other. The New America Foundation advocates for a middle-income social contract. It assumes that many service industries won't offer workers middle-income salaries, which means that the government will have to take a more active role in making essential services like education, childcare, and healthcare affordable. Universal pre-k, single-payer health insurance, raising the federal minimum wage to a true living wage, and expanding education at all levels will be essential in a system more suited to the current economy and needs of workers and citizens (Freedman and Lind 2013).

These reports explore the universality in providing social assistance, social insurance, and quality basic services, the presence of both horizontal and vertical inequalities, how emerging economic distributional tensions have given rise to populism, and how political, economic, and social forces give rise to preventable individual and community woes. They argue how a new social contract could support healthier people, stronger societies, and a future of sustained shared prosperity.

Certain things are clear – the trend of low wages, high goods and services, and insecure employment patterns can exist only if there are major and substantial government assistance programs that are available to all. People are dispirited and conflict between us increasing. Children's health in the US is lowest of any developed nation and is behind many underdeveloped nations. Hunger, homelessness, and economic distress for the average household are increasing. Household and community stability are shaky. None of this is good for a healthy society's future. A new ethical, moral, just social contract is long past due – it would help not just those who are homeless, but it could help us all.

Trauma Prevention Approach

Trauma is both a cause of homelessness and an effect of insecure housing and homelessness. As a cause, many children grew up in situations that created trauma for them; into their adulthood, they experienced additional traumas. These predisposed them toward homelessness. Trauma is also a consequence of being homeless, as people struggled with financial problems and personal chaos until they could no longer function and became homeless. Poverty breeds a host of preventable traumas. As homeless parents, no matter how hard they try to buffer their children from the adverse realities of it, they are being exposed to trauma, thereby setting into course a set of conditions that makes homelessness in their own children a possibility throughout their lives. This replication of homelessness from one generation to the next could stop of appropriate interventions were put into place when a child was young. If they are not, trauma's effects can become intergenerational (Finkelhor 2013).

Poverty and homelessness are regarded as traumatogenic forces (Bloom 2019). Lack of housing is an isolated, lonely, alienated, and abandoned situation.

It subjects people who are doing their best to degrading stigma. Homelessness becomes their master status as people respond to what they lack, rather than to what one gifts and talents they have. Homelessness enhances vulnerability and makes the cuts deeper in one's already raw and abused physical, psyche, and social worlds.

What is needed is a new paradigm that connects cause and consequence throughout the human lifespan – from before birth through adulthood. In order to prevent homelessness, the complexity of homelessness must be considered – its many causes, layers, and impacts – and how it sets children up for a lifetime of poverty and housing distress. While housing is a critical need of homeless families, it is not their only need (Duffield 2016).

Addressing children's developmental needs is the keystone to this paradigm. Children's well-being should be our national priority. One cannot have a healthy, functioning society without having healthy children from environments that function well to meet their needs. Research substantiates that homeless children have poorer socio-emotional, physical, and cognitive development compared with peers. Early deficits are shown to have long-term consequences in health, school, work, criminal justice contact, and reliance upon social programs for assistance. Homelessness presents preventable trauma and perils for children and youth, necessitating different standards for care and for assessing risk. Their brains, bodies, and spirits are developing in ways that will impact them for the rest of their lives. They cannot wait to become a priority or for solutions that meet their unique and comprehensive needs. It is foundational to not miss nurturing major developmental touchpoints when they occur (Duffield 2016; Shonkoff 2019).

Trauma as a Cause of Homelessness

Homelessness is a form of emotional trauma. For every visible homeless person there are hundreds that we do not recognize, and for every homeless person we don't see there are many more precariously housed, often suffering more than or equal to those out on the street (Muller 2013). Many experts consider trauma to be the root cause of homelessness, and that most cases of homelessness result from a series of losses so severe and betraying, so devastating, that these individuals cannot even tolerate the idea of hope.

Background causes of homelessness include poverty, substance abuse, violence, physical and mental disorders, family, work, school, and community problems people face and suffer. Not knowing where you are going to sleep, if you will get anything to eat, how you are going to pay bills or buy anything, what people think of you, or what is waiting to destroy you is highly stress producing. Homeless individuals, young and old alike, are routinely stigmatized because they are poor.

In a review of homeless literature, researchers identify vulnerability trends in both childhood and adulthood that contribute to homelessness, trends that correlate from what we have independently observed in our work (Anda 2006; Dube 2001; Felitti 1998; Herman 1997; Muñoz et al. 2019; Nurius 2012; Patterson 2014; Roos 2013; Vernon-Feagans et al. 2013). Toxic stressors homeless children face can be understood from an Adverse Child Experiences (ACEs) perspective. ACEs are stressful or traumatic events that are strongly related to the development and prevalence of a wide range of both physical and mental health problems that can last throughout a person's lifetime. Homeless children are likely to have experienced ACEs that include poverty, transiency, parental separation, economic hardship, physical, sexual or emotional abuse, domestic violence, cultural violence, threats and actual violence, neglect, incarceration of a household member, substance misuse within the home, or parents who were ill or unable to care for them. Negative outcomes associated with ACEs include some of society's most intractable health issues such as homelessness, alcoholism, drug abuse, depression, suicide, behavioral and emotional challenges, physical health, and obesity. Averse child experiences put children at risk of a wide range of physical, mental, and social health problems, including homelessness. These include child abuse (physical, sexual, or emotional/verbal), being expelled from school, running away or being kicked out of the home, being in foster care, having lower self-esteem, lower grades, and ultimately lower educational and career attainment. There is evidence that children who experience high ACEs are more likely to experience poverty (SAMHSA 2019).

Exposure to adverse experiences even very early in children's lives, even before they are mobile and verbal, have been shown to lead to a variety of preventable problems that may cause lifelong physical, emotional, cognitive, and behavioral problems, as shown in Figure 10.1. Quality of life may be drastically impaired, chronic diseases are likely, and an early death may occur (Murphey and Sacks 2019).

Children who grow up homeless carry its impact into adulthood. It's important to ensure that children grow up in safe and secure homes. The intergenerational negative impacts of poverty and homeless are significant and preventable. Children need safe affordable housing. They need education and employment opportunities. Children are resilient and can recover from homelessness, but foundational abilities are set in the early months of their lives. Services for children must be provided as soon as families enter shelters and follow them into permanent housing (American Institutes for Research 2018a).

Trauma as an Effect of Homelessness

Homelessness almost always leads to trauma. Loss of a home is accompanied by loss of status, community, possessions, and security. The regular routine that families had disappears as schedules become unpredictable

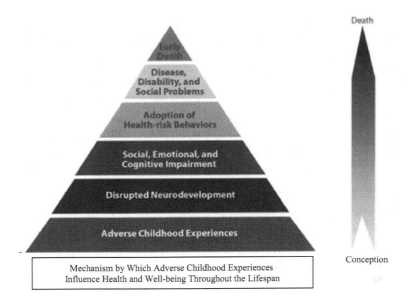

Figure 10.1 Adverse Childhood Experiences (ACES) Model of Early Risk Factors. Source: Center for Disease Control (CDC). Downloaded from www.cdc.gov/violence prevention/acesstudy/index.html, July 2019.

since one may not know where they are going to be that night, how they will obtain money, food, childcare, transportation, or daily essentials. Lowered self-esteem and personal control are inevitable. Ability to have credibility declines with one's own family, workers, friends and neighbors, or with those whom are being asked for assistance. Families that were intact before becoming homeless may not be able to withstand the pressures. Living on the street increases opportunity for illness, rape, assaults, having possessions stolen or destroyed, substance use, and crime. It's harder to hold important relationships together. Housing insecurity leads to work and school troubles. Existing material and nonmaterial resources evaporate. Stress may increase emotional outbursts, mental illnesses, substance abuse, or violence (as victims or perpetrators). These behaviors may then be used to blame people for being out of control. This can lead to police or cut intervention and potentially legal actions or even institutionalization (Muller 2013).

Recovering from Homeless Trauma

Muñoz et al. (2019) reviewed different models analyzing homelessness and found no agreement on how best to address the problem. Many programs hold potential. SAMHSA provides a list of trauma-sensitive recovery programs for homeless families here.[1] Providers aren't always aware of the impact homelessness has and need more training in trauma-informed care. Extensive work has been done by homeless-trauma experts to help workers implement this approach here[2] (Hopper et al. 2009). Bloom's Sanctuary model provides details on how organizations can address trauma successfully.[3] Boston Healthcare for the Homeless[4] and Boston's Healthcare without Walls[5] programs go into the community providing both routine and sophisticated care to homeless individuals. Clinicians, case managers, and behavioral health professionals work in 45 locations delivering healthcare to some of the community's most vulnerable, and most resilient, citizens. They go into homes, under bridges, into parks, doing preventive care, diagnoses, and treatments, including dialysis and chemotherapy, without people having to come into clinics. Their philosophy treats patients with dignity and quality professional care (O'Connel 2015).

These programs realize homeless people haven't been treated with dignity and respect by others in the past. Seeking care itself can pose trauma. All families and individuals who have experienced homelessness benefit from trauma-focused care. When someone is homeless, even seemingly helpful suggestions may inadvertently cause harm and direct pain. It is important for professionals working with people in need to be trauma informed (Muller 2013).

Homeless individuals have suffered immense pain and trauma. Breaking through barriers of distrust, trauma and pain takes time, energy, and compassionate hearts. To heal trauma, one must be treated like they have value and be given skills on how to overcome traumas, many of which first occurred during childhood (Career and Recovery Resources 2018). Services must incorporate trauma-informed care, with attention to the identification, prevention, and treatment of major depression in both children and parents.

Without early care and education, today's homeless children are more likely to become tomorrow's homeless adults. A multi-generational approach to preventing homelessness calls for access to quality childcare, early learning programs, schools, and other children's services as essential parts of anti-poverty and homelessness assistance services. As Duffield notes (2016), if the nation's approach to homelessness is constrained solely to housing, or directed at HUD's outdated definition of homelessness, and if education and essential well-being services are ignored,

> we will be generating poverty, [trauma] and homelessness for the foreseeable future. We will not truly end chronic homelessness, or any other kind of homelessness, until the complex realities and comprehensive needs of homeless children and youth take a front seat in federal homelessness policy. Only then will we see true cost savings and real homelessness prevention.
>
> (Duffield 2016)

Human Rights Approach

Housing is a human right, and homelessness is a violation of that right (National Law Center on Homelessness and Poverty 2011 & 2018b). All human rights treaties affirm an individual's right to have dignity and be treated fairly, irrespective of age, gender, race, religion, nationality, and other factors. The following address the right to housing:

Roosevelt's 1944 Second Bill of Rights

In his 1944 State of the Union address, President Franklin D. Roosevelt announced the nation needed a Second Bill of Rights. He felt that the original Bill of Rights was written when the nation was young and its creators didn't envision the challenges that the nation came to face. Additional rights were needed to protect and preserve the values of our great nation. Here are excerpts from it that lay the foundation for housing to be a right of all Americans. [6]

Therefore, in order to concentrate all our energies and resources on winning the war, and to maintain a fair and *stable economy at home, I recommend that the Congress adopt:*

1 *A realistic tax law – which will tax all unreasonable profits, both individual and corporate, and reduce the ultimate cost of the war to our sons and daughters. The tax bill now under consideration by the Congress does not begin to meet this test.*
2 *A continuation of the law for the renegotiation of war contracts – which will prevent exorbitant profits and assure fair prices to the Government. For two long years I have pleaded with the Congress to take undue profits out of war.*
3 *A cost of food law – which will enable the Government (a) to place a reasonable floor under the prices the farmer may expect for his production; and (b) to place a ceiling on the prices a consumer will have to pay for the food he buys. This should apply to necessities only; and will require public funds to carry out. It will cost in appropriations about 1% of the present annual cost of the war.*
4 *Early reenactment of the stabilization statute of October, 1942. This expires June 30, 1944, and if it is not extended well in advance, the country might just as well expect price chaos by summer.*
5 *A national service law which, for the duration of the war, will prevent strikes, and, with certain appropriate exceptions, will make available for war production or for any other essential services every able-bodied adult in this Nation.*

These five measures together form a just and equitable whole. I would not recommend a national service law unless the other laws were passed to keep down the cost of living, to share equitably the burdens of taxation, to hold the stabilization line, and to prevent undue profits. The Federal Government already has the basic power to draft capital and property of all kinds for war purposes on a basis of just compensation.

He continues:

As our Nation has grown in size and stature, however – as our industrial economy expanded – these political rights proved inadequate to assure us equality in the pursuit of happiness.

We have come to a clear realization of the fact that true individual freedom cannot exist without economic security and independence. "Necessitous men are not free men." People who are hungry and out of a job are the stuff of which dictatorships are made.

In our day these economic truths have become accepted as self-evident. We have accepted, so to speak, a second Bill of Rights under which a new basis of security and prosperity can be established for all regardless of station, race, or creed.

Among these are:

The right to a useful and remunerative job in the industries or shops or farms or mines of the Nation;

The right to earn enough to provide adequate food and clothing and recreation;

The right of every farmer to raise and sell his products at a return which will give him and his family **a decent living;**

The right of every businessman, large and small, to trade in an atmosphere of freedom from unfair competition and domination by monopolies at home or abroad;

The right of every family to a decent home;

The right to adequate medical care and the opportunity to achieve and enjoy good health;

The right to adequate protection from the economic fears of old age, sickness, accident, and unemployment;

The right to a good education.

All of these rights spell security. And after this war is won we must be prepared to move forward, in the implementation of these rights, to new goals of human happiness and well-being.

America's own rightful place in the world depends in large part upon how fully these and similar rights have been carried into practice for our citizens. For unless there is security here at home there cannot be lasting peace in the world.

Roosevelt died in office the following year before he could instill this bill. His widow, Eleanor Roosevelt, made sure that housing was included as a basic human right alongside food, clothing, and medical care in the Universal Declaration of Human Rights.

The US has either failed to sign or ratify at least six international treaties in which housing was declared a human right. When given the opportunity in 2009, Shaun Donovan, President Obama's HUD secretary, shied away from declaring housing a human right. In 2010, the UN Human Rights Council subjected the US government to a first-ever review, and UN envoys heard testimony across the country, and housing was the # 1 human rights issue mentioned. Even so, the US's Human Rights Council response "carefully sidestep[ped] naming housing and other economic and social rights as rights," according to the National Law Center on Housing and Poverty. The same year, Obama released his Strategic Plan to End Homelessness, which contained no action plan and no funding (Callahan 2013).

National Economic and Social Rights Initiative

The National Economic and Social Rights Initiative (NESRI)[7] identifies seven fundamental principles of the right to housing in the US. These include (1) security of tenure to be protected against evictions, harassment, predatory redevelopment and displacement; (2) essential facilities for safe drinking water, heating and lighting, washing facilities, food storage, and sanitation; (3) affordability in housing so people don't have to choose between paying rent and buying food; (4) structurally decent and safe homes that protect residents from cold, damp, heat, rain, wind, or other threats to health, structural hazards, and disease; (5) accessible housing; (6) built on land and locations that ensure safety and access to other social facilities; and (7) housing polices respect expression of cultural identity and diversity. These would be elaborations and additions to rights endorsed by FDR.

Universal Declaration of Human Rights

The Universal Declaration of Human Rights (UDHR)[8] was created after World War II by the United Nations. It outlined 30 fundamental rights that all nations should honor, with hopes that the violence and oppression of war wouldn't occur again. Article 25.1 protected the right to housing –

> Everyone has the right to a standard of living adequate for the health and wellbeing of himself and of his family, including food, clothing, housing and medical care and necessary social services, and the right to security in the event of unemployment, sickness, disability, widowhood, old age or other lack of livelihood in circumstances beyond his control.

Convention on the Rights of the Child

The Convention on the Rights of the Child (CRC)[9] is the most ratified of all human rights treaties in the world; all UN member nations have ratified it with only one exception – the US. The 54 articles outline protections, provisions, and participations of children, age birth – 18. Article 27.3 speaks directly to children's right for secure housing:

> States Parties, in accordance with national conditions and within their means, shall take appropriate measures to assist parents and others responsible for the child to implement this right and shall in case of need provide material assistance and support programmes, particularly with regard to nutrition, clothing and housing.

International Covenant on Economic, Social and Cultural Rights

This 1966 UN International Covenant on Economic, Social, and Cultural Rights codified the right to housing.[10] The US and Thailand are the only two UN member states who have failed to ratify it. Article 11.1 states that "States Parties to the present Covenant recognize the right of everyone to an adequate standard of living for himself and his family, including adequate food, clothing and housing, and to the continuous improvement of living conditions. The States Parties will take appropriate steps to ensure the realization of this right." In addition, the Committee on Economic, Social, and Cultural Rights has issued general comments on the right to housing, #4 and #7.

Convention on the Elimination of All Forms of Racial Discrimination

Article 5 of this UN treaty prohibits racial discrimination in all its forms and guarantees rights to everyone, without distinction as to race, color, or national or ethnic origin, to equality before the law.[11] It pertains to a set of civil rights, including employment and healthcare. Article 5.d.iii designates the right to housing.

Convention on the Elimination of All Forms of Discrimination against Women

In this treaty, there are many protections and provisions for women identified.[12] Article 14(h) specifies that women have the right "To enjoy adequate living conditions, particularly in relation to housing, sanitation, electricity and water supply, transport and communication."

The American Declaration on Rights and Duties of Man

This declaration was signed in 1948 in Columbia.[13] Article XI (11) states that "Every person has the right to the preservation of his health through sanitary and social measures relating to food, clothing, housing and medical care, to the extent permitted by public and community resources."

Application of Human Rights to Homeless Individuals

These treaties reflect the different dimensions outlined in Maslow's hierarchy of needs (1954). Housing is a fundamental human need. It allows for people to meet basic physiological needs such as sleep, cleanliness, and cooking food. In these human rights treaties, people have a right to health care, education, living wages and safe work conditions, and just interactions with the criminal justice systems. People are entitled to respect and dignity. They should be allowed the right to participate in civic and governmental decisions and to have their interests addressed in the same manner as other people. If people have their physiological needs met, if they feel safe and secure, feel they matter and belong to their community, their self-esteem can become greater, which hopefully will lead to self-actualized individuals and world.

Homeless children and families are often denied these basic rights outlined in these international human rights treaties. If they have no home, they have nowhere to sleep, get clean, or access nutritious food. Being transient increases insecurity and risks to violence, and children can't feel safe. Not belonging to a neighborhood or community is challenging for children who live a transient or nomadic life. If children are separated from their families and reside in shelters, foster care, or with others who don't have kinship affection for them, they naturally experience emotional challenges. It's hard to make school a priority when you're scared, tired, hungry, and don't know where you're going to be sleeping that night. This makes it very challenging for children to achieve high self-esteem or the self-actualization that Maslow promotes as signs of well-being. If enough individuals are denied these opportunities, communities cannot become self-actualized places to live for anyone. Therefore, providing safe and secure permanent housing for children is foundational for the creation not just of healthy, well-adjusted children but for healthy, well-adjusted societies as well.

Homeless Person's Bill of Rights

The Homeless Bill of Rights is a legislative proposal that would protect the civil and human rights of people who are homeless. It is a response to the increased criminalization of homeless people. It is not a federal bill but needs to be enacted at the state level. The National Coalition for the Homeless[14] advocates for the passage of this rights bill that is designed to protect the rights of homeless individuals to vote, have medical care, opportunities for education and employment, free movement, and privacy. The laws would give them the right to use public spaces without fear of discrimination, criminalization, or harassment by law enforcement; the right to non-obstructively seek shelter, social services, legal aid, and education; the right to privacy of property in public spaces; and the right to feel safe and not be subject to physical, verbal, or emotional violence. It would also protect people against segregation, laws targeting homeless people for their lack of housing and not their behavior, and restrictions on the use of public space. Passage of the bill would encourage states to increase dialogue about how better to address the needs of homeless individuals and families. A Homeless Bill of Rights has become law in Connecticut, Rhode Island, and Illinois. It is under consideration by California, Colorado, Delaware, Hawaii, Massachusetts, Michigan,

Minnesota, Missouri, Oregon, Pennsylvania, Tennessee, and Vermont, as well as Washington, DC. A template for a homeless bill of rights can be found here.[15]

Summary

Options on how to prevent homelessness exist. We need to start viewing and treating poverty and homelessness as what they are: human and civil rights issues (Abro 2014). There are plenty of national and international treaties, research, and rationales for housing to be considered a human right. Given the well-documented negative consequences of poverty and homelessness on children's development and well-being, their human right to housing is of utmost importance.

Maria Foscarinis (2011a) at the National Law Center on Poverty and Homelessness (2011; 2018c) sees housing as a human rights issue. Many research-based ideas exist on how to prevent homelessness. However, the government has never fully invested in them; if there were sufficient resources and support, the current programs may actually work. She states

> it's not enough to say we know how to end and prevent homelessness — and to then make available the resources to do so for a fraction of the homeless population. It's not enough to say that ending and preventing homelessness makes moral and fiscal sense — and then not do it. We have the data and we have the program models. What's missing are the policies and funding needed to bring those models to scale.... Now we need a new paradigm shift. Homelessness cannot be solved by funding a few good programs. Rather, law and policy must ensure that everyone has a safe, affordable place to live. That basic value and principle is a matter of fundamental human rights. It's time to make those rights real.
>
> Foscarinis 2011b

We are amazed that so many people naively believe that with a little tweaking and adjusting here and there, the current policies addressing homelessness and poverty could be made to work. They can't. The programs that we have in place aren't working because their fundamental assumptions make it impossible for them to work. There is a de-evolution of the public's response to public problems. Philanthropy, business, and privatization won't solve social problems. Public programs have in the past and could today if we truly invested in them. Instead, many programs are designed to look good on the surface so the public can point to them and say, "see, there are programs that work," and if they don't, homeless people get blamed for what is essentially a system failure.

As this pertains to family homelessness, it's easier for the public to point to unwed mothers, lack of education, mental illness, drug use, and domestic problems rather than focus on unsustainable economic systems and the lack of attainable housing, childcare, and jobs that pay living wages. If benefit-based programs existed to help people obtain healthcare, housing, food, childcare, and education, that would help enormously. In the scales of justice, one can't have all the costs high and the incomes and benefits low and think things are going to work out for someone to live a balanced life.

The current paradigm is not working and unless we try some new and innovative strategies, homelessness is going to increase in amount and severity. We need to consider different types of data collection and program innovations. Shifting how we look at and treat each other is of utmost importance. Programs of all sorts can follow the lead our heads, hearts, and good-quality data so indicate. The biggest cost if we don't is to our youngest citizens, who are going to be the parents, workers, leaders, criminals, and inheritors of tomorrow.

As you consider what new approaches and paradigms to try, we hope you hold in your mind's eye that all children are our children, that all children inherit the earth and have the potential to change the world for the better, or not. Give them a fighting chance to be their best, and enable them to create a world in which we will all like to live. The future depends on us.

Notes

1 www.prainc.com/wp-content/uploads/2012/01/trsrvcsfinaldoc.pdf
2 www.traumacenter.org/products/pdf_files/shelter_from_storm.pdf
3 http://sanctuaryweb.com/TheSanctuaryModel.aspx
4 www.bhchp.org/
5 www.healthcarewithoutwalls.org/our-work/bridges
6 www.fdrlibrary.marist.edu/archives/address_text.html
7 www.nesri.org/programs/what-is-the-human-right-to-housing
8 www.nesri.org/sites/default/files/Universal_Declaration.pdf
9 https://www.nesri.org/sites/default/files/Convention_on_the_Rights_of_the_Child.pdf
10 www.nesri.org/programs/what-is-the-human-right-to-housing
11 www.nesri.org/sites/default/files/International_Convention_on_the_Elimination_of_All_Forms_of_Racial_Discrimination.pdf
12 www.nesri.org/sites/default/files/Convention_on_Elimination_of_All_Forms_of_Discrimination_Against_Women.pdf
13 www.nesri.org/sites/default/files/American_Declaration_of_the_Rights_and_Duties_of_Man.pdf
14 https://nationalhomeless.org/campaigns/bill-of-right/
15 www.housingrightswatch.org/sites/default/files/Template%20Homeless%20Bill%20of%20Rights%20EN.pdf

Appendix

Business Plan for Building a Shelter

Homelessness can be a money-maker for some entrepreneurs and organizations, as seen in the emergence of the shelter industrial complex. While some people and organizations start shelters with good intentions to help folks who are in housing distress, others may do so because they see it as a profit-making venture. This is especially the case when there is a pot of government money to tap and a growing population whose needs are unmet. Creating shelters requires professionalization, training, monitoring, and diligent dedication to help others using best practices and prudent financial decisions. Yet some people are scam-artists in their pursuit of pilfering dollars designed to help homeless people find shelter. Providing high-quality care or advocating for people to prevent or limit their housing distress may not be their raison d'etre. We believe that creating high-quality shelters is not something that just anyone can do. Yet websites like Profitableventure.com (https://www.profitableventure.com/starting-a-homeless-shelter-business/) make it seem like anone can set up a homeless shelter and access grants and government funding. We believe that such an approach exploits homeless individuals, taxpayers, and agencies who have moneys designated to help people in distress. Below is an entrepreneurial site that makes it seem that anyone, with no knowledge of the housing industry at all, can make money by sheltering people who are homeless. The wording is verbatim from their website:

Are You Interested in Starting a Homeless Shelter? If YES, Here Is a Complete Guide to Starting a Homeless Shelter Business with Government Fund and No Experience.

Okay, so we have provided you an in-depth sample homeless shelter business plan template. We also took it further by analyzing and drafting a sample homeless shelter marketing plan backed up by actionable guerrilla marketing ideas for homeless shelter companies. In this article, we will be considering all the requirements for starting a homeless shelter business. So put on your entrepreneurial hat and let's proceed.

What is a Homeless Shelter?

Homeless shelters give momentary habitation to homeless people or families who are not capable of paying their own rent by themselves. These shelters are in existence to give protection to homeless people against harsh weather conditions.

By starting a homeless shelter, you are helping people who are in the need of a home. To start a homeless shelter, you need to have compassion for people in need to be able to run a homeless shelter successfully. You help to provide the needy with a roof over their head and you give them food to eat when you start it.

Why Start a Homeless Shelter?

People come to stay in the homeless shelters for short periods and the homeless shelter offer helps them with how they can get their life back on track and go back to living independently again. Most homeless shelters are associated with municipal governments or churches and they fund their activities by getting funds from government and other donors that support their cause.

Many people in the United States are spending a lot of their income on only rent and this makes them vulnerable to becoming homeless. This has led to a rise in demand for the services of homeless shelters but there are low resources to run these shelters. A lot of shelters have also had to turn people away from their shelters because of this reason.

The concept of homeless shelter began to gain ground in the United States in the seventies because of the high rate of unemployment at the time. The cost of housing was on the rise and the people that had serious cases of serious mental illness were being deinstitutionalized. When the cases of homeless people was becoming a case of a national epidemic, the professionals who were helping them then created shelters as a form of temporary refuges for the homeless to occupy.

Homeless shelters also house asylum seekers from other countries and provide outreach to people who choose not to make use of a shelter or who are unable to use the shelter. The outreach that is provided includes provision of items of food and provision of clothing for people that are housed.

The way most of these shelters operate is that the people that are housed in these shelters are expected to vacate the shelter in the morning and get something with which to keep them busy during the course of the day. They then return later in the evening for a meal and a roof over their head so they can sleep. There are curfews in these shelters and they are fixed at early hours than is typical for people who return back to their homes.

Some shelters run as only daytime alone homeless shelters, where homeless people can stay when they can't stay at their shelters that are operated as night time shelters.

The homeless shelter industry provides several community housing services which includes short-term emergency shelter for victims of child abuse or sexual assault and domestic violence; temporary residential shelter for runaway youths, families that are caught up in medical crises and the homeless; transitional housing and assisted living for people with low level of income and other volunteer repair and construction work needed by low-cost housing.

Starting a Homeless Shelter Business With Government Fund – A Complete Guide

The Homeless Shelter Industry Overview

There are about 3.5 million people that are homeless in the United States. The number is expected to keep rising and there are not enough homeless shelters to help house these people.

The population of the homeless shelter has remained the same over the past five years despite the fact that there is a decrease in population of the homeless people. As a result of this, the demand for the services in this industry is still high. The United States still has a lot of need for the services of homeless shelter therefore this will lead to further growth of the revenue in the industry.

Interesting Statistics About the Homeless Shelter Construction Industry

The recession in the United States economy caused a boom in the funding of the Homeless Shelter industry as the high rate of unemployment and the credit freeze left a lot of people homeless or in need of temporary accommodation. This made the government to increase the funding of the projects for homeless shelters.

As a result of this, there was a strong growth rate witnessed in the industry during the worst period of recession. The revenue for homeless shelter increased from 8.1% in 2008 and another 11.2% in 2009. The demand for the services of the industry also grew subsequently in 2007. In the five years to 2012, the industry revenue grew as a result of funding by the government.

In this industry, there is heavy reliance on voluntary help, as a result of this; the pay rates are often low. There are about 120,000 workers in this industry. The revenue in the industry is about $10 billion but the industry is highly fragmented and no single player can account for the significant share of the revenue in the industry. Distribution of federal funding among the different shelters and organizations that exist is carried out by the Department of Housing and Urban Development (HUD).

The continuous recovery of the United States economy will slow down the funding of this industry as more Americans find jobs and are able to get permanent housing. The industry revenue is expected to increase at a marginal average annual rate through 2017.

The factors and incentives that make people want to start a homeless shelter arise from the desire to help other people and the community at large. You need to be kind and have a compassionate spirit to help other people. As an individual, you will then be able to live with purpose, do your job with passion and it will also be a way of giving back to the society.

Starting a Homeless Shelter Business – Market Research and Feasibility Studies

Demographics and Psychographics

The demographic and psychographic composition of those who need the services of homeless shelters cuts across a lot of sectors such as the public sector, families, communities and different kinds of people from all walks of life. The following is a list of the people that need the services of Homeless Shelters:

- Child abuse victims
- Victims of sexual assault
- Domestic violence victims
- Runaway youths
- Families caught up in medical crises
- People with low income

List of Niche ideas Within the Homeless Shelter Business That You Can Specialize in

In setting up a homeless shelter business, there are some niche ideas in the industry that an entrepreneur can choose from. The following are the list of niche ideas that a homeless shelter business can be specialized in:

- Youth homeless shelter
- Women only homeless shelter
- Men only homeless shelter
- Family with income homeless shelter
- Homeless shelters for couples
- Homeless shelter for single women and men
- Low income people homeless shelter
- Sexual assault homeless shelter
- Domestic violence homeless shelter
- Disaster and emergency relief shelter
- Pregnant women shelter

The Level of Competition in the Homeless Shelter Industry

Surviving in the homeless shelter is more than having the requisite expertise as there is increased competition and homeless shelter businesses need to confront mounting pressures to show how effective they are. These days, there is a need for home shelters to be accountable for all the funds they are given as opposed to the days when they were left to do what they wanted with the funds they were given.

There is also a need for the performances of these shelters to be evaluated. As a result of this, there have been great efforts made to see to it that there are ways that the performances of these organizations can be measured. This way the funding agencies can take more active roles in the way the shelters are run and also insist on getting results that can be measured.

List of Well – Known Brands in the Homeless Shelter Industry

There are several homeless shelters in the United States that give housing solution to people that are in need. The following is a list of homeless shelter in the United States:

- Back On My Feet
- Carrfour Supportive Housing
- Coalition on Homelessness
- Interagency Council on Homelessness
- National Alliance to End Homelessness
- Operation Sacred Trust
- Pathways to Housing
- Rosewater
- Rosies Place
- Saint Francis House

Economic Analysis

Setting up a homeless shelter is a very serious business and as such ought to be treated as such. There is a need to carry out serious economic analysis to find out the threats and other risks that are associated with starting a homeless shelter.

As a homeless shelter business owner, you should be concerned about how to get funding for the shelter apart from getting the location for the business. Other things that you need to concern yourself with when setting up a homeless shelter is how to get volunteers to work at the shelter and how to get the needed resources for the shelter.

Even though running a homeless shelter can be a cost effective venture because you do not need to hire a lot of workers because of the voluntary workers that come out to help do work there, you still need to get some staff that you need to pay salaries, though the salary is low when compared to other organizations that are run for profit.

An important factor is to have the people working in these shelters well trained so that when their performances are appraised, companies that fund the shelters will be impressed and help to continue with the upkeep of the people that needs the services of the homeless shelters.

Is a Homeless Shelter Business Worth Starting from Scratch or is Buying a Franchise Better?

If you are concerned about the plight of the homeless people in your community, then you should consider setting up a homeless shelter. This you can do in with the support and help of your family and friends. One thing that motivates people to start this kind of business is largely as a result of a passion for helping other people that are homeless in the society.

You can also get the franchise of an already established homeless shelter so that you do not go through all the problems associated with starting the homeless shelter from scratch. If you don't know how to run a shelter, they can give you training on how to run it.

Another thing that can be done in this business is to partner with other institutions such as charity groups, religious institutions and other non-profit organizations in setting up your own homeless shelter.

Possible Threats and Challenges You Will Face When Starting a Homeless Shelter Business

In the homeless shelter industry, there are threats and challenges that these organizations are subjected to and some of these include the problem of overcrowding in the facilities that are used to house homeless individuals as there are a large number of people that require shelter.

Another problem that a homeless shelter can face is the problem of hygiene and the problem of some of the inhabitants engaging in the use of hard drugs in these shelters. At times, homeless shelters are faced with the challenges of security in a case where the homeless shelter is used to house victims of domestic violence; it could be faced with the threat of being attacked by the men that the ladies have been rescued from.

Starting a Homeless Shelter Business With Government Fund – Legal Matters

Best Legal Entity To Use for a Homeless Shelter Business

You need to incorporate your homeless shelter business so that it can have a legal entity. This way the business can have its personal bank account and property. The business will also be able to go on when you are not there and it will separate you from any liability of the business. With the incorporated non-profit business, you will need a board of directors for your homeless shelter business.

Catchy Business Name ideas Suitable for a Homeless Shelter Business

If you have to name your homeless shelter business, there are really no rules for you to follow to do this. You might just want to ensure that the name you choose takes into consideration what the business is about. The following are catchy name ideas that you can choose for your homeless shelter clients:

- House the Nation
- House Support for All
- Candy's Housing
- Road to End Homelessness
- Homeless Eradication
- Give Me A Place
- Coalition for Support
- Support the Shelter
- Sheltered Abode

The Best Insurance Needed for a Homeless Shelter Business

In order to set up a business in the United States of America, you need to put some insurance in place according to the requirements of the industry you want to set up your business in:

You cannot run a business if you do not possess most of the required insurance as dictated by the industry you want to set up your business in. In order to get your insurance, make an allowance for it in your budget and get the services of an insurance broker to help you in choosing the right insurance policies that are suited to the kind of business you are running. They will guide you in evaluating the risks associated with your business and give you the appropriate advice.

The following insurance covers are necessary if you are considering setting up a homeless shelter business in the United States of America:

- General liability insurance
- Workers compensations insurance
- Commercial property insurance
- Umbrella insurance
- Unemployment insurance
- Business owner's policy
- Sexual abuse liability
- Social work, foster care and counselling liability

Intellectual Property Protection and Trademark

To set up a homeless shelter, you should think of filing for intellectual property protection so as to protect the documents of the business and your business logo. It will also enable you to protect your business name and any software application that you might own.

To go about the process of filing for intellectual property protection and doing the registration of the trademark for your homeless shelter business. You have to begin the procedure at the USPTO where you are expected to file an application. You will then get the final approval for the trademark of your homeless shelter once it has been subjected to the evaluation of attorneys which is a requirement by the USPTO.

Is Professional Certification Needed to Start a Homeless Shelter Business?

If you are starting a homeless shelter, then you and your staff can consider getting some certifications to give your business an edge over your competitors in the same business. Once you and your staff have relevant certifications, people will take you seriously as an outfit that knows a lot about improving the lives of other people.

The following professional certifications will be relevant for you and your members of staff if you intend setting up a homeless shelter and they are as follows:

- The Certified Social Work Case Manager
- Case Manager Certification
- Certified Advanced Practise Social Worker
- Certified Independent Practise Social Worker
- Commission for Case Manager Certification

List of Legal Documents You Need to Run a Homeless Shelter Business

If you want to set up a homeless shelter business, you need to get all the necessary paperwork in place in order to be able to carry out your operations legally. The following legal documents are some of the legal documents that you should have in place if you intend starting a homeless shelter in the United States:

- Certificate of Incorporation
- Business License
- Business Plan
- Insurance Policy
- Tax exemption

- DBA Business Name
- Seller Permit
- Federal EIN
- State EIN

Writing a Business Plan for your Homeless Shelter Business

Even though you are starting a non-profit business, you still need to write a business plan for your homeless shelter business. The business plan will help your homeless shelter describe how it plans to go about implementing the mission of the business and also how it will achieve the goals and objectives that it has set for the business. In order to do these successfully, contact an expert to help you in writing a business plan that you can work with.

To be successful in the management of the homeless shelter business you want to set up, the business plan is the blue print you need to achieve this. It will help you conduct the business properly. At any given period of time, you will know what to do in the course of running this business both in terms of handling the challenges that comes with growth and expansion.

In the business plan, the process that will be used in conducting researches for the service that the business intends to do will be written there. How to investigate the resources that you will need to render the service, devising how to implement the marketing strategies to be used, how to assess the risk involved and the ways you will evaluate the success of the business.

The business plan for a homeless shelter takes account of other factors like the vision statement, the role of the board members and environmental factors. Potential changes in revenue should also be put into consideration. Plans on how to prepare for risks in the future are also included in the plan.

The essence of putting down a business plan is to have a detailed guide to help you in running your business effectively. Try to be realistic in your projections when putting figures on your profits and income. Do not underestimate so that you do not get disappointed when your business operation starts.

Detailed Cost Analysis fo Starting a Homeless Shelter Business

There are some expenses that you have to incur in the event of launching your homeless shelter business. Do your feasibility studies properly prior to making a budget and getting funding for the business. The following are some of the cost that you will incur in the process of starting a homeless shelter in the United States:

- Fee for incorporating a Business in the United States of America – $750
- Money to pay for permits, insurance and license – $5,000

- The Amount needed to get a place to be used as the shelter – $0 – $50,000.
- The Cost for equipping the shelter with beddings$0 – $15,000
- The Cost of owning a website $0 – $700
- Other Expenditure (business cards, signage, adverts and promotions et al) – $2,500
- Miscellaneous- $1,000

According to the report from the research and feasibility studies carried out, starting a homeless shelter does not cost much because most of the things needed is likely to come from donations. The location needed might be donated by churches, hotel and other well-meaning people.

A small scale homeless shelter will cost from $0 – $500 to set up. To set up a medium scale homeless shelter, you will need $0–20,000,000 to set it up To set up a large scale homeless shelter, you will need $0 – $1,000,000 million to do so.

Financing Your Homeless Shelter Business

When you want to start a homeless shelter, you do not need much resource to set it up as majority or almost all of your needs will be provided through donations, grants and so on. Once you are able to secure the location for the business, you are on your way to starting the business. Most of the staff that will be working at the shelter will also be working on a voluntary basis so you might just need to hire a few people that you will need to pay salaries to.

To get the necessary funding for your homeless shelter, a good business plan is important. Once you have it in place, it won't take you long to convince people to give donations to your homeless shelter.

You should explore the following options as avenues to get funds for your homeless shelter:

- Raising money from churches, mosques and other religious organizations
- Raising money from non-profit organizations
- Raising money from charity groups
- Raising money from big stores
- Raising money from public and private grants
- Funding from federal government
- Funding from state governments
- Funding from city governments
- Funding from county

Choosing a Location for Your Homeless Shelter Business

It is important to choose the right location for a homeless shelter because you have to consider the fact that it is human beings that are going to be staying in these shelters. You have to make sure that the location you are choosing has adequate ventilation so that in summer the people there do not suffer from heat. Consider getting a place that will be equally easy to keep warm during winter period as well. Put into consideration getting lockers for people so that they can keep their belongings.

Hygiene is also another important factor in getting a location; get a place that will be easy to clean so that insects don't infest the shelters. The list is endless as there are a lot of factors to be considered to ensure that people are comfortable in the shelters.

To choose a location for a homeless shelter, you have to consider the following factors:

- The safety of the location because of people that are victims of domestic violence
- The availability of a location that has space as a place that has too much built-in furniture is not usable
- A place that has a minimum of 10 hours for people to use so that they can get a minimum of 8 hours of sleep.
- Availability of bathroom facilities
- The local laws and regulations in the community or state where your homeless shelter resides
- Availability of security for the shelter members
- Traffic
- parking

Starting a Homeless Shelter Business With Government Fund – Technical & Manpower Details

To set up a homeless shelter, you will need to get some software, security camera and other accessories. To get a place to locate your homeless shelter, you can get people to donate the land for the building of the shelter. You can get churches, mosques and other religious institutions to donate their buildings as well. In the case that you cannot get a building for free, you might have to rent or buy a place to locate the homeless shelter.

You need people that will work at the shelter but you can get people who will offer their services voluntarily at your homeless shelters. On the average, you need a shelter director, case manager, group facilitator, counsellor, literacy tutor, social worker and house manager.

As a homeless shelter business, you will also need the services of an accountant, lawyer and some other professionals who you can hire on an as needed basis. You also have to put together a board of directors for the business.

Make sure you hire the right people and get volunteers that are really committed to the business as these individuals are important to the image you want to portray to people about the kind of homeless shelter business you are running.

The Services process Involved in the Homeless Shelter Industry

The service process that is involved in the running of a homeless shelter depends on the niche the business is into. Once a homeless shelter has got the necessary funding for the business and everything has been put in place. It is then ready to take in homeless people.

If it is a homeless shelter for individuals to sleep in at night, then people start arriving at the time that the shelter opens to accommodate people. They are assessed and given a place where they can spend the night. Blankets, toiletries, coffee and light refreshment or food are served to the inhabitants. Generally, there is a curfew in homeless shelters that the individuals have to adhere to. Once it is morning, the people in the shelter have to leave the shelter and find something with which to occupy them during the day before they return to the shelter again in the night.

Starting a Homeless Shelter Business With Government Fund – The Marketing Plan

Marketing Ideas and Strategies for a Homeless Shelter Business

When you are writing the marketing plan for your homeless shelter, make sure that you write a convincing profile for the company. Include the profile of the board of directors and the members of the management team. These marketing strategies will help you to get donors.

Create the right awareness to capture the interest of your donors. Include the message that makes your homeless shelter different and makes it a worthy enough cause that needs to be supported. If you have well trained and dedicated members on your team, your homeless shelter is off to a good start and it will thrive and flourish.

You can use the following platform to put out the word about your homeless shelter business:

- Spread word about your homeless shelter by informing other homeless shelters to put out the word
- Spread the word at community outreach programs
- Traditional advertising
- Use of the internet through your website
- By direct mail
- Through telemarketing
- Through the use of newsletters and press releases
- Make use of blogs and social media
- Organise events, galas and fundraising gatherings

Possible Competitive Strategies for Winning your Competitors in the Homeless Shelter industry

Competing with other homeless shelters in the industry might be challenging, therefore you need to choose your board members carefully and also build the people that you are going to be working with.

Once you have the requisite expertise to run a homeless shelter, then you are in business. Whenever homeless people come to your shelter, endeavour to treat them right so that they can help you spread the word about your shelter so as to get more people off the streets especially during the cold freezing nights of winter.

A lot of people are afraid of shelters because of the bad stories they have heard about them. Make yours exceptional and you will succeed in getting more people off the streets and also have success in convincing the donors that you are doing something worthy that they need to donate their money to.

You can also form partnerships with religious institutions, other non-profit organizations and charity groups that can help you start up the business by being a fiscal sponsor for your business.

Possible Ways to Increase Customer Retention for a Homeless Shelter Business

Customer satisfaction is a very important aspect of any business you are running as it will help you to retain the clients of your business and it will restore investor confidence in your business. When your clients are satisfied, they will stickwith your brand and will not look for your competitor to do business with.

As a homeless shelter business, once you are able to satisfy the people that take refuge in your shelter then you will have good testimonials as these are the proof that you are rendering a service that is of high quality to the people that patronize your business.

Make sure that you are sending the correct message at all times to the right people by giving good customer service always. This way you will be able to get a large percentage of the donor money as you have been able to position yourself properly in the minds of your donors and you will have proved the value of the service that you provide.

Available statistics show that the reason why customers got for alternative services is as a result of poor quality of service delivery. If you keep improving on the quality of your service, then you will keep attracting funds for your homeless shelter.

Strategies to Boost your Brand Awareness and Create a Corporate identity

In order to create a brand identity for your homeless shelter, make sure you do it well so that your constituents can support your cause. Let your strategies include the message that makes your homeless shelter different from other worthy causes that equally needs to be supported. Make sure it addresses the issue of donor loyalty because it is important for retained supporter.

You should therefore map out a publicity plan and the right advertising strategy that will help you in your cause. Since your donors know that the best way of supporting worthy causes does not necessarily mean that they should also open up their own homeless shelter but to put together the resources they have and make it available for the use of people that have a similar mind set with theirs.

The following are some of the platforms you can use to boost your brand awareness and create the corporate identity for your homeless shelter:

- Spread word about your homeless shelter by informing other homeless shelters to put out the word
- Spread the word about your homeless shelter business at community outreach programs
- Traditional advertising
- Use of the internet to advertise your business through your website
- Make use of direct email marketing
- Through telemarketing
- Through the use of newsletters and press releases
- Make use of blogs and social media to promote your homeless shelter
- Organise events, galas and fundraising gatherings with the aim of creating awareness and to promote your brand.
- Make branded shirts for your employees and volunteers and also brand the official vehicles of your business.

Creating a Suppliers / Distribution Network for your Homeless Shelter Business

Running a homeless shelter business makes it possible for networking in the homeless shelter business industry and with the government since the issue of housing homeless people cannot be carried out alone by only the people running the business.

They need to get help from other well-meaning people such as volunteers, donors and the government to be able to be in business. There is also room for strategic partnership to be formed by the homeless shelter and other institutions like churches, mosques, supermarkets and other charity groups. They can help to support the cause of the homeless shelter by making donations of clothes, food, toys, books, sponsorship and money.

Tips for Running a Homeless Shelter Business Successfully

To run your homeless shelter business successfully, you need to get all the people working with you in your team to be in synch with you at all times. This will help your business to succeed. As the founder of the business, you should endeavour to steer the business in the right direction. Find time to hold meetings and deliberate on issues and get feedbacks from the meetings. Also make sure that the meetings are held regularly.

Give staff appraisals regularly and train your employees and volunteers so that they can help you to run the homeless shelter effectively. Give them encouragement to get certified in the areas that they have specialization. If possible, offer to sponsor them partially or fully for the certifications they want to take. Listen to your workers when they have suggestions on how to make the business better. Reward excellent performance so as to encourage healthy competition.

References

ABC. 2018. "Made in America Christmas." https://abcnews.go.com/WN/mailform?id=14998335.

Abel, D. 2003. "Study Finds Use of Food Pantries Soaring in Massachusetts. www.boston.com/news/local/massachusetts/articles/2010/02/03/study_finds_use_of_food_pantries_soaring_in_mass/.

Abro, James. 2014. Poverty and homelessness are human and civil rights issues. *Talk Poverty.* https://talkpoverty.org/2014/10/09/poverty-and-homelessness/.

Addressi, Frank. 2018. "The 50 Worst Charities in America – How to Keep from Being Scammed." SmartAsset.com, May 21. https://smartasset.com/mortgage/the-50-worst-charities-in-america-how-to-keep-from-being-scammed.

Adorno, Theodor W., Else Frenkel-Brunswik, Daniel Levinson and Nevitt Sanford. 1950. *The Authoritarian Personality.* New York: Harper & Brothers.

Almendrala, Anna. 2014. The Disturbing Link between Brain Injury and Homelessness. *Huffington Post.* www.huffpost.com/entry/traumatic-brain-injury-homelessness_n_5227637.

Almendrala, Anna. 2018. Hospitals are Releasing Homeless Patient Back to the Streets: There must be a Better Way. *Huffington Post.* www.huffpost.com/entry/homeless-patients-hospitals-recuperative-care_n_5ad91023e4b03c426dacc350.

Amadeo, Kimberly. 2018a. "Living Wage and How It Compares to the Minimum Wage: How Much Do You Need to Live?" TheBalance.com. Last updated March 26. www.thebalance.com/living-wage-3305771.

Amadeo, Kimberly. 2018b. "Universal Basic Income, Its Pros and Cons with Examples: Should Everyone Get a Guaranteed Income?" TheBalance.com. September 5. www.thebalance.com/universal-basic-income-4160668.

American College of Obstetricians and Gynecologists. 2013. "Health Care for Homeless Women." Committee Opinion No. 576. American College of Obstetricians and Gynecologists (October). *Obstet Gynecol* 122: 936–40. www.acog.org/Clinical-Guidance-and-Publications/Committee-Opinions/Committee-on-Health-Care-for-Underserved-Women/Health-Care-for-Homeless-Women.

American Institutes for Research. 2017. "Pay for Success/Social Impact Bonds at AIR." AIR.org, June. www.air.org/sites/default/files/downloads/report/Pay-for-Success-Brief-update-January-2018-rev.pdf.

American Institutes for Research. 2018a. "National Center on Family Homelessness." *American Institutes for Research.* www.air.org/center/national-center-family-homelessness.

American Institutes for Research. 2018b. National Poverty Study. www.air.org/project/national-poverty-study.

Americans for Tax Fairness. 2014. "Tax Fairness Briefing Booklet." https://americansfortaxfairness.org/tax-fairness-briefing-booklet/fact-sheet-taxing-wealthy-americans/.

Anda, Robert. 2006. "The Enduring Effects of Abuse and Related Adverse Experiences in Childhood: A Convergence of Evidence from Neurobiology and Epidemiology." *European Archives of Psychiatry and Clinical Neurosciences* 256(3): 174–186.

Anderson, Nels. 1923. *The Hobo: The Sociology of the Homeless Man.* Chicago: University of Chicago Press.

Arthur, W. Brian. 1990. "Positive Feedbacks in the Economy." *Scientific American* 262(2): 92–99.

Bachega, Hugo. 2018. Homelessness in US. *BBC.* www.bbc.com/news/world-us-canada-45442596.

Badger, Emily. 2013. Why Homelessness Is a Transportation issue. www.citylab.com/solutions/2013/02/why-homelessness-transportation-issue/4577/.

Badger, Emily and Christopher Ingraham. 2015. "The Rich Get Government Handouts Just Like the Poor. Here are 10 of Them." *The Washington Post*, April 9. www.washingtonpost.com/news/wonk/wp/2015/04/09/the-rich-get-government-handouts-just-like-the-poor-here-are-10-of-them/?utm_term=.16f1b3a3bc0e.

Badger, Emily and Quoctrung Bui. 2018. "In 83 Million Eviction Records, a Sweeping and Intimate New Look at Housing in America." *The New York Times*, April 7. www.nytimes.com/interactive/2018/04/07/upshot/millions-of-eviction-records-a-sweeping-new-look-at-housing-in-america.html.

Baker, Peter C. 2018. "How Much is an Hour Worth? The War Over the Minimum Wage." *The Guardian*, April 13. www.theguardian.com/news/2018/apr/13/how-much-is-an-hour-worth-the-war-over-the-minimum-wage.

Baldari, Cara. 2019. "We Know we Can Cut Poverty in Half so Why Aren't we?" First Focus. https://firstfocus.org/blog/we-know-we-can-cut-child-poverty-in-half-so-why-arent-we.

Barak, Gregg. 1992. *Gimme Shelter: A Social History of Homelessness in Contemporary America.* New York: Praeger.

Barnes, Mo. 2018. "The Return of Government Cheese, Canned Beef, and Stigmatizing the Poor." RollingOut.com, February 16. https://rollingout.com/2018/02/16/return-government-cheese-canned-beef-stigmatizing-poor/.

Bassuk Center. 2018a. "Letter: Data Vastly Underestimates the Number of Homeless Children and Families". *Boston Globe.* www.bostonglobe.com/opinion/letters/2018/12/21/data-vastly-underestimate-number-homeless-kids-families/asfFt5J0uC8A3j7SHhREbI/story.html.

Bassuk Center. 2018b. "Family Homelessness." www.bassukcenter.org/.

Bassuk Center. 2018c. "The Bassuk Center on Homeless and Vulnerable Children and Youth." Bassuk Center. www.bassukcenter.org/.

Bassuk, Ellen L., Carmela J. DeCandia, Corey Anne Beach and Fred Berman. 2014. "America's Youngest Outcasts: A Report Card on Child Homelessness." Waltham, MA: The National Center on Family Homelessness at American Institutes for Research. www.air.org/sites/default/files/downloads/report/Americas-Youngest-Outcasts-Child-Homelessness-Nov2014.pdf.

Bassuk, Ellen L. and Jeffrey Olivet. 2016. "The Trauma of Homelessness." Presentation for the Center for Social Innovation, June 22. www.masspartnership.com/pdf/TraumaofHomelessness6-22-16.pdf.

Bauer, Lauren. 2019. "Who Was Poor in the US in 2017?" Brookings. www.brookings.edu/blog/up-front/2019/01/03/who-was-poor-in-the-united-states-in-2017/.

Baum, Alice and Burns, Donald. 1994. "A Nation in Denial: The Truth About Homelessness." *Sociology and Social Welfare* 21(2): 23 https://scholarworks.wmich.edu/cgi/viewcontent.cgi?article=2152&context=jssw.

Baumberg, Ben, Kate Bell and Declan Gaffney. n.d. "Benefit System Riddled with 'Stigma'." Poverty.ac.uk. www.poverty.ac.uk/report-benefits-attitudes/benefit-system-riddled-%E2%80%98stigma%E2%80%99.

Bayer, Israel. 2014. "Paul Boden and the History of Homelessness as we Know It Today." StreetRoots.org, July 2. https://news.streetroots.org/2014/07/02/paul-boden-and-history-homelessness-we-know-it-today.

BBC. 2018. "Homelessness Could End in a Decade, says Charity Crisis." *BBC*, June 11. www.bbc.com/news/uk-44434481.

BeBusinessEd. 2018. "History of Minimum Wage." BeBusinessEd.com. https://bebusinessed.com/history/history-of-minimum-wage/.

Beck, Elizabeth and Pamela C. Twiss. 2018. *The Homelessness Industry: A Critique of U.S. Social Policy.* Denver, CO: Lynne Reinner Press.

Berchick, Edward. 2019. "Uninsured Rate for Children Lower. Census Bueau. www.census.gov/library/stories/2019/09/uninsured-rate-for-children-in-2018.html.

Berman, Ana. 2018. "Venezuela to Fund Housing for Homeless with National Cryptocurrency Petro." CoinTelegraph.com, July 6. https://cointelegraph.com/news/venezuela-to-fund-housing-for-homeless-with-national-cryptocurrency-petro.

Berman, Annie. 2019. San Francisco Homeless Policy Assailed as Cruel and Ineffective. https://missionlocal.org/2019/08/san-francisco-homeless-policy-assailed-as-cruel-ineffective/.

Bertalanffy, Ludwig. 1974. "General Systems Theory and Psychiatry." In *American Handbook of Psychiatry*, vol. 1, 2nd edition, edited by Silvano Arieti. New York: Basic Books.

Bhattrai, Gandhi Raj, Patricia A. Duffy and Jennie Raymond. 2005. "Use of Food Pantries and Food Stamps in Low- Income Households in the United States." *The Journal of Consumer Affairs* 39(2): 28–37.

Biello, Peter. 2016. "A Promise Infulfilled". NHPR.www.nhpr.org/post/promise-unfulfilled-where-homelessness-nh-stands-today#stream/.

Blenford, Adam. 2019. "Global Wellness Rankings." www.bloomberg.com/news/articles/2019-03-04/global-wellness-rankings-these-are-the-best-places-to-live.

Bloom, Alan. 2005. "Review Essay: Toward a History of Homelessness." *Journal of Urban History* 31(6): 907–17. doi: 10.1177/0096144205276990.

Bloom, Sandra. 2019. "Sanctuary Model." www.sanctuaryweb.com.

Blumberg, Antonia. 2019. "Amazon to Pay $0 in Federal Tax in 2019: Report." *HuffingtonPost.com*, February 14. www.huffpost.com/entry/amazon-federal-taxes-2019_n_5c660227e4b01757c369c5b3.

Boettke, Peter J. and David Prychitko. n.d. "Is an Independent Nonprofit Sector Prone to Failure? An Austrian School Analysis of the Salamon Paradigm and the Lohmann Challenge." Working Paper. http://mercatus.org/uploadedFiles/Mercatus/Publications/Failure.pdf.

Booker, Brakken. 2018. "HUD Unveils Plan to Increase Rent on Millions Receiving Federal Housing Assistance. NPR. www.npr.org/2018/04/25/605900171/hud-unveils-plan-to-increase-rent-on-millions-receiving-federal-housing-assistan.

Boone, Alistair. 2019. "Why Can't We Get an Accurate Count of The Homeless Population?" Pacific Standard. https://psmag.com/social-justice/why-cant-we-count-the-homeless-population.

Bosman, Julie. 2009. "Newly Poor Swell Lines at Food Banks." *New York Times*, February 19. www.nytimes.com/2009/02/20/nyregion/20food.html.

Bouchard, Mikayla. 2015. "Transportation Emerges as Crucial to Escaping Poverty." *The New York Times*, May 7. www.nytimes.com/2015/05/07/upshot/transportation-emerges-as-crucial-to-escaping-poverty.html.

Bregman, Rutger. 2016. "The Bizarre Tale of President Nixon and His Basic Income Bill". The Correspondent. https://thecorrespondent.com/4503/the-bizarre-tale-of-president-nixon-and-his-basic-income-bill/173117835-c34d6145.

Brenner, Harvey. 1973. *Mental Illness and the Economy*. Cambridge, MA: Harvard University Press.

Brickell, Katherine, Melissa Fernández Arrigoitia and Alex Vasudevan. 2017. "Geographies of Forced Evictions." https://link.springer.com/chapter/10.1057/978-1-137-51127-0_1.

Bronfenbrenner, Urie. 2005. *Making Human Beings Human: Bioecological Perspectives on Human Development*. Thousand Oaks, CA: Sage Publications.

Bruder, Jessica. 2017. *Nomadland*. New York: W. W. Norton & Company.

Burt, Martha. 1999. *Homelessness: Programs and the People They Serve*. Diane Press

Bussolo, Maurizio. 2019. "Do We Need a New Social Contract?" www.brookings.edu/blog/future-development/2019/04/11/do-we-need-a-new-social-contract/.

Callahan, David. 2013. "How the GI bill left out African Americans." https://www.demos.org/blog/how-gi-bill-left-out-african-americans.

Camarota, Steven A. and Karen Zeigler. 2018. "63% of Non-Citizen Households Access Welfare Programs." Center for Immigration Studies, December 2. https://cis.org/Report/63-NonCitizen-Households-Access-Welfare-Programs.

Cammarosano, Louis. 2015. "Bankruptcy in America." Inman.com, June 2. www.inman.com/2015/06/02/bankruptcy-in-america/.

Caplovitz, David. 1967. *The Poor Pay More: Consumer Practices of Low-Income Families*. New York: Free Press.

Capps, Kriston. 2016. "Nationwide, Homelessness Plunged Under Obama." CityLab.com, November 18. www.citylab.com/equity/2016/11/homelessness-obama-trump/508223/.

Career and Recovery Resources. 2018. "Emotional Homelessness: It's Causes and Cures." Career and Recovery Resources, Inc. www.careerandrecovery.org/emotional-homelessness-its-causes-and-cures/.

Carrier, Scott. 2015. The Shockingly Simple Surprisingly Cost Effective Way to End Homelessness. www.motherjones.com/politics/2015/02/housing-first-solution-to-homelessness-utah/.

Carroll, Archie. 1991. "The Pyramid of Corporate Social Responsibility: Toward the Moral Management of Organizational Stakeholders." *Business Horizons* 34: 39–48. www.researchgate.net/publication/4883660_The_Pyramid_of_Corporate_Social_Responsibility_Toward_the_Moral_Management_of_Organizational_Stakeholders.

Casselman, Ben. 2018. "The Economy Hits a High Note and Trump Takes a Bow. *New York Times.* www.nytimes.com/2018/07/27/business/economy/economy-gdp.html.

Caton, Carol. 1990. *Homeless in America.* Oxford: Oxford University Press.

CBS. 2018. Ben Carson. www.cbsnews.com/pictures/donald-trumps-14-billion-cabinet/10/.

Charity Choices. 2018. "How Much is Given? By Whom? For What?" CharityChoices.com. www.charitychoices.com/page/how-much-given-whom-what.

chiefmappster. 2017. "POINTS Cryptocurrency Joins the Fight Against Homelessness." Steemit post, August 29. https://steemit.com/points/@chiefmappster/points-cryptocurrency-joins-the-fight-against-homelessness.

Child Trends. 2019a. Youth Homelessness. www.childtrends.org/indicators/homeless-children-and-youth.

Child Trends. 2019b. Youth Suicide. www.childtrends.org/indicators/suicidal-teens.

Children's Defense Fund. 2016. Ending Poverty is a Moral and Economic Necessity. www.childrensdefense.org/child-watch-columns/health/2016/ending-child-poverty-a-moral-and-economic-necessity.

Christian Science Monitor Editorial Board. 2010. "Obama Builds on Bush Success to Help the Homeless." *The Christian Science Monitor,* June 22. www.csmonitor.com/Commentary/the-monitors-view/2010/0622/Obama-builds-on-Bush-success-to-help-the-homeless.

Christian Science Monitor Editorial Board. 2018. "Amazon's Bezos Clicks on Homelessness." *The Christian Science Monitor,* September 17. www.csmonitor.com/Commentary/the-monitors-view/2018/0917/Amazon-s-Bezos-clicks-on-homelessness?j=91414&sfmc_sub=13810897&l=1222_HTML&u=3088096&mid=10979696&jb=9&cmpid=ema:Commentary:20180920&src=newsletter.

Christie, Les. 2009. "Foreclosures Up a Record 81% in 2008." CNN.com, January 15. https://money.cnn.com/2009/01/15/real_estate/millions_in_foreclosure/.

Cohen, Rick. 2015. Stories of Those Who Don't Fit the Housing First Model. *Nonprofit Quarterly.* October28. https://nonprofitquarterly.org/what-is-homelessness-those-who-dont-fit-the-housing-first-model/.

Coleman-Jensen, Alisha, Mark Nord, Margaret Andrews and Steven Carlson. 2011. "Household Food Security in the United States in 2010." Economic Research Report No. (ERR-125), U.S. Dept. of Agriculture, Econ. Res. Serv. September.

Collatz, Andrea. 2018. "True Costs of Eviction." www.mysmartmove.com/SmartMove/blog/true-cost-eviction.page.

Community First! Village. 2019. "Description." https://mlf.org/community-first/.

Consorte, Dennis. 2018. "Peruvian Economist Hernando de Soto Calls for Blockchain to Bring Wealth to Peru." Cryptosumer.com, July 14. https://cryptosumer.com/2018/07/14/peruvian-economist-hernando-de-soto-calls-for-blockchain-to-bring-wealth-to-peru/.

Cooper, Marianne. 2014. *Cut Adrift: Families in Insecure Times*. Berkeley: University of California Press.

Cooper, Marianne. 2015. "The False Promise of Meritocracy." *The Atlantic*, December 1. www.theatlantic.com/business/archive/2015/12/meritocracy/418074/.

Cooper, P. 2018. "Social Media Advertising Stats that matter to marketers in 2018. Hootsuite." https://blog.hootsuite.com/social-media-advertising-stats/

Cost Helper. 2019. "Fighting Eviction Costs." https://personalfinance.costhelper.com/fighting-eviction.html.

Couch, Robbie. 2014. "Hawaii To Buy 1-Way Tickets to Keep Homeless People Away from Tourists." *HuffingtonPost.com*, updated on December 6, 2017. www.huffingtonpost.com/2014/11/04/hawaii-one-way-flights-homeless_n_6101274.html.

Covert, Bruce. 2014. It would actually be very simple to end homelessness forever. *Think Progress*. https://thinkprogress.org/it-would-actually-be-very-simple-to-end-homelessness-forever-d6f15852b2ec/.

Covert, Bruce. 2018. "A New Deal for Day Care." *The New Republic*, May 1. https://newrepublic.com/article/147802/new-deal-day-care-america-change-care-kids.

Crane, Maureen, Kathleen Byrne, Ruby Fu, Bryan Lipmann, Frances Mirabelli, Alice Rota-Bartelink, Maureen Ryan, Robert Shea, Hope Watt and Anthony M. Warnes. 2005. "The Causes of Homelessness in Later Life: Findings From a 3-Nation Study." *The Journals of Gerontology: Series B* 60(3): S152–S159.

Crenshaw, Kimberlé. 2010. *Critical Race Theory: The Key Writings That Formed the Movement*. New York: New Press.

Crenshaw, Kimberlé. 2019. *On Intersectionality: Essential Writings*. New York: New Press.

Crichton, Danny. 2018. "Austin is Piloting Blockchain to Improve Homeless Services." TechCrunch.com, published in April. https://techcrunch.com/2018/04/14/austin-is-piloting-blockchain-to-improve-homeless-services/.

Cryptocurrency clarified. 2019. "General information." https://cryptoclarified.com/.

Culhane, Dennis and Thomas Byrne. 2010. "Ending Chronic Homelessness: Cost-Effective Opportunities for Interagency Collaboration" Penn School of Social Policy and Practice Working Paper. www.researchgate.net/publication/45181111_Ending_Chronic_Homelessness_Cost-Effective_Opportunities_for_Interagency_Collaboration.

Culhane, Dennis, Metraux, Stephen and Byrne, Thomas. 2011. "A Prevention-Centered Approach to Homelessness Assistance: A paradigm shift?" *Housing Policy Debate* 21: 295–315. 10.1080/10511482.2010.536246. www.researchgate.net/publication/232971846_A_prevention-centered_approach_to_homelessness_assistance_A_paradigm_shift.

Da Costa Nunez, Ralph. 2016. "A housing first approach could actually stimulate homelessness." *Huffington Post*. https://www.huffpost.com/entry/is-hud-stimulating-homele_b_10106572.

Da Costa Nunez, Ralph. 2017a. "Comprehensive Vision on Homelessness is Already Here. *HuffingtonPost.com*, updated on December 13. www.huffingtonpost.com/entry/comprehensive-vision-on-homelessness_b_13533184.

Da Costa Nunez, Ralph. 2017b. "Review of contributions." *Huffington Post*. https://www.huffpost.com/author/media-204.

Da Costa Nunez, Ralph and Ethan G. Sribnick. 2013. *The Poor Among Us: A History of Family Poverty and Homelessness in New York City*. New York: White Tiger Press.

Dain, Amy. 2018. "The State of Zoning for Accessory Dwelling Units/ Pioneer Opportunity." White Paper No. 184/July 2018 Pioneer Institute Public Policy Research. www.facebook.com/pg/PioneerInstitute/about/?ref=page_internal.

Data Lab. 2018. "Homelessness Analysis." https://datalab.usaspending.gov/home lessness-analysis.html.

Dawson, Chrisopher. 2019. A Suburbia for the Homeless. *CNN*. www.cnn. com/2019/03/26/us/iyw-town-for-the-homeless-trnd/index.html.

Day, Eli. 2017. "The Number of Homeless People in America Increased for the First Time in 7 Years." MotherJones.com, December 21. www.mother jones.com/politics/2017/12/the-number-of-homeless-people-in-america-increased-for-the-first-time-in-7-years/.

Deaton, Angus. 2018. "The U.S. Can No Longer Hide From Its Deep Poverty Problem." *New York Times* [Opinion], January 24. www.nytimes. com/2018/01/24/opinion/poverty-united-states.html.

Delaney, Arthur. 2019. "Trump Diligently Slashes Social Programs." www. huffpost.com/entry/donald-trump-social-safety-poverty-welfare_n_5cd5d5e-be4b054da4e895073.

Delaney, Arthur and Scheller, Alissa. 2015. "Who Gets Food Stamps?" *Huffington Post*. www.huffpost.com/entry/food-stamp-demographics_n_6771938.

Democracy Now. 2010. Chilean Economist Manfred Max-Neef on Bare-foot Economics, Povert and Why The U.S. is Becoming an "Under developing Nation. www.democracynow.org/2010/11/26/chilean_economist_manfred_max_neef_on.

DeNavas-Walt, Carmen, Bernadette D. Proctor and Jessica C. Smith. 2011. "U.S. Census Bureau, Current Population Reports, P60-239, Income, Poverty, and Health Insurance Coverage in the United States: 2010." U.S. Government Printing Office, Washington, DC.

Denzin, Norman K. 1978. The Research Act. New York: McGraw-Hill.

Deppen, Colin. 2018. "Bad Public Transportation Keeps Americans Poor. These Folks Won't Tolerate It." *HuffingtonPost.com*, December 12. www.huffingtonpost.com/entry/bad-public-transportation-transit-justice_us_5c0940d6e4b0bf813ef4f219.

Desmond, Matthew. 2017. *Evicted: Poverty and Profit in the American City*. New York: Broadway Books.

Desmond, Matthew. 2019. "Dollars on the Margins." *New York Times Magazine*, February 21. www.nytimes.com/interactive/2019/02/21/magazine/minimum-wage-saving-lives.html.

Diaz, Andrea. 2018. "'Misinformation' is Crowned Dictionary.com's Word of the Year." CNN.com, November 26. www.cnn.com/2018/11/26/us/misinformation-dictionary-word-of-the-year-2018-trnd/index.html.

Dickrell, Stephanie. 2016. "Child Homelessness Can Have Long-Term Consequences." *SC Times*, June 4. www.sctimes.com/story/news/local/homelesskids/2016/06/04/child-homelessness-can-have-long-term-consequences/84902750/.

Dilulio, John J. 2002. "The Future of Compassion: President Bish's Social Program Hasn't Yet Gotten a Chance." Brookings, December 4. www.brookings.edu/

opinions/the-future-of-compassion-president-bushs-social-program-hasnt-yet-gotten-a-chance/.

Dohrenwend, Bruce P., Itzhak Levav, Patrick E. Shrout, Sharon Schwartz, Guedalia Naveh, Bruce G. Link, Andrew E. Skodol and Ann Stueve. 1992. "Socioeconomic Status and Psychiatric Disorders: The Causation-Selection Issue." *Science* 255(5047): 946–952.

Donnella, Leah. 2018. "Why is it Still OK to 'Trash' Poor White People?" *NPR*, August 1. www.npr.org/sections/codeswitch/2018/08/01/605084163/why-its-still-ok-to-trash-poor-white-people.

Dooley, Erin. 2018. "Investigators Probing Ben Carson's Son's Involvement in Father's Official Business." *ABC News*, February 2. https://abcnews.go.com/Politics/investigators-probing-ben-carsons-son-involvement-fathers-official/story?id=52804921.

Doorways. 2018. "The Facts about Family Homelessness." DoorwaysVA.org. www.doorwaysva.org/our-work/education-advocacy/the-facts-about-family-homelessness/.

Doyle, Alison. 2018a. "2018 Federal and State Minimum Wage Rates." TheBalanceCareers.com, last updated August 2. www.thebalance.com/2017-federal-state-minimum-wage-rates-2061043.

Doyle, Alison. 2018b. "Pros and Cons of Raising the Minimum Wage." TheBalanceCareers.com, updated on December 20. www.thebalancecareers.com/pros-and-cons-of-raising-the-minimum-wage-2062521.

Drier, Peter. 2011. "Reagan's Real Legacy." TheNation.com, February 4. www.thenation.com/article/reagans-real-legacy/.

Dube, S. 2001. "Childhood Abuse, Household Dysfunction, and the Risk of Attempted Suicide Throughout the Life Span: Findings from the Adverse Childhood Experiences Study." *JAMA* 286(24): 3089–3096.

Duchscherer, Heather. 2016. "A Continuum Divided: Breaking Down Silos and Setting Up Tables between Homelessness and Domestic Violence Services in HEARTH Act Implementation." Master's Thesis, the University of Minnesota. University of Minnesota Digital Conservancy. http://hdl.handle.net/11299/182607.

Duffield, Barbara. 2016. "Helping Homeless Students Step out of the Shadows." *Education Week*. September.6. www.edweek.org/ew/articles/2016/09/07/helping-homeless-students-step-out-of-the.html.

Duffield, Barbara and Phillip Lovell. 2008. "The Economic Crisis Hits Home: The Unfolding Increase in Child & Youth Homelessness." Washington, DC: National Association for the Education of Homeless Children and Youth/First Focus. Google Scholar. https://eric.ed.gov/?redir=http%3a%2f%2fwww.naehcy.org%2fsites%2fdefault%2ffiles%2fimages%2fdl%2fTheEconomic-CrisisHitsHome.pdf.

Duke, Marshall. 1994. *Chaos Theory and Psychology*. Belmont, CA: Wadsworth.

Dunn, Amina. 2018. "Partisans Are Divided over Fairness of the US Economy." *Pew Research Center*. www.pewresearch.org/fact-tank/2018/10/04/partisans-are-divided-over-the-fairness-of-the-u-s-economy-and-why-people-are-rich-or-poor/.

Dupere, Katie. 2015. "6 Welfare Myths we All Need to Stop Believing." Mashable.com (blog), July 27. https://mashable.com/2015/07/27/welfare-myths-debunked/#l9a6gAd6YZqU.

Ebbinghaus, Bernhard. 2015. Welfare Retrenchment. International Encyclopedia of the Social & Behavioral Sciences (Second Edition). pp: 521–527. www.sciencedirect.com/topics/economics-econometrics-and-finance/welfare-state.

Economic Policy Institute. 2018. Twelve Charts that Show How Policy Could Reduce Inequality but is Making it Worse Instead. www.epi.org/publication/top-charts-of-2018-twelve-charts-that-show-how-policy-could-reduce-inequality-but-is-making-it-worse-instead/.

Edelman, Peter. 1997. "The Worst Thing Bill Clinton Has Done." *The Atlantic*, March Issue. www.theatlantic.com/magazine/archive/1997/03/the-worst-thing-bill-clinton-has-done/376797/.

Edelman, Peter. 2017. *Not A Crime to Be Poor: The Criminalization of Poverty in America*. New York: The New Press.

Eden, Elana. 2018. "How Transportation Assistance Can Fight Homelessness." www.planetizen.com/news/2018/09/100753-how-transportation-assistance-can-fight-homelessness.

Egan, Matt. 2014. "2008: Worse than the Great Depression?" CNN.com, August 27. https://money.cnn.com/2014/08/27/news/economy/ben-bernanke-great-depression/index.html.

Ehrenfreund, Max. 2016. "The Poor Pay More for Everyday Purchases, a New Study Warns." *The Washington Post*, May 20. www.washingtonpost.com/news/wonk/wp/2016/05/20/the-poor-pay-more-for-everyday-purchases-and-its-getting-worse-a-new-study-warns/?utm_term=.e4c1a67844d5.

Ehrenfreund, Max. 2017. "How Trump's Budget Helps the Rich at the Expense of the Poor." *The Washington Post*, May 23. www.washingtonpost.com/news/wonk/wp/2017/05/23/how-trumps-budget-helps-the-rich-at-the-expense-of-the-poor/?utm_term=.db8d641afb6c.

Ehrenreich, Barbara. 2011. *Nickel and Dimed: On (not) Getting by in America*. New York: Picador.

Eidelson, Josh. 2018. "America's Wage Growth Remains Slow and Uneven". Bloomberg. https://www.bloomberg.com/news/articles/2018-03-01/america-s-wage-growth-remains-slow-and-uneven.

Elhage, Alysse. 2014. "To Fight Child Homelessness, Strengthen Families." Institute for Family Studies, December 4. https://ifstudies.org/blog/to-fight-child-homelessness-strengthen-families/.

Ellen, Barbara. 2017. "The Warped Logic of Making the Poor Pay More." *The Guardian*, October 14. www.theguardian.com/commentisfree/2017/oct/15/the-warped-logic-of-making-the-poor-pay-more.

Elliott, Lynda Thistle. 2018. "Homeless Students." New Hampshire Department of Education.

Encyclopedia.com. 2001. "Social Forecasting." www.encyclopedia.com/social-sciences/encyclopedias-almanacs-transcripts-and-maps/social-forecasting.

Enzer, Selwyn. 1984. "Anticipating the Unpredictable." *Technological Forecasting and Social Change* 26: 201–204.

Eskes, Donald. 2017. "The Housing First Model for Homelessness isn't Working." https://gvwire.com/2017/10/24/housing-first-model-for-fresno-homeless-isnt-working/.

Family Promise of Davie County. 2018. "HUD Homeless Data Don't Add up: Children and Youth Pay the Price." FamilyPromiseDC.org, December 19.

http://familypromisedc.org/hud-homeless-data-dont-add-up-children-and-youth-pay-the-price/.

Fantuzzo, John, Whitney LeBoeuf, Benjamin Brumley and Staci Perlman. 2013. "A Population-Based Inquiry of Homeless Episode Characteristics and Early Educational Well-being." *Children and Youth Services Review* 35(6): 966–972.

Farrugia, David. and Gerrard, Jessica. 2015. Academic Knowledge and Contemporary Poverty: The Politics of Homelessness Research, *Sociology* 50(2): 267–284.

Feeding America. 2014a. "Fact Sheet." *Feeding America.* www.feedingamerica.org/hunger-in-america/impactof-hunger/child-hunger/child-hunger-fact-sheet.html.

Feeding America. 2014b. "Hunger in America 2014." *Feeding America.* www.feedingamerica.org/hunger-inamerica/our-research/the-hunger-study/.

Feeding America. 2019. "Backpack program". www.feedingamerica.org/our-work/hunger-relief-programs/backpack-program.

Feiner, Lauren. 2019. "Amazon is the Most Valuable Public Company in the World After Passing Microsoft." *CNBC,* January 7. www.cnbc.com/2019/01/07/amazon-passes-microsoft-market-value-becomes-largest.html.

Feldman, David. 2017. "Why Do People Believe Things that Aren't True? *Psychology Today.* www.psychologytoday.com/us/blog/supersurvivors/201705/why-do-people-believe-things-aren-t-true.

Felitti, Vincent. 1998. "Relationship of Childhood Abuse and Household Dysfunction to Many of the Leading Causes of Death in Adults." *American Journal of Preventive Medicine* 14(4): 245–258.

Fessler, Pam. 2015. "Sanctuary, Not Just Shelter. NPR. www.peconicpublicbroadcasting.org/post/quest-end-homelessness-some-developers-are-going-high-end.

Filipovic, Jill. 2018. "Trumps Tax Cuts are a Bust." CNN.com, updated on December 24. www.cnn.com/2018/12/18/opinions/trump-tax-cuts-fed-interest-rate-jill-filipovic/index.html.

Find Law. 2018. "Movie Day at the Supreme Court or "I Know It When I See It: A History of the Definition of Obscenity." FindLaw.com. https://corporate.findlaw.com/litigation-disputes/movie-day-at-the-supreme-court-or-i-know-it-when-i-see-it-a.html.

Finkelhor, David. 2013. "Improving the ACES Study Scale." https://jamanetwork.com/journals/jamapediatrics/fullarticle/1393429.

Finn, Joseph. 2018. "The Massachusetts PFS Story." https://govlab.hks.harvard.edu/files/govlabs/files/ma_pfs_ABA_article.pdf.

Finn, Joseph. 2019. Personal Communication with Author Yvonne Vissing, January 2019.

Fischer, Robert. 2011. "The History of Homelessness in America 1640s to Present." Downtown Congregations to End Homelessness, November 16. www.dceh.org/the-history-of-homelessness-in-america-1640s-to-present/.

Fisher, Mark. 2019. "7 Practical Ways we Can Bless Someone Experiencing Homelessness". www.samekindofdifferentasmefoundation.org/blog/7-practical-ways-we-can-bless-someone-experiencing-homelessness.

Fischer, Will and Barbara Sard. 2017. "Cart Book: Federal Housing Spending is Poorly Matched to Need." Center on Budget and Policy Priorities, last updated March 8. www.cbpp.org/research/housing/chart-book-federal-housing-spending-is-poorly-matched-to-need?fa=view&id=4067%20.

Fitzpatrick, S. 2005. Explaining Homelessness: A Critical Realist Perspective. *Housing, Theory and Society* 22(1): 1–17.

Foley-Keene, Max. 2017. "Violence Against Homeless People is an American Epidemic." *The Diamondback*, October 23. www.dbknews.com/2017/10/24/hate-crimes-homeless-poverty-richard-collins-fbi/.

Fontenot, Kayla, Jessica Semega and Melissa Kollar. 2018. "Income and Poverty in the United States: 2017." United States Census Bureau, September 12. www.census.gov/library/publications/2018/demo/p60-263.html.

Forbes, Steve. 2015. "How Bitcoin Will End World Poverty." *Forbes*, April 2. www.forbes.com/sites/steveforbes/2015/04/02/how-bitcoin-will-end-world-poverty/.

Foscarinis, Maria. 2011a. The human right to housing. Shelter Force. https://shelterforce.org/2011/12/14/the_human_right_to_housing.

Foscarinis, Maria. 2011b Homelessness Policy: Time for another paradigm shift. *Huffington Post*. February 8, 2011. https://www.huffpost.com/entry/homelessness-policy_b_907397.

Freed, Ben. 2017. "Jeff Bezos Won't Entirely Rule Out Running for President." *Washington Post*. www.washingtonian.com/2017/02/09/jeff-bezos-wont-entirely-rule-running-president/.

Freedman, Josh. and Michael Lind. 2013. New Social Contract. *The Atlantic*. Available at www.theatlantic.com/business/archive/2013/12/the-past-and-future-of-americas-social-contract/282511/.

Freedman, Michael. 2019 . *A Magna Carta for Children?* Cambridge: Cambridge University Press.

Frey, William H. 2010. "Five Myths about the 2010 Census and the U.S. Population." *The Washington Post*, February 14. www.washingtonpost.com/wp-dyn/content/article/2010/02/11/AR2010021103898.html?noredirect=on.

Friedman, Milton. 1962. *Capitalism and Freedom*. Chicago: University of Chicago Press.

Friedrich, Bob. 2019. "Causes of Homelessness are Going Unaddressed." *Queens Chronicle*, February 28. www.qchron.com/editions/queenswide/causes-of-homelessness-are-going-unaddressed/article_df55166c-2b46-594e-815f-0a9ec4e1ab01.html.

Friere, Paulo. 1968. *Pedagogy of the Oppressed*. New York: Continuum.

Friesen, Justin P., Campbell, Troy H., and Kay, Aaron. C. 2015. "The Psychological Advantage of Unfalsifiability: The Appeal of Untestable Religious and Political Ideologies." *Journal of Personality and Social Psychology* 108(3), 515–529. https://psycnet.apa.org/record/2014-48913-001.

Froelich, Thomas C., Michael B Sauter and Alexander Kent. 2018. "Poverty in America." 247WallSt.com, November 9. https://247wallst.com/special-report/2018/11/09/poverty-in-america-2/.

Frum, David. 2013. "Fewer Homeless, a Bush Legacy." *CNN.com*, updated on April 29. www.cnn.com/2013/04/29/opinion/frum-less-homelessness/index.html.

Fukuda-Parr, Sakiko. 1999. "What Does Feminization of Poverty Mean? It Isn't Just Lack of Income." *Feminist Economics* 5(2): 99–103.

Fuller, Carey. 2011. "Homeless Shelter Systems and What They Don't Tell You." *HuffingtonPost.com*, December 27. www.huffingtonpost.com/carey-fuller/homeless-shelter-parents_b_1035952.htmlhttps://www.huffingtonpost.com/carey-fuller/homeless-shelter-parents_b_1035952.html.

Fulton, Margaret. 2010. "A Study of Homelessness." PhD diss., Worcester Polytechnic Institute. https://web.wpi.edu/Pubs/E-project/Available/E-project-031610-141453/unrestricted/A_Study_of_Homelessness.pdf.

Galatzer-Levy, Robert. 2016. "The Edge of Chaos: A Nonlinear View of Psychoanalytic Technique." *The International Journal of Psychoanalysis* 97(2): 409–427. doi: 10.1111/1745-8315.12363.

Gans, Herbert J. 1971. "The Uses of Poverty: The Poor Pay All." *Social Policy* 2: 21–23.

Gans, Herbert J. 2012. "The Benefits of Poverty." *Challenge* 55(1): 114–125. doi: 10.2753/0577-5132550106.

Garton, Eric. 2017. "The Case for Investing More in People." *Harvard Business Review*. https://hbr.org/2017/09/the-case-for-investing-more-in-people.

Gatto, Mike. 2018. "Opinion: Why Building More Shelters Won't Solve Homelessness." *Mercury News*, June 14. www.mercurynews.com/2018/06/14/opinion-why-building-more-shelters-wont-solve-homelessness/amp/.

Gee, Alastair, Julia Carrie Wong, Paul Lewis, Adithya Sambamurthy and Charlotte Simmonds. 2017. "Bussed Out." *The Guardian*, December 20. www.theguardian.com/us-news/ng-interactive/2017/dec/20/bussed-out-america-moves-homeless-people-country-study.

Gentzel, Thomas. 2017. Public Education Must Be Our New Frontier. *Huffington Post*. www.huffpost.com/entry/public-education-must-be_b_9839506.

Gilson, Dave and Edwin Rios. 2016. "11 Charts Show Income Inequality Isn't Getting Better." *Mother Jones*. www.motherjones.com/politics/2016/12/america-income-inequality-wealth-net-worth-charts/.

Godoy, Maria and Allison Aubrey. 2017. "Trump Wants Families on Food Stamps to Get Jobs. The Majority Already Work." NPR.com, May 24. www.npr.org/sections/thesalt/2017/05/24/529831472/trump-wants-families-on-food-stamps-to-get-jobs-the-majority-already-work.

Goldberg, Eleanor. 2015. "We're Not Trash." *Huffington Post*. www.huffpost.com/entry/were-all-human-were-nottrash-homeless-people-would-like-you-to-know_n_560e24d0e4b0dd85030b88fc.

Gotsis, Chloe. 2012. "Need Increasing at Newton's Food Pantries." WickedLocal.com, updated on January 31. www.wickedlocal.com/newton/news/x1622349128/Need-increasing-at-Newtons289food-pantries#axzz1mTmpFcfb.

Gould, Elise and Schneider, Jessica. 2018. "Poverty persists 50 years after Poor People's Campaign. Economic Policy Institute." www.epi.org/publication/poverty-persists-50-years-after-the-poor-peoples-campaign-black-poverty-rates-are-more-than-twice-as-high-as-white-poverty-rates/.

Green Doors. 2019. "Family Homelessness Facts." Green Doors. www.greendoors.org/facts/family-homelessness.php.

Greenberg, Greg A. and Robert A. Rosenheck. 2008. "Jail Incarceration, Homelessness, and Mental Health: A National Study." *Psychiatric Services* 49(2): 170–177. https://ps.psychiatryonline.org/doi/full/10.1176/ps.2008.59.2.170.

Griffin, Anna. 2015. "Our Homeless Crisis: A Timeline of Shifting Federal Philosophies and Approaches Toward Poverty." *The Oregonian* (OregonLive), updated on March 1. www.oregonlive.com/portland/index.ssf/2015/02/timeline_of_federal_housing_ef.html.

Gripp, Andrew. 2014. "America's Welfare System is Failing Those Most in Need." IVN.us, July 16. https://ivn.us/2014/07/16/americas-welfare-system-failing-need/.

Guardian, The. 2017. Bussed out: How American Moves its Homeless. www. theguardian.com/us-news/ng-interactive/2017/dec/20/bussed-out-america-moves-homeless-people-country-study.

Gustafson, Kaaryn. 2009. "The Criminalization of Poverty." *Journal of Criminal Law and Criminology* 99(3): 643–715. https://scholarlycommons.law.northwestern.edu/cgi/viewcontent.cgi?article=7330&context=jclc.

Gusfield, Joseph.1984. *The Culture of Public Problems*. Chicago: University of Chicago Press.

Hacker, Jacob. 2016. *American Amnesia: How the War on Government Led us to Forget What Made America Prosper*. New York: Simon & Schuster.

Hagle, Courtney. 2019. "Fox Has Spent Months Demonizing Homeless." *Media Matters*. www.mediamatters.org/fox-news/fox-news-has-spent-months-demonizing-homelessness-california-now-trump-wants-major.

Harrington, Michael. 1997/1962. *The Other America*. New York: Scribner.

Harvard University. 2018. "State of the Nation's Housing 2018" Joint Center for Housing Studies. Access Date. www.jchs.harvard.edu/state-nations-housing-2018.

Hatcher, Dan. 2016. *The Poverty Industry*. New York: NYU Press.

Hecht, Heidi. 2017. "Technology Is Helping the Homeless Get Out of Poverty." Foundation for Economic Education, December 4. https://fee.org/articles/technology-is-helping-the-homeless-get-out-of-poverty/.

Heiby, E. M. 1995. Chaos Theory, Nonlinear Dynamical Models, And Psychological Assessment. *Psychological Assessment*, 7(1): 5–9. doi: 10.1037/1040-3590.7.1.5.

Heller, Nathan. 2018. "Who Really Stand to Win from Universal Basic Income." *The New Yorker*, July 16. www.newyorker.com/magazine/2018/07/09/who-really-stands-to-win-from-universal-basic-income.

Henry J. Kaiser Family Foundation. 2018. "Key Facts About the Uninsured Population." KFF.org, December 7. www.kff.org/uninsured/fact-sheet/key-facts-about-the-uninsured-population/.

Henry, Meghan, Rian Watt, Lily Rosenthal and Azim Shivji. 2017. "The 2017 Annual Homeless Assessment Report (AHAR) to Congress." *The U.S. Department of Housing and Urban Development*, December. www.hudexchange.info/resources/documents/2017-AHAR-Part-1.pdf.

Herman, Daniel B. 1997. "Adverse Childhood Experiences: Are They Risk Factors for Adult Homelessness?" *American Journal of Public Health* 87(2): 249–255.

Higginbotham, Peter. 2014. *The Workhouse Encyclopedia*. Charleston, SC: History Press.

Higgins, Jane. 2018. "Farmers' Struggle to Legally Import Workers Threatens U.S. Crops." *UPI*, September 19. www.upi.com/Farmers-struggle-to-legally-import-workers-threatens-US-crops/3711537355230/.

Hiltzik, Michael. 2018. "The Truth About Income Inequality. *Los Angeles Times.* www.latimes.com/business/hiltzik/la-fi-hiltzik-inequality-20180807-story.html.

Himmelfarb, Gertrude. 1983. *The Idea of Poverty: England in the Early Industrial Age*. New York: Knopf.

History. 2010. "Hoovervilles." History.com, last updated November 2, 2018. www.history.com/topics/great-depression/hoovervilles.

History. 2018. Recession. www.history.com/topics/21st-century/recession.

Hobbes, Michael. 2018. "America's Housing Crisis is a Ticking Time Bomb." *HuffingtonPost.com*, Updated on June 19. www.huffingtonpost.com/entry/housing-crisis-inequality-harvard-report_us_5b27c1f1e4b056b2263c621e.

Hobbes, Michael. 2019. Why America Can't Solve Homelessness. *Huffington Post.* www.huffpost.com/entry/homeless-utah-end-america-salt-lake-city_n_5c d1cac0e4b04e275d511aba.

Hobbes, Thomas. 1652. Leviathan. New York: Oxford University Press.

Hobson, Jeremy and Serena McMahon. 2019. "This New Jersey County was the 1st in the U.S. to End Chronic Homelessness." *WBUR*, February 20. www.wbur. org/hereandnow/2019/02/20/bergen-county-new-jersey-homelessness?fbclid= IwAR0T0zPrf_t4I52H99wH7_tl8ZLuc62PX4rcBEoroft8Ds63pFEffXcECcI.

Hoffer, Eric. 1951. *The True Believer: Thoughts on the Nature of Mass Movements.* New York: Harper and Brothers.

Holroyd, P. 1978. Change and Discontinuity. *Futures* 10: 31–43.

Hopper, Elizabeth, Ellen Bassuk and Jerry Oliver, J. 2009. Shelter from the Storm. www.traumacenter.org/products/pdf_files/shelter_from_storm.pdf.

Hopper, Kim and Jill Hamburg. 1986. "The Making of America's Homeless: From Skid Row to New Poor, 1945–1984." In *Critical Perspectives on Housing*, edited by Rachel G. Bratt, Chester Hartman and Ann Meyerson, 12–40. Philadelphia: Temple University Press.

HUD. 2018. "Funding Availability." www.hud.gov/grants.

HUD Exchange. 2017. "2017 AHAR: Part 1 – PIT Estimates of Homelessness in the U.S." The United States Department of Housing and Urban Development, December. www.hudexchange.info/resource/5639/2017-ahar-part-1-pit-estimates-of-homelessness-in-the-us/.

HUD Exchange. 2018. "Homeless Emergency Assistance and Rapid Transition to Housing Act." HUDExchange.info. www.hudexchange.info/ homelessness-assistance/hearth-act/.

Hudson, Christopher G. 1998. *An Interdependency Model of Homelessness: The Dynamics of Social Disintegration.* Lewiston: Edwin Mellin.

Hudson, Christopher G. 2004. "The Dynamics of Self-Organization: Neglected Dimensions." *Journal of Human Behavior in the Social Environment* 10(4): 17–38.

Hudson, Christopher G. 2010. *Complex Systems and Human Behavior.* Chicago: Lyceum.

Hudson, Christopher G. 2012. "Patterns of Residential Mobility of People with Schizophrenia." *Journal of Sociology & Social Welfare* 39(3): 149–179.

IBISWorld. 2018. "Community Housing & Homeless Shelters Industry in the US." IBISWorld.com, October. www.ibisworld.com/industry-trends/market-research-reports/healthcare-social-assistance/social-assistance/community-housing-homeless-shelters.html.

Inequality.org. 2018. Wealth inequality in the US. https://inequality.org/facts/ wealth-inequality/.

Institute for Children, Poverty and Homelessness. 2012. "A New Path: An Immediate Plan to Reduce Family Homelessness. ICPHUSA.org, February 1. www.icphusa.org/reports/a-new-path/.

Institute for Children, Poverty and Homelessness. 2014. "United States of Homelessness." ICPHUSA.org. www.icphusa.org/interactive_data/the-united-states-of-homelessness/.

Institute for Children, Poverty and Homelessness. 2017. "Out of the Shadows: A State-By-State Ranking of Accountability for Homeless Students." Institute for Children, Poverty, and Homelessness, June 9. www.icphusa.org/national/ shadows-state-state-ranking-accountability-homeless-students/.

Institute for Children, Poverty and Homelessness. 2018a. "Are We Really Counting America's Homeless Families?" ICPHUSA.org, January 19. www. icphusa.org/reports/really-counting-americas-homeless-families/#a-more-comprehensive-picture.

Institute for Children, Poverty and Homelessness. 2018b. "New Jersey's Student Homelessness Grew the Most of Any State Over 3 Years." ICPHUSA.org, March 23. www.icphusa.org/reports/new-jerseys-student-homelessness-grew-the-most-of-any-state-over-3-years/.

Institute for Children, Poverty and Homelessness. 2018c. "One-Third of Georgia's Homeless Students Live in Rural Areas." ICPHUSA.org, September 11. www.icphusa.org/reports/one-third-of-georgias-homeless-students-live-in-rural-areas/.

Insurance Business. 2016. "Shelters are a Nonprofit Segment that Reaps Big Revenue for Agents." *Insurance Business America*, February 4. www.insurance businessmag.com/us/news/non-profits/shelters-are-a-nonprofit-segment-that-reaps-big-revenue-for-agents-28177.aspx.

Isenberg, Nancy. 2017. *White Trash: The 400-year Untold History of Class in America.* London: Atlantic Books.

Isidore, Chris. 2019. "JPMorgan is Creating Its Own Cryptocurrency." CNN. com, February 14. www.cnn.com/2019/02/14/investing/jpmorgan-jpm-coin-cryptocurrency/index.html.

Jaeger, Max. 2018. "Universal Basic Income Would Cost Taxpayers $3.8T Per Year: Study." *New York Post*, July 12. https://nypost.com/2018/07/12/universal-basic-income-would-cost-taxpayers-3-8t-per-year-study/.

James, Adam. 2018a. "Berkeley Hopes to Tackle Homelessness with Its Own Cryptocurrency." Bitcoinist.com, February 9. https://bitcoinist.com/berkeley-hopes-to-tackle-homelessness-with-its-own-cryptocurrency/.

James, Cody. 2018. "Coins4Clothes Toronto – Bitcoin Cash." Medium.com, March 29. https://medium.com/bitcoin-cash-fund/coins4clothes-toronto-bitcoin-cash-78a903429bf5.

Janosko, Jackie. 2018. "CCEH Track Summary." From the 2018 National Conference on Ending Homelessness, Connecticut Coalition to End Homelessness. http://cceh.org/wp-content/uploads/2018/08/Racism-Homelessness-Track-v2.pdf.

Janus, Kathleen Kelly. 2013. "Not All Social Problems Can Be Solved by Business." www.huffpost.com/entry/social-problems_b_4171598.

Johnson, Allie. 2019. "40 Year Mortgages." www.lendingtree.com/home/mortgage/40-year-mortgage/.

Johnson, Becky. 2006. "Least, the Last, and the Lost." *The StreetSpirit.org*, accessed on. www.thestreetspirit.org/Feb2005/pr-least.htm.

Jones, Sarah. 2018. "Ben Carson: A Quiet Scandal." *New Republic*. https://newre public.com/minutes/151322/ben-carsons-hud-quiet-scandal.

Karpman, Michael, Stephen Zuckerman and Dulce Gonzalez. 2018. "The Well-Being and Basic Needs Survey." Urban Institute, August 28. www.urban. org/research/publication/well-being-and-basic-needs-survey.

Kaser, Rachel. 2018. "This 3D Printed House Aims to End Homelessness: Could it work?" TheNextWeb.com, April 20. https://thenextweb.com/tech/2018/04/20/3d-printed-house-aims-end-homelessness-work/.

Katz, Michael B. 1996. *In the Shadow of the Poorhouse: A Social History of Welfare in America*. New York: Basic Books.

Kavoussi, B. 2012. US Could End Homelessness with Money Spent to Buy Christmas Decorations. *Huffington Post*. www.huffpost.com/entry/homelessness-christmas-decorations_n_2276536.

Katayama, Devin. 2017. "The Suburbs: The New Face of Homelessness." www.kqed.org/news/11533683/the-suburbs-the-new-face-of-bay-area-homelessness.

Kennedy, Mavis. 2015. "Homelessness in Victorian London." *The Guardian*. www.theguardian.com/artanddesign/2015/jan/02/homelessness-victorian-london-exhibition-geffrye-museum.

Kelleher, Kevin. 2019. "Gilded Age 2.0: U.S. Income Inequality Increases to Pre-Great Depression Levels." *Fortune*, February 13. http://fortune.com/2019/02/13/us-income-inequality-bad-great-depression/.

Kessler, Ronald C., Matthias Angermeyer, James C. Anthony, Rod De Graaf, Koen Demyttenaere, Isabelle Gasquet, Giovanni De Girolamo, Seymon Gluzman, Oye Gureje, Josep Maria Haro, Norito Kawakami Aimee Karam, Daphna Levinson, Maria Elena Medina Mora, Mark A. Oakley Browne, Jose Posada-Villa, Dan J. Stein, Cheuk Him Adley Tsang, Sergio Aguilar-Gaxiola, Jordi Alonso, Sing Lee, Steven Heeringa, Beth-Ellen Pennell, Patricia Berglund, Michael J. Gruber, Maria Petukhova, Somnath Chatterji and T. Bedirhan Ustun. 2007. "Lifetime Prevalence and Age-of-Onset Distributions of Mental Disorders in the World Health Organization's World Mental Health Survey Initiative." *World Psychiatry: Official Journal of the World Psychiatric Association (WPA)* 6(3): 168–176.

Keyes, Scott. 2013. "Everything You Think You Know About Panhandlers is Wrong." ThinkProgress.org, October 30. https://thinkprogress.org/everything-you-think-you-know-about-panhandlers-is-wrong-36b41487730d/.

Keyes, Scott. 2014. It saves millions to simply give homeless people a place to live. *Think Progress*. https://thinkprogress.org/it-saves-millions-to-simply-give-homeless-people-a-place-to-live-e18ddbc1146d/.

Khandelwal, Neha. 2016. "Maslows Hierarcny of Needs vs Max Neef Model. https://medium.com/@hwabtnoname/maslow-s-hierarchy-of-needs-vs-the-max-neef-model-of-human-scale-development-9ebebeabb215.

Kimura, Donna. 2017. "Trump Budget Would Escalate Homelessness." HousingFinance.com, June 1. www.housingfinance.com/policy-legislation/trump-budget-would-escalate-homelessness_o.

Kitson, Kayla. 2018. "Scoring Trump's Tax Cuts So Far: $280K for Rich Lawmakers, Pennies for Working People." TruthOut.org, August 25. https://truthout.org/articles/scoring-trumps-tax-cuts-280k-for-rich-lawmakers-pennies-for-working-people/.

Knight, Heather. 2018. "What It Really Costs to Help the Homeless. And How Business Can Do More." *San Francisco Chronicle*, August 24. www.sfchronicle.com/bayarea/heatherknight/article/Businesses-must-contribute-more-to-city-s-13178743.php.

Konczal, Mike. 2014. "The Voluntarism Fantasy." *Democracy Journal*, 32. https://democracyjournal.org/magazine/32/the-voluntarism-fantasy/?page=all.

Korten, David 2019. "A Living Wealth Money System." https://davidkorten.org/the-new-economy/money-rules/.

Kowalchuk, Michael. 2018. "NYC's 'Shelter-Industrial Complex' Makes Money over Rising Homelessness." LiberationNews.org, May 3. www.liberationnews. org/nycs-shelter-industrial-complex-makes-money-rising-homelessness/.

Krippner, S. 1994. "Humanistic Psychology and Chaos Theory: The Third Revolution And The Third Force." *Journal of Humanistic Psychology*, 34(3): 48–61. doi: 10.1177/00221678940343005.

Krishnamurthy, Prabhakar. 2010. "Social Forecasting – Relevance in Strategic Planning for Corporate Sector." *SSRN Electronic Journal*. doi: 10.2139/ssrn.1632506. www.researchgate.net/publication/228319991_Social_Forecasting_-_Relevance_in_Strategic_Planning_for_Corporate_Sector.

Kuhn, Thomas. 2012. *The Structure of Scientific Revolutions*. Chicago: University of Chicago Press.

Kusmer, Kenneth L. 2003. *Down and Out, on the Road: The Homeless in American History*. New York: Oxford University Press.

Kuznetsov, Nikolai. 2017. "How Emerging Markets and Blockchain Can Bring an End to Poverty." *Forbes*, July 24. www.forbes.com/sites/nikolai kuznetsov/2017/07/24/how-emerging-markets-and-blockchain-can-bring-an-end-to-poverty/#16e1e6814a0c.

LaMagna, Maria. 2018. "The American Dream May Be Dead." *NY Post*, August 22. https://nypost.com/2018/08/22/the-american-dream-may-be-dead/.

LaMarche, Pat. 2014. Dying Homeless. https://us.thinkt3.com/blog/dying-homeless/.

Laughlin, Jason. 2018. "Panhandlers in Philly Traffic Ply a Lucrative, but Dangerous, Trade." *The Inquirer*, January 31. philly.com/philly/news/ pennsylvania/philadelphia/in-traffic-philly-highway-panhandlers-beg-police-homeless-scullion-heroin-addiction-arrest-20180131.html.

Levitz, Eric. 2019. "Ocasio-Cortez's 70 Percent Top Tax Rate Is a Moderate, Evidence-Based Policy." *New York Magazine*, January 4. http://nymag.com/ intelligencer/2019/01/alexandria-ocasio-cortez-70-top-tax-rate-60-minutes-green-new-deal.html.

Lewin, Roger. 2000. *Complexity: Life at the Edge of Chaos*. Chicago: University of Chicago Press.

Lewis, David. 1994. *W.E.B. Du Bois: Biography of a Race, 1868–1919*. New York: Holt Paperbacks.

Lichtenstein, Nelson. 2018. "A Fabulous Failure." https://prospect.org/article/ fabulous-failure-clinton%E2%80%99s-1990s-and-origins-our-times.

Link, Bruce. 1995. "Study Finds More Homeless than Ever." *Columbia University Record 20*, 14. www.columbia.edu/cu/record/archives/vol20/vol20_iss14/re-cord2014.30.html.

Loehwing, Melanie. 2018. *Homeless Advocacy and the Rhetorical Construction of the Civic Home*. University Park, PA: Penn State University Press.

Lorenz, Edward N. 1972. "Predictability: Does the Flap of a Butterfly's Wings in Brazil Set Off a Tornado in Texas?" Paper presented at the AAA's Convention of the Global Atmospheric Research Program. Cambridge, MA: MIT.

Louis, Errol. 2017. "Trump Hires the Wedding Planner – To Oversee NY Federal Housing Program." CNN.com, updated on June 17. www.cnn.com/2017/06/16/ opinions/patton-urban-development-louis-opinion/index.html.

Lowrey, Annie. 2017. "The People Left Behind When Only the 'Deserving' Poor Get Help." *The Atlantic*, May 25. www.theatlantic.com/business/

archive/2017/05/the-people-who-are-left-behind-when-only-the-deserving-poor-get-help/528018/.

Ludwig, Mike. 2018. "Under Trump, More People Live Without Health Coverage." TruthOut.org, December 11. https://truthout.org/articles/under-trump-more-people-live-without-health-coverage/.

Mabli, James, Rhoda Cohen, Frank Potter, and Zhanyun Zhao. 2010. "Hunger in America 2010 National Report Prepared for Feeding America." https://www.mathematica.org/our-publications-and-findings/publications/hunger-in-america-2010-national-report-prepared-for-feeding-america.

MacKay-Tisbert, Tully. 2016. "Homelessness Industry Manages, Doesn't Fix Problem." *SF Gate*, February 18. www.sfgate.com/opinion/article/Homelessness-industry-manages-doesn-t-fix-6841264.php.

Mandel, David. 1995. "Chaos Theory, Sensitive Dependence, and the Logistic Equation." *American Psychologist*, 50(2): 106–107. doi: 10.1037/0003-066X.50.2.106.

Manduca, Robert. 2018. "How Rising US Income Inequality Exacerbates Racial Economic Disparities." Washington Center for Equitable Growth, August 23. https://equitablegrowth.org/how-rising-u-s-income-inequality-exacerbates-racial-economic-disparities/.

Manstead, Antony S.R. 2018. "The Psychology of Social Class: How Socioeconomic Status Impacts Thought, Feelings, and Behaviour." *The British journal of Social Psychology* 57(2): 267–291. doi: 10.1111/bjso.12251.

Marsh, Rene and Wallace, Gregory. 2018. "Emails show Ben and Candy Carson spent $31,000 on Dining Table." *CNN*. www.cnn.com/2018/03/14/politics/emails-ben-candy-carson-dining-set/index.html.

Martin, Emmie. 2018a. "This Map Shows How Much a Single Person Needs to Earn to Live Comfortably in Every US State." *CNBC*, July 20. www.cnbc.com/2018/07/19/living-wage-for-a-single-person-in-every-us-state.html.

Martin, Emmie. 2018b. States with the highest levels of income inequality. CNBC. https://www.cnbc.com/2018/03/12/us-states-with-the-highest-levels-of-income-inequality.html.

Marx, Karl. 1964; original 1848. *Communist Manifesto*. New York: Washington Square Press.

May, Lucy. 2012. "3CDC: Cost to Build Homeless Shelters Now $40M." *Cincinnati Business Courier*, September 12. www.bizjournals.com/cincinnati/news/2012/09/12/3cdc-cost-to-build-homeless-shelters.html.

McDonald, Mary. 2017. "From Shell Hock to PTSD." *The Conversation*. https://theconversation.com/from-shell-shock-to-ptsd-a-century-of-invisible-war-trauma-74911.

McLeod, Saul. 2018. "Maslow Hierarchy of Needs." www.simplypsychology.org/maslow.html.

McMahon, John. 2018. "Berkeley to Launch ICO for the Homeless." *News BTC*, February 13. www.newsbtc.com/2018/02/13/berkeley-launch-ico-homeless/.

McSwain, Dan. 2017. Homelessness is Solvable But Won't Yield to Political Timidity. *San Diego Union Tribune*. www.sandiegouniontribune.com/business/columnists/dan-mcswain/sd-fi-mcswain-homeless-mayor-20170126-story.html.

Meni, David 2018. *Suprise: The mortgage interest deduction is now even more of a handout to the wealth*. Greater Washington. https://ggwash.org/view/67481/surprise-the-mortgage-interest-deduction-is-now-even-more-of-a-handout-to-the-wealthy.

Mercatus Center. 2018. "How Effective are HUD Programs?" No One Knows. https://neighborhoodeffects.mercatus.org/tag/cdbg/.

Merton, Robert King. 1976. *Contemporary Social Problems*. New York: Harcourt Brace.

Merton, Robert. 1968. *Social Theory and Social Structure*. New York: Free Press.

Milligan, Susan. 2018. "Building a Legacy: Former President Jimmy Carter Talks of His Life's Work on Affordable Housing and the Future of Public Service." *U.S. News*, August 31. www.usnews.com/news/the-report/articles/2018-08-31/jimmy-carter-on-affordable-housing-and-public-service.

Mills, C. Wright. 1956. *The Power Elite*. New York: Oxford University Press.

Millsap, Adam. 2016. "How Ben Carson can improve HUD." *Forbes*. www.forbes.com/sites/adammillsap/2016/12/07/how-ben-carson-can-improve-hud/#540c74191138.

Mitchell, Mindy. 2018. "Homelessness and Incarceration are Linked." https://endhomelessness.org/homelessness-incarceration-intimately-linked-new-federal-funding-available-reduce-harm/.

Mo's Heroes. 2019. "Helping Homeless Heroes." MosHeros.org. http://mosheros.org/?gclid=Cj0KCQiAzKnjBRDPARIsAKxfTRA3t8DrBuzHQ0G2R9PXnI3UcO_pO4Pr5IJigHqG6cv31DG3WHTJp14aAkCEEALw_wcB.

Moon, Chris and Madison Miller. 2018. "How Long Homeowners Stay." www.valuepenguin.com/how-long-homeowners-stay-in-their-homes.

Morris, Andrew J.F. 2008. *The Limits of Voluntarism: Charity and Welfare from the New Deal through the Great Society*. Cambridge: Cambridge University Press.

Muller, Robert T. 2013. "Homelessness as Trauma." PsychologyToday.com, August 16. www.psychologytoday.com/us/blog/talking-about-trauma/201308/homelessness-trauma-0.

Muñoz, Manuel, Carmelo Vazquez, Sonia Panadero and Aida de Vicente. 2019. "Theoretical Models in the Homeless Population." 5th Meeting Constructing Understanding of the Homeless (CUPH) Network. Milan, Italy, 21–22 April. www.researchgate.net/publication/255588272_THEORETICAL_MODELS_IN_THE_HOMELESS_POPULATION.

Murdock, Sebastian. 2019. "Black HUD Official Lynne Patton Used as a Political Prop in Attempt to Prove Trump Isn't Racist." *Huffington Post.com*, February 27. www.huffpost.com/entry/lynn-patton-trump-racist_n_5c76cf61e4b062b30eba641f.

Murphey, David and Sacks, Vanessa. 2019. "Supporting Students With Adverse Child Experiences. www.aft.org/sites/default/files/ae_summer2019_aces.pdf.

Murphy, Justin. 2018. School Lunch Shaming. www.democratandchronicle.com/story/news/2018/01/19/school-lunch-shaming-what-do-schools-do-when-student-accounts-dont-have-money/1012590001/.

Mutz, Diana. 2019. Status Threat, Not Economic Hardship, Explains the 2016 Presidential Vote. *Proceedings of the National Academy of Science*. www.pnas.org/content/115/19/E4330.

Nadasen, Premilla. 2016. "How a Democrat Killed Welfare." *Jacobin*. www.jacobinmag.com/2016/02/welfare-reform-bill-hillary-clinton-tanf-poverty-dlc/.

Nasheed, Jameelah. 2019. When You Can't Afford School Lunch the Toll Is More Than Just Physical. www.teenvogue.com/story/physical-emotional-academic-effects-lunch-shaming.

National Alliance to End Homelessness. 2012. "Changes in the HUD Definition of Homelessness". EndHomelessness.org, January 18. https://endhomelessness.org/resource/changes-in-the-hud-definition-of-homeless/.

National Alliance to End Homelessness. 2018. "Family Homelessness in the United States: A State-By-State Snapshot." National Alliance to End Homelessness, February 20. https://endhomelessness.org/resource/family-homelessness-in-the-united-states-state-by-state-snapshot/.

National Alliance to End Homelessness. 2019. "Federal Funding for Homelessness Programs." EndHomelessness.org. https://endhomelessness.org/ending-homelessness/policy/federal-funding-homelessness-programs/.

National Center for Homeless Education. 2018. "Other Resources" section. NCHE.ed.gov. https://nche.ed.gov/data-collection/.

National Center for Homeless Education. 2019. "Federal Data Summary, School Years 2014–15 to 2016–17." National Center for Homeless Education at the University of North Carolina Greensboro, February. https://nche.ed.gov/wp-content/uploads/2019/02/Federal-Data-Summary-SY-14.15-to-16.17-Final-Published-2.12.19.pdf.

National Coalition for Homeless Veterans. 2019. "FAQ About Homeless Veterans." NCHV.org. http://nchv.org/index.php/news/media/background_and_statistics/.

National Coalition for the Homeless. 2018. "Vulnerable to Hate: A Survey of Bias-Motivated Violence Against People Experiencing Homelessness in 2016–2017." NationalHomeless.org, December 21. https://nationalhomeless.org/category/civil-rights/violence-against-the-homeless/.

National Conference of State Legislatures. 2016. "Homeless and Runaway Youth." NCSL.org, April 14. www.ncsl.org/research/human-services/homeless-and-runaway-youth.aspx.

National Health Care for the Homeless Council. 2018. "What is the Official Definition of Homelessness?" NHCHC.org. www.nhchc.org/faq/official-definition-homelessness/.

National Law Center on Homelessness and Poverty. 2011. "Simply unacceptable: Homelessness and the human right to housing in the US." https://nlchp.org/wp-content/uploads/2018/10/Simply_Unacceptable.pdf.

National Law Center on Homelessness and Poverty. 2018a. "No Safe Place: The Criminalization of Homelessness in U.S. Cities." *National Law Center on Homelessness and Poverty.* https://nlchp.org/wp-content/uploads/2019/02/No_Safe_Place.pdf.

National Law Center on Homelessness and Poverty. 2018b. *Human rights to human reality.* http://nlchp.org/wp-content/uploads/2018/10/Human_Rights_to_Human_Reality.pdf.

National Low Income Housing Coalition. 2018. "Study Finds Significant Racial Disparities in Homelessness Rates." *National Low Income Housing Coalition,* April 9. https://nlihc.org/resource/study-finds-significant-racial-disparities-homelessness-rates.

Navarez, Ailana. 2017. "An Economic Answer to Terrorism: Re-Visiting De Soto's 'The Other Path'." *International Policy Digest,* August 12. https://intpolicydigest.org/2017/08/12/an-economic-answer-to-terrorism-re-visiting-de-soto-s-the-other-path/.

Nelson, Andrew. 2018. "De Soto Inc.: Where Eminent Domain Meets the Blockchain." *Bitcoin Magazine*, March 5. https://bitcoinmagazine.com/articles/de-soto-inc-where-eminent-domain-meets-blockchain/.

Nelson, G., and Prilleltensky, I. 2010. *Community Psychology: In Pursuit of Liberation and Well-being.* New York: Palgrave.

Neubeck, Kenneth and Cazenave, Noel. 2001. *Welfare Racism.* New York: Routledge.

Newswires 2018. House Financial Services Subcommittee Issues Testimony From Family Promise of Colorado Springs. https://insurancenewsnet.com/oarticle/house-financial-services-subcommittee-issues-testimony-from-family-promise-of-colorado-springs#.XX5V_ShKhPZ.

New York Times. 2017. "Don't Make Housing for the Poor too Cozy. www.nytimes.com/2017/05/03/us/politics/ben-carson-hud-poverty-plans.html.

New York Times. 2018. Fighting Back Against the War on Homeless Shelters. www.nytimes.com/2018/07/20/nyregion/fighting-back-against-the-war-on-homeless-shelters.html.

Nonko, Emily. 2016. "Tiny Home Zoning Regulations: What You Need to Know." Curbed.com, September 22. www.curbed.com/2016/9/22/13002832/tiny-house-zoning-laws-regulations.

Nooe, Roger M. and David A. Patterson. 2010. "The Ecology of Homelessness." *Journal of Human Behavior in the Social Environment* 20(2): 105–152. doi: 10.1080/10911350903269757.

Northwestern Institute for Policy Research. 2014. "The Great Recession: Over But Not Gone." IPR.Northwestern.edu. www.ipr.northwestern.edu/about/news/2014/IPR-research-Great-Recession-unemployment-foreclosures-safety-net-fertility-public-opinion.html.

Nunez, Ralph de Costa. 2016. A housing first approach could actually stimulate homelessness. *Huffington Post.* https://www.huffpost.com/entry/is-hud-stimulating-homele_b_10106572.

Nunez, Ralph de Costa. 2017. Review of contributions. Huffington Post. https://www.huffpost.com/author/media-204.

Nurius, Paula. 2012. "ACEs Within a Social Disadvantage Framework: Distinguishing Unique, Cumulative, and Moderated Contributions to Adult Mental Health." *J Prevention and Intervention in the Community* 40(4): 278–290.

O'Brien, Andy. 2018. "Rockland Software Developer Unveils New Cryptocurrency "Mined" with the Power of Doing Good." *The Free Press*, December 6. https://freepressonline.com/Content/Top-Scrolling-Area/Top-Scrolling-Area/Article/Rockland-Software-Developer-Unveils-New-Cryptocurrency-Mined-with-the-Power-of-Doing-Good-/126/724/62211.

O'Connell, James. 2015. *Stories from the Shadows: Reflections of a Street Doctor.* Boston, MA: Boston Healthcare for the Homeless.

O'Flaherty, B. 2004. "Wrong Person and Wrong Place: For Homelessness, the Conjunction is what Matters." *Journal of Housing Economics* 13(1): 1–15.

O'Hara, Mary. 2019. "Lesson from America: Social Exclusion." *The Guardian.* www.theguardian.com/society/series/mary-o-hara-lesson-from-america+socialexclusion.

O'Kane, Sean. 2019. "Jeff Bezos and Space." www.theverge.com/2019/5/11/18564655/blue-origin-jeff-bezos-space-moon-new-glenn.

O'Sullivan, E. 2008. Pathways Through Homelessness: Theoretical and Policy Implications, in: J. Doherty and B. Edgar (Eds.) 'In My Caravan, I Feel Like Superman': Essays in Honour of Henk Meert, 1963-2006, pp.79–108. (Brussels: FEANTSA/Centre for Housing Research, University of St. Andrews).

Olasky, Marin. 1994. *The Tragedy of American Compassion*. Washington D.C.: Regnery Publishing.

Olivet, Jeff. 2016. "Homelessness Is a Symptom of Racism." *HuffingtonPost*.com, updated on October 28. www.huffingtonpost.com/jeff-olivet/homeless-ness-is-a-symptom_b_8409582.html.

Orrenius, Pia. 2016. "Benefits of Immigration Outweigh the Costs." The Catalyst (Spring 2016, Issue 2). www.bushcenter.org/catalyst/north-american-century/benefits-of-immigration-outweigh-costs.html.

Osili, Una and Sasha Zarins. 2018. "Fewer Americans are Giving Money to Charity but Total Donations are at Record Levels Anyway." The Conversation. com, July 3. http://theconversation.com/fewer-americans-are-giving-money-to-charity-but-total-donations-are-at-record-levels-anyway-98291.

Packard, Norman. 1988. *Adaptation Towards The Edge of Chaos*. Urbana: University of Illinois at Champagne-Urbana, Center for Complex Systems Research.

Paddlson, Laura. 2019. "Finland Gave People $640 a Month, No Strings Attached. Here's What Happened." *HuffingtonPost.com*, February 8. www.huffingtonpost.com/entry/universal-basic-income-finland-ontario-stockton_us_5c5c3679e4b00187b558e5ab.

Paddock, Anne. 2015. "Where Does Your $1 to the March of Dimes go?" https://paddockpost.com/2015/10/28/where-does-your-1-to-march-of-dimes-go/.

Palta, Rina. 2018. "Here's What It Would Cost to Shelter Every Homeless Person – And Why LA Will Never Do It." LAist.com, June 22. https://laist.com/2018/06/22/heres_what_it_would_cost_to_shelter.php.

Papenfuss, Mary. 2018. "On Strike! Amazon Workers Walk Out in Germany, Spain, Italy and the UK." *HuffingtonPost.com*, November 23. www.huffing-tonpost.com/entry/amazon-workers-walk-out-in-germany-spain-italy-uk_us_5bf8c36fe4b03b230fa193d7.

Papenfuss, Mary. 2019a. "400 Richest Americans Own More Than 150 Million of the Nation's Poorest: Study." *HuffingtonPost.com*, updated on February 11. www.huffingtonpost.com/entry/400-richest-own-more-than-150-million-poorest_us_5c60f627e4b0eec79b250c34.

Papenfuss, Mary. 2019b. "Trump Vowed to Wipe Out National Debt; Deficit Soars 41.8 Percent." *HuffingtonPost.com*, February 15. www.huffpost.com/entry/trump-national-debt-deficit-soars_n_5c662ccae4b05c889d1d9ea6.

Patterson, Michelle. 2014. "Setting the Stage for Chronic Health Problems: Cumulative Childhood Adversity among Homeless Adults with Mental Illness in Vancouver, British Columbia." *BMC Public Health* 14: 350–350.

Patton, Stacy. 2012. "The Ph.D Now Comes with Food Stamps." *The Chronicle of Higher Education*, May 6. www.chronicle.com/article/from-graduate-school-to/131795?sid=at&utm_medium=en&utm_source=at.

Paul, Kari. 2019. "Amazon Cancels New York HQ2." Market Watch. www.marketwatch.com/story/amazon-hq2-could-push-800-people-into-homeless-ness-economist-says-2018-11-16.

Pay Wizard. 2018. Ben Carson. https://paywizard.org/salary/vip-check/ben-carson.

Pearce, Diane. 1978. "The Feminization of Poverty: Women, Work, and Welfare." *Urban and Social Change Review* 11: 1–2, 28–36.

Peoples, Angela and Montgomery, Mariah. 2018. Amazon to Seattle: The housing crisis is not our problem. Prospect. https://prospect.org/article/amazon-seattle-housing-crisis-not-our-problem.

Picture the Homeless. 2019. Housing. http://picturethehomeless.org/.

Pleace, Nicholas. 2012. Housing First. European Observatory on Homelessness. https://www.feantsaresearch.org/en/other-observatory-publications/2012/11/29/housing-first-2012?bcParent=764.

Pleace, Nicholas. 2016. "Researching Homelessness in Europe: Theoretical Perspectives." *European Journal of Homelessness* 10(3): 19–44. www.feantsaresearch.org/download/10-3_article_11612162762319330292.pdf.

Poor People's Campaign. n.d. "Poor People's Campaign." www.poorpeoplescampaign.org/.

Porter, Michael E. and Mark R. Kramer. 2002. "The Competitive Advantage of Corporate Philanthropy." *Harvard Business Review*, December Issue. https://hbr.org/2002/12/the-competitive-advantage-of-corporate-philanthropy.

Powell, John A. and Marguerite L. Spencer. 2003. "Giving Them the Old "One-Two": Gentrification and the K.O. of Impoverished Urban Dwellers of Color." *Howard Law Journal* 46(3): 433–490. https://heinonline.org/HOL/Landing-Page?handle=hein.journals/howlj46&div=21&id=&page=

PR Newswire. 2011. "Food Bank Use Skyrockets 26% Since 2008." PRNewswire.com, March 26, 2012. www.prnewswire.com/news-releases/food-bank-use-skyrockets-by-26-since-2008-132989278.html.

Qu, Genesis and Stephanie Lai. 2019. "Latino Homeless Population Found to be at Disadvantage in Outreach Programs." *Daily Bruin*, February 18. https://dailybruin.com/2019/02/18/latino-homeless-population-found-to-be-at-disadvantage-in-outreach-programs/.

Quigley, Bill. 2014. "Ten Examples of Welfare for the Rich." *HuffingtonPost*.com, updated on March 16. www.huffingtonpost.com/bill-quigley/ten-examples-of-welfare-for-the-rich-and-corporations_b_4589188.html.

Quigley, Bill. 2016. "6 Billion Dollar Industries." www.alternet.org/2016/03/six-billion-dollar-industries-make-their-profits-exploiting-poor/.

Radocchia, Samantha. 2018. "Blockchain Builds Trust in Food Industry. *Medium*. https://medium.com/betterkinds/3-innovative-ways-blockchain-will-build-trust-in-the-food-industry-3cbb46f83d9b.

Radzicki, Michael J. and Robert A. Taylor. 2008. "Origin of System Dynamics: J.W. Forrester and the History of System Dynamics." In *U.S. Department of Energy's Introduction to System Dynamics*. https://scholar.google.com/citations?user=kSXHvWQAAAAJ&hl=en&oi=sra.

Rae, Barney. 2018. "Propy to Apply Blockchain To Solve Homelessness." http://icoscientist.com/propy-to-apply-blockchain-technology-to-solve-homelessness-crisis-in-california/.

Ramrayka, Liza. 2019. "Students Are Missing School for Lack of Hygiene Products." www.huffpost.com/entry/hygiene-pantries-child-poverty-public-school-teachers_n_5cd2ec92e4b07ce6ef790381.

Ramsey, Dave. 2019. "Against 30 Year Mortgages." www.daveramsey.com/blog/why-daves-against-30-year-mortgages.

Rascon, Jacob. 2015. "Utah's Strategy for the Homeless: Give Them Homes." *NBC News*, May 3. www.nbcnews.com/news/us-news/utahs-strategy-homeless-give-them-homes-n352966.

Raskin, David. 2012. "Revisiting the Hope VI Public Housing Program's Legacy." *Governing*, May Issue. www.governing.com/gov-revisiting-hope-public-housing-programs-legacy.html.

Ratson, Moshe. 2016. "Why is it Important to Live a Meaningful Life?" *HuffingtonPost.com* (blog), last updated December 6, 2017. www.huffingtonpost.com/moshe-ratson/why-is-it-important-to-li_b_9044030.html.

Reich, Robert B. 2010a. *The Work of Nations: Preparing Ourselves for 21st Century Capitalism*. New York: Random House.

Reich, Robert. 2010b. "The Super Rich Get Richer, Everyone Else Gets Poorer, and the Democrats Punt." Robert Reich's professional website, September 24. http://robertreich.org/post/1178374104.

Reich, Robert. 2015. "The Rich Don't Work Anymore; Working Is for Poor People." https://www.alternet.org/2015/03/robert-reich-rich-dont-work-anymore-working-poor-people/.

Reuters. 2014. "US House Speaker Boehner Bemoans Work." https://www.reuters.com/article/us-usa-congress-poverty/u-s-house-speaker-boehner-bemoans-notion-i-dont-have-to-work-idUSKBN0HD2OC20140918.

Rhodan, Maya. 2018. "Trump Administration Targets Immigrants Who Receive Public Benefits." *Time*, September 24. http://time.com/5384007/trump-administration-public-charge-rule/.

Rhule, James. 2017. "Homelessness Is Everybody's Problem." https://medium.com/@jamesrhule/why-homelessness-is-an-everybody-problem-not-their-problem-99a127a842c8.

Rice, Douglas. 2017. "Trump Budget Would Increase Homelessness and Hardship in Every State, End Federal Role in Community Development." *The Center on Budget and Policy Priorities*, May 23. www.cbpp.org/blog/trump-budget-would-increase-homelessness-and-hardship-in-every-state-end-federal-role-in.

Riley, Parker. 2018. "Ben Carson's Unqualified Son and Wife Work at HUD and People are Pissed." *Radio One*. https://woldcnews.com/1609185/ben-carsons-unqualified-son-and-wife-work-at-hud-and-people-are-pissed/.

Rikken, Maarten. 2016. "Two in One." *New York Times*. www.researchgate.net/blog/post/two-in-one-differences-in-the-us-justice-system-for-the-rich-and-the-poor.

Robb, Dean. 2009. "The Old vs New Social Contract." www.academia.edu/7481492/The_Old_Vs._New_Social_Contract.

Roberts, Chris. 2016. "The Great Eliminator: How Ronald Reagan Made Homelessness Permanent." *SF Weekly*, June 29. www.sfweekly.com/news/the-great-eliminator-how-ronald-reagan-made-homelessness-permanent/.

Roberts, David. 2018. "Friendly Policies Keep Oil and Coal afloat." *Vox*. www.vox.com/energy-and-environment/2017/10/6/16428458/us-energy-coal-oil-subsidies.

Roberts, Joel. 2011. "Five Reasons Why Politicians Ignore Homelessness." *Huffington Post*. www.huffpost.com/entry/five-reasons-why-politici_b_765353.

Roberts, Steve, Jr. 2018. "Tipping the Scales: Trump Administration Looks to Change Rules on Tipping at Restaurants." *Williamsburg Yorktown Daily*, February 12. https://wydaily.com/local-news/2018/02/12/tipping-the-scales-trump-administration-looks-to-change-rules-on-tipping-at-restaurants/.

Robin, Vickie and Dominquez, Joe. 2018. "Humans Once Worked Only Three Hours A Day And Now We Are Always Working. https://bigthink.com/big-think-books/vicki-robin-joe-dominguez-your-money-or-your-life.

Robinson, R. 1993. "Chaos or Nonlinear Dynamics: Implications for Reading Research." *Reading Research and Instruction*, 32(4), 15–23. doi: 10.1080/19388079309558129.

Roman, Nan. 2007. Keynote Address. Presented at the National Alliance to End Homelessness Conference, Washington, DC. July 9.

Roos, Leslie. 2013. "Relationship Between Adverse Childhood Experiences and Homelessness and the Impact of Axis I and II Disorders." *American Journal of Public Health* 103(Suppl 2): S275–S281.

Rosenbaum, Dottie, Stacy Dean, Ed Bolen, Elizabeth Wolkomir, Brynne Keith-Jennings, Lexin Cai and Catlin Nchako. 2018. "President's Budget Would Cut Food Assistance for Millions and Radically Restructure SNAP." *Center on Budget and Policy Priorities*, February 15. www.cbpp.org/research/food-assistance/presidents-budget-would-cut-food-assistance-for-millions-and-radically.

Rosenburg, Stephanie. 2013. "Volunteerism: History of an American Value." VolunteerMatch.org, April 18. https://blogs.volunteermatch.org/engagingvolunteers/2013/04/18/volunteering-history-of-an-american-value/.

Rosser, Ezra. 2017. "Exploiting the Poor: Housing, Markets, and Vulnerability." *The Yale Law Journal Forum* 126: 458

Rossi, Peter Henry. 1989. *Down and Out in America: The Origins of Homelessness.* Chicago: The University of Chicago Press.

Rossi, Peter Henry. 1990. "The Old Homeless and the New Homelessness in Historical Perspective." *American Psychologist* 45(8): 954–959.

Rothrie, Sarah. 2018. "How Blockchain Can Help the Homeless." CoinCentral.com, August 5. https://coincentral.com/how-blockchain-can-help-the-homeless/.

Rubinow, Isaac Max. 1934. *The Quest for Security.* New York: H. Holt and Company.

Ruiz-Grossman, Sarah. 2018. "Hundreds Protest in Cities Across U.S. for 'Poor People's Campaign'." *HuffingtonPost.com*, May 14. www.huffingtonpost.com/entry/poor-peoples-campaign-protests-nationwide_us_5afa0792e4b09a94524b4de7.

Ryan, William. 1971. *Blaming the Victim.* New York: Pantheon Books.

Salam, Reihan. 2019. "Los Angeles is in Crisis." *The Atlantic.* https://www.theatlantic.com/ideas/archive/2019/06/how-solve-los-angeless-homelessness-crisis/591976/.

Salamon, Lester. 1987. "Of Market Failure, Voluntary Failure, and Third-Party Government: Toward a Theory of Government-Nonprofit Relations in the Modern Welfare State." *Nonprofit and Voluntary Sector Quarterly* 16(1–2): 29–49. doi: 10.1177/089976408701600104.

Saltsman, Michael. 2017. "Why the $15 Minimum Wage Will Cost California 400,000 Jobs." *Forbes*, December 15. www.forbes.com/sites/michaelsaltsman/2017/12/15/why-the-15-minimum-wage-will-cost-california-400000-jobs/#2d423d8843b9.

SAMHSA. 2019. "ACES and Trauma." www.integration.samhsa.gov/clinical-practice/trauma-informed.

Santens, Scott. 2017. "The Cost of Universal Basic Income is Less Than You Might Think." Futurism.com, July 23. https://futurism.com/cost-universal-basic-income-less-you-might-think.

Savage, Meabh. 2016. "Gendering Women's Homelessness." *Irish Journal of Applied Social Studies*. 16(2): 43–64 https://pdfs.semanticscholar.org/f4c0/74275497d45abebe3a8e2524e5dc9f2e9517.pdf.

School House Connection. 2018a. "Educating Students Experiencing Homelessness: A Primer on Legal Requirements and Implementation Strategies for Educators, Advocates and Policymakers." SchoolHouseConnection.org, October 22. www.schoolhouseconnection.org/educating-students-experiencing-homelessness-a-primer-on-legal-requirements-and-implementation-strategies-for-educators-advocates-and-policymakers/.

School House Connection. 2018b. "House Hearing on Homeless Children and Youth." SchoolHouseConnection.org, June 8. www.schoolhouseconnection.org/house-hearing-on-homeless-children-and-youth/.

School House Connection. 2018c. "Risk and Resilience: Differences in Risk Factors and Health Outcomes Between Homeless and Non-Homeless Students in 2017 YRBS Data." SchoolHouseConnection.org, November 9. www.schoolhouseconnection.org/risk-and-resilience-differences-in-risk-factors-and-health-outcomes-between-homeless-and-non-homeless-students-in-2017-yrbs-data/.

School House Connection. 2019. "McKinney-Vento Act Summary." www.schoolhouseconnection.org/wp-content/uploads/2019/05/McKinney-Vento_2Pager_May2019.pdf.

Schiff, Jeannette Waegemakers and Schiff, Rebecca 2014. Housing First: Paradigm or Program? *Journal of Social Distress and the Homeless* 23(2): 80–104. doi: 10.1179/1573658X14Y.0000000007. www.tandfonline.com/doi/abs/10.1179/1573658X14Y.0000000007.

Scott, J. 1993. Homelessness and Mental Illness. *The British Journal of Psychiatry*, 162, 314–324. doi: 10.1192/bjp.162.3.314 https://psycnet.apa.org/record/1993-37666-001.

Sellars, Frances Stead, Karen Weintraub, Cleve R. Wootson Jr. and Kevin Sullivan. 2018. "Thousands of Residents Still Out of Their Homes After Gas Explosions Trigger Deadly Chaos in Massachusetts." *The Washington Post*, September 14. www.washingtonpost.com/national/thousands-of-residents-still-out-of-their-homes-after-gas-explosions-trigger-deadly-chaos-in-massachusetts/2018/09/14/802ff690-b830-11e8-94eb-3bd52dfe917b_story.html?utm_term=.dd6c2f883a51.

Severance, Cristin. 2017. "Consumer Justice Investigates Network of Professional Panhandlers." *CBS Dallas*, May 24. https://dfw.cbslocal.com/2017/05/24/consumer-justice-investigates-professional-panhandlers/.

Shambaugh, Jay. 2017. "Who are the Poor Americans?" *BBC News*, December 11. www.bbc.com/news/world-us-canada-41930107.

Shaw, Sara. 2019. "To understand Early Childhood Homelessness We Need To Look Across Data Systems." Child Trends. www.childtrends.org/to-understand-early-childhood-homelessness.

Shonkoff, Jack. 2019. Importance of Brain Development in Children. https://developingchild.harvard.edu/.

Sink, Justin. 2019. "Trump Redefine Poverty." www.bloomberg.com/news/articles/2019-05-06/trump-poverty-line-inflation.

Smith, Noah. 2018a. "Homelessness Is a Tragedy the US Can Afford to Fix." *Bloomberg*, May 21. www.bloomberg.com/opinion/articles/2018-05-21/ending-homelessness-is-a-job-for-the-federal-government.

Smith, Noah. 2018b. "Ending Homelessness Is a Job for the Federal Government." *Bloomberg*. www.bloomberg.com/opinion/articles/2018-05-21/ending-homelessness-is-a-job-for-the-federal-government.

Social Solutions. 2016. "2016's Shocking Homelessness Statistics." SocialSolutions. com(blog),June21.www.socialsolutions.com/blog/2016-homelessness-statistics/.

Sommeiller, Estelle and Price, Mark. 2018. "The New Gilded Age. Economic Policy Institute. www.epi.org/publication/the-new-gilded-age-income-inequality-in-the-u-s-by-state-metropolitan-area-and-county/.

Spellman, Brooke, Jill Khadduri, Brian Sokol, Josh Leopold and Abt Associates Inc. 2010. "Costs Associated with First-Time Homelessness for Families and Individuals." Report prepared for the U.S. Department of Housing and Urban Development, the Office of Policy Development and Research, and the Office of Special Needs Assistance Programs, March. www.huduser.gov/publications/pdf/costs_homeless.pdf.

Spielberg, Ben. 2017. "Think a $15 Minimum Wage is Too High? Think Again." *HuffingtonPost.com*, last updated January 23. www.huffingtonpost.com/ben-spielberg/think-a-15-minimum-wage-i_b_9062534.html.

Squire, Heather. 2018. "A Brief-ish History of Housing Policy in the United States." HeatherSquire.com, April 24. https://heathersquire.com/2018/04/24/a-brief-ish-history-of-housing-policy-in-the-united-states/.

Stanford Encyclopedia of Philosophy. 2018. "Socrates." *Stanford Encyclopedia of Philosophy*, updated on February 6. https://plato.stanford.edu/entries/socrates/.

Statista. n.d. "Estimate Number of Homeless People in the United States in 2017, by Race." Statista.com. www.statista.com/statistics/555855/number-of-homeless-people-in-the-us-by-race/.

Statista.2018."NumberofHomelessPeopleintheU.S.byRace2018."Statista.com.www.statista.com/statistics/555855/number-of-homeless-people-in-the-us-by-race/.

Stephans, Morgan. 2019. "It's Not Just a Homelessness Crisis, It's An Eviction Crisis Too." Huffington Post. www.huffpost.com/entry/los-angeles-evictions_n_5ccc8b02e4b0e4d757325671.

Stewart, Emily. 2018a. "Americans Are Losing Faith to Solve Their Problems." www.vox.com/business-and-finance/2018/3/20/17107626/corporate-america-nra-guns-daca-trump.

Stewart, Emily. 2018b. "Ben Carson's Family Ethics Drama, Explained." *Vox*, February 3. www.vox.com/policy-and-politics/2018/2/3/16967628/ben-carson-ethics-hud-son-baltimore.

Stribley,Robert.2017.No,UndocumentedImmigrantsAren'tStealingYourBenefits. *Huffington Post*. www.huffpost.com/entry/no-undocumented-immigrants-arent-stealing-your-benefits_b_5a144263e4b010527d6780b0.

Stroh, David Peter and Michael Goodman. 2007. "A Systemic Approach to Ending Homelessness." *Applied Systems Thinking Journal* (Tropical Issues No. 4).

Suliman,Adela.2017."DisastersMake14MillionPeopleHomelessEachYear:U.N." *Reuters*, October 12. www.reuters.com/article/us-un-disaster-displacement/disasters-make-14-million-people-homeless-each-year-u-nidUSKB-N1CH35D.

Super Scholar. 2018. "Homelessness in America." https://superscholar.org/homeless/.

Taylor, Ryan. 2018. "Can Cryptocurrencies Solve the Humanitarian Crisis?" *The Hill*, July 13. https://thehill.com/opinion/cybersecurity/396909-can-crypt ocurrencies-solve-the-humanitarian-crisis.

Tetlock, Phil. 2016. *Superforecasting*. New York: Broadway Books.

The Nation. 2018. "151 Years of America's Housing History." *The Nation*, May 24. www.thenation.com/article/americas-housing-history/.

Tiehen, Laura. 2002. "Use of Food Pantries by Households With Children Rose During the Late 1990s." *Food Review* 25(3): 44–50.

Teitelbaum, Joel and Wilinsky, Sarah. 2017. *Health Policy and Law*. Boston, MA: Jones and Bartlett.

Tobias, Jimmy. 2018. "Meet the Rising New Housing Movement that Wants to Create Homes for All." *The Nation*, May 24. www.thenation.com/article/the-way-home/.

Torrey, E. Fuller. 2013. "Fifty Years of Failing America's Mentally Ill." RealClearPolitics.com, February 5. www.realclearpolitics.com/2013/02/04/fifty_years_of_failing_america039s_mentally_ill_301246.html.

Tran, Linda Diem, Zimmerman, Frederick. J. and Fielding, Jonathan E. 2017. "Public Health and the Economy Could Be Served by Reallocating Medical Expenditures to Social Programs." *SSM – Population Health* 3: 185–191. doi: 10.1016/j.ssmph.2017.01.004. www.ncbi.nlm.nih.gov/pmc/articles/PMC5769015/.

Uchitelle, Louis. 2001. "How to Define Poverty". *New York Times*. https://www.nytimes.com/2001/05/26/arts/how-to-define-poverty-let-us-count-the-ways.html.

US Conference of Mayors. 2014. "Mayors Hunger and Homelessness Report." USMayors.org. www.usmayors.org/pressreleases/uploads/2014/1211-release-hh.pdf.

U.S. Department of Health and Human Services. 2019. "2019 Poverty Guidelines." https://aspe.hhs.gov/2019-poverty-guidelines.

US Department of Agriculture. 2014. "Faith Based and Neighborhood Partnerships." *U.S. Department of Agriculture*. www.usda.gov/wps/portal/usda/usda-home?contentidonly=true&contentid=fnp_page01-4C.xml.

Vallas, Rebecca. 2014. "A New Social Contract for the 21st Century." https://talkpoverty.org/2014/08/13/new-social-contract-21st-century/.

Van Buren, Peter. 2016. "You Can't Earn a Living on the Minimum Wage." *HuffingtonPost.com*, updated on December 6. www.huffingtonpost.com/peter-van-buren/you-cant-earn-a-living-on-minimum-wage_b_9242970.html.

van der Leum, Justine. 2018. "'You Descend Into Hell By Coming Here': How Texas Shut the Door on Refugees." *The Guardian*, November 2. www.theguardian.com/us-news/2018/nov/02/you-descend-into-hell-by-coming-here-how-texas-shut-the-door-on-refugees.

Vernon-Feagans, Lynne, Martha J. Cox and Rand D. Conger 2013. *The Family Life Project: An Epidemiological and Developmental Study of Young Children Living in Poor Rural Communities*. Boston, MA: Wiley.

Vissing, Yvonne. 1997. *Out of Sight, Out of Mind: Homeless Children and Families in Small Town America*. Lexington: University of Kentucky Press.

Vissing, Yvonne, Joann Gu, Andrea Jones, Sue Gabriel. 2017. Preserving Dignity in the Face of Hunger: A Study of Food Pantry Utilization. *Humanity and Society*. 41(4): 461–481.

Voice, Kensington. 2019. "How Hard is it to Convert Vacant Buildings into Affordable Homes for Kensington Residents in Need." generocity.org, February 18. https://generocity.org/philly/2019/02/18/how-hard-is-it-to-convert-vacant-buildings-into-affordable-homes-for-residents-in-need-kensington-voice-homelessness/.

Waldrop, M. Mitchell. 1992. Complexity: The emerging science the edge of order and chaos. New York: Simon and Schuster.

Wallace, Gregory and Rene Marsh. 2018. "Son of Close CArson Friend Hired at HUD." CNN.com, updated on May 31. www.cnn.com/2018/05/30/politics/ben-carson-aide/index.html.

Walker, Alissa. 2018. Why isn't Homelessness Seen as a National Crisis? www.curbed.com/2018/2/1/16956732/homelessness-hud-housing-mayors

Wamhoff, Steve. 2018. "Congress Should Reduce Not Expand Tax Breaks." *Institute on Taxation and Economic Policy.* https://itep.org/congress-should-reduce-not-expand-tax-breaks-for-capital-gains/.

Wang, Lucy. 2017. "3D Printed Pod Homes For The Homeless". https://inhabitat.com/3d-printed-pod-homes-for-the-homeless-could-cling-to-nyc-buildings/.

Weber, Max. 2002/1905. *The Protestant Ethic and the "spirit" of Capitalism and Other Writings.* Translated by Peter Baehr, and Gordon C. Wells. New York: Penguin Books.

Wehner, Peter. 2018. "Why People Are Wired to Believe What They Want To Believe. Medium. https://medium.com/trust-media-and-democracy/why-people-are-wired-to-believe-what-they-want-to-believe-4d9b4e161eb5.

Wetsman, Nicole. 2018. "The Public Health Crisis Facing Homeless Children." www.thedailybeast.com/the-public-health-crisis-facing-homeless-children.

White, Chelsea. 2015. "Five Ways Poor Pay More." GlobalCitizen.org, January 30. www.globalcitizen.org/en/content/five-ways-the-poor-pay-more-everyday/.

Wier Kirsten. 2017. "Why We Believe Alternative Facts." *American Psychological Association.* 48(5): 24. www.apa.org/monitor/2017/05/alternative-facts.

Williams, Adam. 2013. "Cardboragami Fuses Cardboard And Origami To Shelter The Homeless. https://newatlas.com/cardborigami-homeless-shelter/26437/.

Wilson, Reid. 2017. "Homelessness Rises for the First Time since Recession." *The Hill*, December 6. http://thehill.com/homenews/state-watch/363599-homelessness-rises-for-first-time-since-recession.

Woiem, S. 2018. "Americans Spend $70 Billion on Pets." *The Conversation.* https://theconversation.com/americans-spend-70-billion-on-pets-and-that-money-could-do-more-good-102467.

Wogan, J. 2018. "Can Homeless Programs Make Money And Should They?" www.governing.com/topics/health-human-services/gov-money-for-home less.html.

Wolfe, Liz. 2017. "The Laws Cities Use to Make Homelessness a Crime." *The Daily Beast*, April 30. www.thedailybeast.com/the-laws-cities-use-to-make-homelessness-a-crime.

World Hunger.org. 2011. "Hunger in America: 2011 United States Hunger and Poverty Facts." WorldHunger.org, April 2, 2012. www.worldhunger.org/articles/Learn/us_hunger_facts.htm.

Wray, Matt. 2006. *Not Quite White: White Trash and the Boundaries of Whiteness.* Durham, NC: Duke University Press.

Yglesias, Matthew. 2015. "Giving Housing to the Homeless is Three Times Cheaper than leaving them on the Streets." *Vox*, February 4. www.vox.com/2014/5/30/5764096/its-three-times-cheaper-to-give-housing-to-the-homeless-than-to-keep.

Yglesias, Matthew. 2019. "The Most Cost-Effective Way to Help the Homeless is to Give Them Homes." *Vox*, February 20. www.vox.com/2014/5/30/5764096/homeless-shelter-housing-help-solutions.

Young, Michael Dunlop. 1958. *The Rise of the Meritocracy, 1870–2033.* London: Thames and Hudson.

Zillman, Claire. 2018. "Childcare Costs More Than College Tuition in 28 States. *Fortune.* https://fortune.com/2018/10/22/childcare-costs-per-year-us/.

Zint, Mike. 2017. "The Real Plight of The Homeless Told By The Homeless." *People's Tribune.* http://peoplestribune.org/pt-news/2017/04/real-plight-homeless-told-homeless/.

Index